Samuel Colcord Bartlett

The Veracity of the Hexateuch

A Defence of the Historic Character of the First Six Books of the Bible

Samuel Colcord Bartlett

The Veracity of the Hexateuch
A Defence of the Historic Character of the First Six Books of the Bible

ISBN/EAN: 9783337100162

Printed in Europe, USA, Canada, Australia, Japan

Cover: Foto ©Lupo / pixelio.de

More available books at **www.hansebooks.com**

The Veracity of the Hexateuch

A Defence of the Historic Character of the First Six Books of the Bible

By

Samuel Colcord Bartlett, D.D., LL. D.
Ex-President of Dartmouth College

Fleming H. Revell Company

Chicago   New York   Toronto

Publishers of Evangelical Literature

*To
My Former Pupils
At
Western Reserve College
Chicago Theological Seminary
And Dartmouth College
This Witness to THE TRUTH
Is Affectionately
Dedicated*

PREFACE

CONSERVATIVE discussions of the Hexateuch have not of late been much in vogue. We have been abundantly notified that modern scholarship is on the other side. However this may be, the recent movement of Homeric scholarship is significant. The reign of Wolf began in 1795, and for much of the intervening century the "scholar" has been constrained to accept the Homeridæ and a compilation of rhapsodies from nameless independent authors. But since the labors of Schliemann and Dörpfeld, even Germany is beginning with some unanimity, we are told, to give us back one Homer, one Iliad, and an actual Trojan war. Perhaps the time has come to say something for Moses and Joshua. Evidently a volume of the right kind in behalf of the views that were universally held for two or three thousand years is still in order.

Such a volume for general use needs to be sufficiently compact to invite a reading, sufficiently clear to be readily followed, broad enough in its scope to recognize the various aspects of the case, and in its statements to rest on trustworthy authorities, while not overweighed with wearisome and repellent details. To meet all these requirements is no easy undertaking. The literature of the subject is almost hopelessly vast, and is constantly increasing. The conflict on some important points still continues.

The work of archæological research, remarkable as it has lately been, and pointing steadily and decisively in one direction, is yet progressive and incomplete. Its further results must be patiently awaited rather than predicted. But while occasional new perplexities may be looked for, and minor modifications of fact and opinion may be expected, there is little reason to anticipate any reversal of the main historic results already established by concurrent evidence from so many different sources.

No one can be more sensible of the difficulty of meeting the requirements above indicated than the present writer, and he by no means claims to have accomplished it. For a long course of years, however, he has followed the discussion, examining all available materials for the solution of the question, while waiting for the light that was to come from further discoveries. But the process of research is a stream that never ceases to flow on; and the call for some practical showing of its combined results up to the present time seems to be urgent.

For the gravity of the real issue is beginning to be more generally understood. It is not chiefly a question of authorship and mode of composition, nor of minor inexactness or "inerrancy," which has come to the front, but of the fundamental veracity of the Old Testament from the beginning of it. Direct and open denials, and charges of being "unhistorical," "fictitious," and "false," have hitherto been more abundant in Germany. But they have made their way into England; and in this country we have begun to hear the same things, usually, though not always, in more decorous language, yet in unexpected quarters.

Meanwhile the religious community are entertained with assurances of the new light and impressiveness thus brought to the sacred volume, and that its "inspired authority," in the words of Dr. Driver, is not impaired. But when we are informed by the same writer that we have but "traditions modified and colored by the associations of the age in which the author lived," and that the author used his "freedom in placing speeches in the mouths" of the several characters, such as "he deemed to be consonant"; when we are told by other writers, English and American, that the early chapters of Genesis are a "myth," and that we have "not the history of Abraham and Jacob, of Moses and Joshua," but of "religious ideas," that the account of the conquest of Palestine is "essentially false," and the like, what becomes of the "inspired authority" and the religious lessons of such a book?

Many, no doubt, are induced to give a general assent to the positions taken by this class of writers by the constant and confident assurance that they are approved and accepted facts. They have not been able to sift the elaborate and wearisome discussions for themselves, and they fail to recognize, beneath these bold pretensions, the unfounded assumptions, the unwarranted methods and inferences, and the ultimate incompatibility of the conclusions with confidence in the Scriptures. The New Testament, also, is so related to the Old, as the basis on which in an important sense it is built, that the attack on the truthfulness of the Hexateuch is a flank movement on the Gospels and the Epistles. In some quarters it seems to have been made a substitute for a direct assault. Slowly and surely foiled and driven back in the attempt to detrude the date of the Gospels far down in the second century, by such newly discovered obstacles as the Diatesseron, the Didache, the Greek text of Barnabas, the Apology of Aristides, the "Gospel of Peter," the identifying of Hippolytus containing the witness of Basilides, and the like, they have transferred the attack to a region where collateral evidence is more difficult of attainment. But the good providence of God has been doing much within a few years past to cast light on those far distant periods, until the time has come when explorers in oriental lands are placing facts against speculations. The speculators do not seem to be fully aware of it.

Meanwhile this agitation tends to produce uneasiness and embarrassment in the minds of many Christians, and unsettlement in the views of many who are not Christians. The object of the present volume is to relieve these difficulties, presenting some of the reasons for holding fast the belief of the ages in the historic truthfulness of the Hexateuch. The aim has been to do it as compactly as is consistent with a clear and satisfactory presentation. With this view, considerable matter by way of illustration and confirmation has been thrown into notes in the appendix, and some accumulated material withheld.

Direct and positive evidence of fact best disposes of speculative objections. It is not necessary, nor would it be possible within reasonable compass, to follow the critical analysis through all its winding course, inasmuch as it only indirectly and inferentially concerns the question of veracity, would require many hundred pages, and probably would find few readers. For the present purpose, if not for all purposes, it is better dealt with by an examination of its methods and principles, together with adequate illustrations, illustrative and representative, and some comparison with other literary procedures and experiences, showing the failure to stand the experimental test. So far as it comes under consideration, while the author has had access to most of the several forms of division of the text, he has referred chiefly to the comparatively conservative representation in Kautzsch's "Die Heilige Schrift des Alten Testament" (1894). He is not confident that he has escaped the charge of tediousness in the references and citations he has made. Those who may wish to follow out this line of the subject in minute and protracted detail are referred to the recent volumes of Dr. W. H. Green, which it has hitherto apparently been found easier to ignore than to answer.

The questions of fact passing under review in this discussion are of very wide range, and involve the investigations and testimony of a host of writers and explorers. On all important points the references are given, which those familiar with the subject will recognize as comprising the highest authorities in their several departments. They are cited, it will be observed, for their testimony rather than for their opinions.

One minor point occasions a slight embarrassment. As to the orthography of many oriental names confusion now reigns. Each modern writer is a law unto himself. In recent volumes of some prominence we find, for example, six ways of spelling Thothmes, four each of Rameses, Usertasen, Menephtah, Assurbanipal. Sennacherib is changed to Sinacherib; the old English word Jehovah is replaced by Jahve, Jahveh, Yahveh, Yahweh, and Yahwè; and what all English readers well know as the Koran has been transformed into the English anomaly and incompatibility of Qur'ān. One can but take his choice, with the prospect of inconsistency when he quotes directly. But it would seem to be a sound principle of English literature that when a foreign name has acquired an established form and held it since the time of King James' Version, an English writer is not called to change it. No perceptible gain would accrue to English literature or Hebrew scholarship by writing Mosheh for Moses, or Yehoshua for Joshua.

Attention is called in conclusion to the fact that the question here discussed is now open to the judgment, not alone of Hebrew scholars, but of intelligent men generally. It has been by modern critics themselves taken off from merely linguistic, and placed on historic, grounds. If other distinct admissions were wanting, as they are not, the confession is found in the revolution which within a few years has transferred the so-called document P, that contains the first chapter of Genesis, from being the oldest to be the youngest of the main constituents.

We are now in the midst and at the height of a great movement against the trustworthiness of the ancient Scriptures. But already there are signs of weakening in some portions of the hostile camp, and in others the very excess and extravagance is a sign of growing weakness. Many of us have read of, and some of us have seen, collapses of popular and even universally accepted movements and theories, both in literature and science. All students of history know how manifold and unceasing have been the efforts to arrest the power and progress of God's Word; and it is easy to see that they will not end so long as men assume as a postulate the denial of the supernatural, or stumble at the "offense of the cross." It is unnecessary to arrange terms of surrender.

Hanover, N. H., June, 1897.

CONTENTS

CHAPTER.		PAGE.
I.	THE CASE STATED	1
II.	THE BOOK OF JOSHUA	13
III.	FROM THE EXODUS TO THE CONQUEST	48
IV.	THE RESIDENCE IN EGYPT	84
V.	THE PATRIARCHAL HISTORY	109
VI.	THE TABLE OF THE NATIONS	137
VII.	THE DELUGE	151
VIII.	ANTEDILUVIAN LIFE	178
IX.	ANTEDILUVIAN OCCUPATIONS	190
X.	THE PRIMITIVE CONDITION	199
XI.	THE TEMPTATION AND THE FALL	214
XII.	THE CREATION NARRATIVE	227
XIII.	THE SABBATH	261
XIV.	THE HISTORIC BASIS	268
XV.	THE LITERARY PROBLEM	283
XVI.	THE ANALYSIS	295
XVII.	UNFOUNDED ASSUMPTIONS	311
XVIII.	UNSUSTAINED DENIALS	322
XIX.	UNSUSTAINED DENIALS: THE PRIESTHOOD	337
XX.	THE CODES	347
	APPENDIX	359
	LIST OF AUTHORS	393
	INDEX	399

CHAPTER I

THE CASE STATED

THE one important question concerning the Hexateuch, as the five books of Moses and the book of Joshua are now called, is this: Is it true history? All others are subordinate and only constructively important. It is comparatively unimportant whether it was the work of various writers, if it be true; not a vital question when it was written, or when it received its present form, if it be valid history. No doubt, could it be shown to have been written many centuries after the events, and without authentic sources, it loses historic weight. But it must be remembered that its composite character, if it were proved, would not carry a determination of its date. That must be shown by distinct evidence. While a very late date of composition would impair its value as a narrative, on the other hand an origin nearly or quite contemporaneous with the events, would, in the absence of conflicting accounts and with the corroboration by such tests as could be applied, render it thoroughly credible.

Two theories of its origin and character are now before the public. They are frequently distinguished as the Traditional and the Critical. Cave terms them the Journal and the Evolution theories; Robertson, the Biblical and the Modern. The latter uses his terms advisedly, because the account given in the Hexateuch, and elsewhere assumed in the Scriptures, as to the law-giving and many earlier transactions, is denied by the Modern theory, though in different degrees by different writers.

The Traditional, Biblical or Journal view holds, as its fundamental point, that the narrative is true history, although written in popular style and method, and that these books were substantially contemporary with Moses and Joshua respectively. As stated in careful form by Ellicott, it would recognize Exodus, Leviticus and Numbers as put in shape by Moses or under his direction, Deuteronomy as manifestly completed by a survivor, and Genesis as compiled by Moses. Joshua is regarded as compiled by some contemporary under the direction of Joshua.[1] It is suggested both by Bishop Ellicott and Professor Leathes (and others) as probable that in the composition of Genesis the lawgiver made use of primeval documents and contemporaneous family records handed down in the line of Abraham and his ancestry. The existence and gradual growth of such records is thought by Leathes to be sustained by such passages as Gen. v. 1; Ex. xvii. 14; xxiv. 7; xxxiv. 27; Num. xxi. 14; xxxiii. 2; Deut. xxxi. 24; Josh. x. 13; xxiv. 26; 2 Sam. i. 18.[2] The chief feature of this view is that it regards the narratives as resting on good and practically contemporaneous authority. But they all show marks of having passed through the hands of editors or revisers.

---

[1] Ellicott, Christus Comprobator, pp. 46-50.
[2] Leathes, The Law in the Prophets, pp. v., vi.

The other view, which we will call the Modern theory, has three prominent features: 1, an analysis of the Hexateuch into the writings of separate and discernible hands, numbering from eight or ten to eighteen or twenty; 2, an assignment of late dates for all these writers, none of them living within less than four or five, some of them not less than ten centuries, of the events; 3, a denial more or less distinct and extensive of the truth of much of the early narrative, as being tradition "modified or colored" by the judgment of the writer, or "mythical" and "unhistorical," or as one writer describes the narrative of the conquest, "essentially false."

The first of these points of itself would be of no special importance. The second is significant as leading to the third. The third is vital. It is with the question of the historic character of the Hexateuch that the present treatise has to do. If that be established, the other points may be disposed of more briefly, and the reader referred to other and more detailed discussions of them.

Meanwhile it may be mentioned as a significant fact what a reaction has begun in Germany against the dissection of Homer and the Iliad, and the extinction of Homer. The anti-Homeric crusade is older and bolder than the anti-Mosaic. For many decades scarcely a scholar dared to question it. But it has had its day. The keen specialist Knoetel has boldly declared that the "theory which cuts the Homeric poems into a larger or smaller number of rhapsodies is unfounded, and such great men and scholars as Wolf, Lachmann, Dissen, Bernhardy and all their followers who undertook the work of literary dissection were entirely in error."[3] And his assertion is said to be substantially and generally accepted. It remains to be seen whether the process of dissecting the Scriptures and excluding Moses may or may not meet a similar fate. Already the excesses of the movement begin to appear like a *reductio ad absurdum* of its methods.

The Pentateuch and the book of Joshua are now commonly treated together as the Hexateuch, on the ground of alleged identity of authorship. Historically they are intimately related. The second is the sequel of the first.

When grave historic treatises present themselves under such remarkable conditions as do these writings, by all the laws of historic reasoning it is incumbent, not on those who accept, but on those who reject, them, to show cause. It is not proposed to dispense with the prestige and power of this position, but to indicate it later, in treating directly of the Pentateuch. Meanwhile we will take our stand on the latest portion of this connected narrative, namely, the book of Joshua, and trace the course of the history upward to the beginning of the stream.

This method undoubtedly has its disadvantages. The transactions in the book of Joshua are not only remote from direct contact with Egypt and its mon-

---

[3] Knoetel, Homeros, der Blinde von Chios, und Seine Werke, 2 vol., Leipzig, 1894-5. In Vol ii., pp. x., xi., he characterizes the process, somewhat too severely, as "carping, chipping and trimming."

uments, but they antedate the evidence which of late years has been coming abundantly from Babylonian and Assyrian discoveries. But though these last-mentioned testimonies fall below the period now in question, they are not to be overlooked, as forming an approach to that period, and as bearing on the general credibility of the Old Testament history. In them we find not only many striking details illustrative of the events in the times of the kings of Israel and Judah, but what is even more weighty, the explanation of that course of events, not otherwise easily intelligible. Indeed the explanation thus gained extends back even to the date of the Exodus, showing the condition and relations of the great nations at that time, which exposed Palestine to invasion and suffered its conquest to take place without hindrance from outside. It has been well said that "the history of Israel, unspeakably interesting and important as it was in itself, may now be seen in its true external setting." It is a fact of the gravest moment that the narrative is not only confirmed in so many of its test details, but that it stands so thoroughly clasped and supported by all its environments. Inasmuch as a full justification of the statement would involve too long a digression from the more direct line of inquiry, the reader is referred to an admirable summary of the situation by Professor J. F. McCurdy.[4]

Proceeding to some of the facts in detail mentioned in the sacred narrative which are contained

---
[4] See Appendix, note I.

also in the Assyrian records, there are found in the latter records six kings of Israel, Omri, Ahab, Jehu, Menahem, Pekah and Hoshea, and four kings of Judah, Azariah, Ahaz, Hezekiah and Manasseh; also Ben-hadad and Hazael of Damascus, and Hiram of Tyre. Tiglath-pileser's movement on Samaria and Syria, Shalmanezer's invasion of Palestine, and Sennacherib's war with Hezekiah have been read from the Assyrian records. Thus Sennacherib relates how he had captured the strong cities of the king of Judah (2 Chron. xxxii. 1), and shut up the king in Jerusalem, where he had given command to strengthen the bulwarks, as the Chronicler also states (ver. 5); and he specifies the amount of tribute exacted, namely, thirty talents of gold, precisely the Scripture number (2 Kings xviii. 14), although the Assyrian monarch claims five hundred talents of silver more than are mentioned in the sacred narrative. Sennacherib's siege of Lachish (2 Chron. xxxii. 9), whither Hezekiah sent his submission (2 Kings xviii. 14), is delineated on thirteen slabs of bas-relief in the palace at Koyunjik, labeled with the name of the monarch and the town.[5] One of the latest discoveries in regard to him (by Father Scheil's excavations)[6] is a mention of his murder by his son, as stated in the Scripture, but not previously known from other sources. The lost and (by some) doubted Belshazzar has been found in three contract tablets dated in the fifth, eleventh and

---

5 Layard's Babylon and Nineveh, p. 154. Records of the Past, i., p. 36.
6 Biblical Science, New York Independent, June 25, 1896.

twelfth years of king Nabonidus, and describing him as "the king's son."[7] The Moabite stone, found in 1868, carries us back to about 900 B. C., and presents to us Mesha king of Moab, otherwise unknown except in the Scriptures (2 Kings iii. 4), Omri king of Judah and his son (Ahab), the heavy tribute exacted from the Moabite king, and at last his rebellion—all as stated briefly in the book of Kings. It also mentions Jehovah as Israel's God, Chemosh as the Moabite deity, and Moab as the "land of Chemosh," just as in Num. xxi. 29 and Jer. xlviii. 46 Moab is called the "people of Chemosh." The script is that of the ancient Hebrew; its vocabulary, with slight exceptions, is that of the Hebrew, as are its syntax and form of sentence also. And what is still more important is its evidence of the power and civilization of Moab at that time, and those of Israel, its neighbor and superior. Says Dr. Driver, "The length and finished literary form of the inscription show that the Moabites in the tenth century B. C. were not a nation that had recently emerged from barbarism; and Mesha reveals himself in it as a monarch capable of organizing and consolidating his dominions by means similar to those adopted by contemporary sovereigns in the kingdoms of Israel and Judah."[8] Another interesting and important inscription, from Jerusalem itself, is the Siloam inscription discovered so recently as

---

7. Records of the Past, New Series, Vol. iii., p. 124.

8 Driver, Notes on the Hebrew Text of Samuel, p xciv. The inscription has been given to the public abundantly, the best form being the fac-simile and translation by Smend and Socin, Freiburg, 1886.

1880. It is cut in the rock sixteen feet from the Siloam entrance of a rock-cut channel which extends to the Fountain of the Virgin, a distance of 1,708 feet. Though the passage winds more or less, following the softer seams of the rock, and was, according to the inscription (and appearances also), excavated from both ends inward, it was so well directed that when three cubits apart the two bands of workmen heard each other's picks and came together. It is regarded for good reasons as dating from about the time of Hezekiah, and it serves two historic purposes: It is a general corroboration of the statement that such water courses (2 Chron. xxxii. 30) or conduits (2 Kings xx. 20) were actually made at Jerusalem during those times; and, still more importantly, it bears witness to the civilization and progress of the nation, since (1) there were workmen competent to do such a piece of engineering, and (2) it presents an inscription of six lines, in Hebrew like that of the Old Testament, containing but one word ("excess"?) not found in the lexicons, and in well-cut Hebrew letters of the archaic form.[9] Somewhat earlier than these is the famous inscription at Thebes in Egypt, of Shishak, the Sheshenk of the monuments, enumerating the places conquered by him or tributary to him, among which is the bearded figure and the name "Judah" —whether rendered king or kingdom—in correspondence to the narrative of 1 Kings xiv. 25, 26,

---

[9] To be found in the Records of the Past, New Series, Vol. 1, p. 174, and elsewhere. A fac-simile and translation was published by the Palestine Exploration fund.

that he carried off the chief treasures of the city and the temple; and in his list of captured places there are certainly identified, among others, the well-known Taanach, Mahanaim, Beth-horon, Beth-tappuah, Ajalon and Shoco.[10] The last two are mentioned in 2 Chron. xi. 5-10 among "fenced cities" which Rehoboam built "for defence"; thus distinctly confirming the statement of 2 Chron. xii. 2-4, that "Shishak took the fenced cities which pertained to Judah, and came to Jerusalem"—the statement of a book (Chronicles) greatly depreciated by some critics. In the history of Joshua (2 Kings xxiii. 29, 30; 2 Chron. xxxvi. 20-24) we get a passing notice of Pharaoh-nechoh of Egypt on his march to Carchemish upon the Euphrates, victorious over Josiah, but to be defeated by the king of Babylon, and also of the effects of that defeat on the history of Palestine, as we learn them from other sources.[11]

Other details of definite corroboration could be given, but these must suffice for the present. Meanwhile it is important to call special attention to the knowledge that has recently come from the investigation of inscriptions in Arabia by Glaser, and elucidated by Hommel, showing an advanced stage of organization, prosperity, if not culture, in that country as early, it is supposed, as the exodus.[12]

---

[10] The latest and probably best list is that of Maspero, given in the Journal of the Victoria Institute, 1894, pp. 93-133. He identifies sixteen places mentioned in Joshua.

[11] Berosus, in Josephus cont. Ap. 1, 19, Josephus Antiq., ch. x., and Jer. xlvi. 2-16.

[12] An excellent popular account of these results was given by Prof. Fitz Hommel in the S. S. Times, October 12 and November 2, 1895.

Thus from these various sources we not only find that in the early days Israel was on all sides surrounded with advanced civilization, but from Assyria, Egypt, Moab, and Jerusalem come evidences extending into the tenth century B. C., touching its history at various points, and abundantly confirmatory of the sacred records. There are minor difficulties, such as are common in historic matters and are easily paralleled, and especially some chronological difficulties, such as are seldom absent from history, whether ancient, medieval or modern. But the substantial facts remain well verified. And with the force of this accumulated preliminary testimony we may approach the times in some of which the external evidences, though not wanting, are less numerous. We are thus far dealing with manifestly true histories which we have tested at various points.

The criteria thus indicated carry us back three-fourths of the interval from the Christian Era to the death of Joshua, or about as near to it as from the present time (1897) to the death of John Carver, the first governor of Plymouth Colony.[13] The weighty bearing of this consideration is not to be overlooked.

For, in truth, the earlier and the later history, as will more fully appear hereafter, are closely interlocked throughout. At every stage the later history and literature are permeated by the facts of the earlier, and cannot be explained without them; related somewhat as is American history and litera-

---
[13] See note ii, Appendix.

ture before and since the Revolution, or as the known origin of Plymouth Colony is presupposed and emphasized in all its subsequent transactions, and never more than in the present day.

After all attempts to discredit the statements of the Pentateuch and Joshua, it has been found impossible to sever the connection of the continuous course of events. Even Wellhausen says: "It is certain that Moses was the founder of the Torah;" "he was the founder of the nation out of which the Torah and the prophecy came as later growths; he laid the basis of Israel's subsequent peculiar individuality, not by any one formal act, but in virtue of his having throughout the whole of his long life been the people's leader, judge and center of union."[14] When these words are carefully weighed, it will be seen that they pretty much surrender the case as a historical issue. Kuenen also, though with cautionary qualifications, declares that "we may not doubt that the exodus is an historical fact," and proceeds unconsciously to show this interlocking of events by arguing that the events ascribed to Moses and Joshua "were, in reality, distributed over a very long period"—"centuries."[15] Dr. Driver, as might be expected, attributes far more to Moses, and dwells much more definitely on the gradual, steady outgrowth of all the civil ordinances, ceremonial observances, and the relations and functions of the priesthood through the entire later history, from the same original agency, declaring in the outset that

---

[14] History of Israel, p. 438.   [15] Religion of Israel, I., p. 117.

"it cannot be doubted that Moses was the ultimate founder of both the religious and national life of Israel."[16]

Such definite tests as have now been cited of the authentic character of the narrative through three-fourths of the interval from Jesus to Joshua, and the inseparable blending of the whole fabric of the earlier and the later history, form not only a legitimate preparation for the discussion of that earlier narrative, but a grave argument for its historic validity. From this standpoint we may proceed to the book of Joshua. Meanwhile, however, it is not to be overlooked that the best evidence of the truth of the early history of Israel, and one not to be set aside except on the best counter evidence, is the fact of its being so embedded in the literature and incorporated in the life of the nation. At whatever point along the course of this history we can apply a test, the history stands the test.

---

16 Introduction, pp. 144-5.

CHAPTER II

THE BOOK OF JOSHUA

In showing the historic character of the Hexateuch it is proposed to make the book of Joshua the starting point, and proceed thence upward. For the present purpose it is unnecessary to enter into any special consideration of the critical analysis of the book—which, though theoretically simple, is actually quite complicated.[1] The question before us, whoever wrote it, is whether it bears the marks of truth. It contains a variety of materials, such as divine utterances, human addresses, land assignments and boundaries, narratives of conquests, and other matters. But it has a distinct unity as a narrative of the establishment of the Israelites in the promised land; and it falls into two main divisions; first, the history of the conquest (Chapters I.-XII.), and second, the allotment of the country (Chapters XIII.-XXIV.), with many subordinate and attendant incidents. It is proposed to call attention to such corroborative circumstances as can be adduced in connection with a series of events so long antecedent to any other continuous written history. It is not proposed to enter on any discussion of the miraculous elements, nor to vouch for the correct transmission of all the numbers contained in the narrative

---

[1] See note iii, Appendix.

—numbers being at all times most difficult of correct preservation.

It must not be forgotten, however, that the effort positively to prove the statements of a reputable and competent witness is a gratuitous proceeding; his testimony stands good and is accepted unless valid reason can be shown for doubting it. Fuller discussion of this point is reserved for later consideration, in connection with the so-called books of Moses. Now there is no claim of any *facts* otherwise known to be in conflict with this narrative. But it is held by the analysts that the writers to whom they ascribe the composition are by a kind of reasoning shown to be of much later date. Some omissions and displacements are also claimed by them, and some alleged discrepancies of no formidable character. The strongest case is made by Dr. Driver when he says, "In point of fact, as some other passages show, the conquest was by no means effected with the rapidity and completeness which some of the passages quoted would imply."[2] But virtually he answers himself, inasmuch as the "other passages" repeatedly affirm that the work was not absolutely complete, and he himself states[3] that according to the writer "the war of conquest occupied about seven years." In other words, the summary statements are explained in detail. We proceed to what should be regarded as the superfluous process of indicating the trustworthiness of the book.

1. The baselessness and unreasonableness of the

---

[2] Introduction, p. 97.   [3] Ib., p. 96.

theory that its events were not put in writing till from three to eight centuries after the death of Joshua. Such is the modern theory; although Dr. Driver, for example, drops a single brief and vague hint of "the compiler of JE utilizing older materials." But let us look at some known facts. The Israelites had come from a long residence among a people where writing had come down from the remotest antiquity, and as Erman well says, the "mania for writing (for we can designate it by no other term) is not a characteristic of the later period only," but prevailed as much under the Middle and Old Empire as under the New Empire. "Nothing was done under the Egyptian government without documents, even in the simplest matters of business."[4] Not only did the victorious monarch inscribe on the walls of his temples the detailed account of his spoils and tributes, but there was a host of scribes in each department of public life. There were inventories of property, orders on the treasury, receipts from workmen, deeds and copies of deeds. The landed proprietors had written reports, made through their stewards, of the respective numbers of their oxen, sheep, cows, asses, goats, geese, and other fowl, and even the number of eggs was ascertained and reported.[5] The Israelites under Joshua also entered a country where it is now proved that the art of writing, and with a very complicated alphabet, had existed before their entrance.

---

4 Life in Ancient Egypt, p. 112-3.
5 Wilkinson's The Ancient Egyptians, II., 445-9.

The Tell Amarna letters to Amenophis IV. of Egypt, written in the wedge-shaped characters of Babylonia, come from Beirut, Sidon, Tyre, and the neighboring cities; also from Accho, Hazor, Joppa, Ascalon, Makkedah, Lachish, Jerusalem, and other cities not so definitely known.

Indeed, there is in the earlier name of Debir, which "before was Kirjath-sepher" (Josh. xv. 15; Judg. i., ii.), an apparent intimation of the art of writing in Palestine prior to the entrance of Joshua. "Book-town" is the literal meaning of the name as given by the lexicographers Gesenius and Fuerst; "city of scribes," as rendered by the Septuagint; "archive-town" in the Targum. The Vatican copy of the Septuagint reads "sophar" instead of "sepher," conforming to the rendering "scribe-town." The name is found by W. M. Mueller also in an Egyptian papyrus.[6]

Now, to suppose that the great minister and successor of Moses, a man born and trained to organize and command, coming from a land where writing was a "mania" to another land where it pervaded the whole region, going through a long series of eventful transactions, having solemn communications to make to a fickle nation, and boundary lines carefully and permanently to assign and define for watchful if not jealous tribes—to suppose that such a man under such circumstances and influences remained there twenty-five years, till his death, and never made the slightest provision to put anything

---

6 Cited by Prof. Moore, Comm. on Judges, p. 27.

on record, is hardly to be called incredulity; it is rather phenomenal credulity. Nothing, therefore, could be more natural than for Joshua to speak of "all that is written" in the book of the law (i. 8), to write upon the stones at Shechem (viii. 32), as was so abundantly done in Egypt, a copy of the law, more or less, and in the last and still more solemn covenant with the people before his death to write the "statute and ordinance" "in the book of the law of God"; and it is quite unnecessary for the analysts to assign the first two passages to a supposed writer some six hundred years later, and to single out the one sentence in the last instance for the still later and more vague personage, the redactor, as they have done.

2. Marks of proximity of date to the events, and of participation in them. These are the more satisfactory because incidental and unobtrusive. One of them occurs in the opening chapter (verses 10, 11), indicating recent contact with Egypt, where, as Erman remarks, "a scribe was an official, and the scribe of the troops was one of the chief officers." The "officers" whom Joshua sent through hosts with commands, were literally writers or scribes, as the word is rendered in the Septuagint.[7] The waters of the Jordan were dried up (v. 1) "till *we were passed over*";[8] and the land they were to

---

[7] In this part of the narrative, Kautzsch, who assigns it to E, would extinguish the reminiscence by having Dt. modify this one verse. Oettli changes it.

[8] This is the reading of the Hebrew text. The Massoretes put "they" in the margin, the reading of the lxx., followed by early translations. The R. V. retains the reading of the text. So does Dillmann, though treating it as spoken communicatively, the writer identifying himself with the people.

enter was the land "which the Lord sware that he would give unto us" (verse 6). The designation of the boundaries of Judah is addressed directly to them; "this shall be your south coast" (xv. 4). It is the language of contemporaneousness with reference to the transactions themselves.

In some cases the proximity of the narrative to the event, and thus its authenticity, are indicated (whether by the author or his annotator) by certain monuments remaining "to this day"; the twelve stones commemorating the crossing of the Jordan (iv. 9), the stones at the cave where the five kings were buried (x. 27), those over the grave of the king of Ai (viii. 29), and also over Achan. The valleys of Achor (vii. 26), and of Gilgal (v. 9), were named from the events that took place at the time, as was the change of Leshem to Dan by the conquering tribe (xix. 47). Whatever date may be assigned to "this day," the existence of the memorial at that date was a voucher for the fact which it commemorated. But in one noteworthy instance the name of the place as known then completely disappeared from that time; Sharahen is mentioned by Thothmes III. as a city of southern Palestine; and a city of the same name is among those assigned by Joshua in the same region to the tribe of Simeon. But the name occurs nowhere in the Old Testament except in this book of Joshua (xix. 6). If the same place was intended by Shilhim (xv. 32), and by Shaaraim (1 Chron. iv. 31), the variation and uncertainty would show still more effectively the antiquity and obsoleteness of the name.

3. The life-like minuteness of much of the narrative marks its original and contemporaneous origin. Thus the account of the spies is not only minute but peculiar in its details: the place of resort, with its unusual location, affording unnoticed access and easy escape; the inquiry and the false reply; the singular concealment; the chase five or six miles to the fords while they are hiding three days in some one of the innumerable caves of the mountains close by, before the shutting of the gate at night-fall; the device for the harlot's protection; the conversation, with its phrase not found elsewhere ("this line of scarlet thread"); the stalks of flax also elsewhere unmentioned, and puzzling to some of the commentators; the panic disclosed in Jericho; the oath and its conditions; the descent by a rope from a window and the binding of the cord in the window—in all this, however it comes to us, we have clearly the very story of the spies themselves.[9]

The account of the crossing of the Jordan, though not constructed on the method of modern composition (and ascribed by Kautzsch to six different writers in twelve distinct portions), is much more circumstantial and complete, and on the whole more easily understood than Cæsar's account of his crossing of the Rhine; the capture of Jericho, and espe-

---

9 It is an interesting fact that in the summer of 1894 the explorer, Mr. F. J. Bliss, found at Tell es Sultan, universally recognized as occupying the site of pre-Israelitish Jericho, traces of a mud-brick wall at the base of the mound, and in it specimens of Amorite or pre-Israelitish pottery, like that found in the oldest stratum at Tell el Hesy. (Quarterly Statement of Palestine Exploration Fund, July, 1894.)

cially the warlike movements attending the conquest of Ai, are given much more vividly and minutely than the account of the first invasion of Britain; while at Ai we can easily fix on a place for the "ambush" and find room for the military operations, whether we locate the ancient Ai exactly at Et Tell (with Grove, Thomson, and others), or at some spot in the vicinity. There is also a touch of our recently acquired oriental history in the "Babylonish garment," or mantle, secreted by Achan.

How can any one take that entire account of the stratagem of the Gibeonites and its issues as other than a living picture? And the battle in their defense afterwards, which Stanley characterizes as one of the most important in the history of the world, is described succinctly and with the minuteness of a personal participation: the assembly of the five hostile kings designated by name and place, the pressing message from Gibeon, Joshua "ascending" from Gilgal up one of the two wadies, the all-night march (some twenty miles), and coming upon them "suddenly," the slaughter on the spot, the chase up and down to Beth-horon, to Azekah (Tell Zakariah) and Makkedah (El Mughar), the caves, the hiding of the kings in the cave, the guarding of the cave till the end of the chase, the production, humiliation and execution of the kings, the taking down of their bodies at sunset, the entombment, and the great stones laid at the cave's mouth.

With greater brevity, but with equal definiteness and exactness of local correspondence, is the other and greater battle at the north described (xi. 1-14): the vast gathering of designated tribes and kings at the waters of Merom, that is, on the broad plain of Huleh (four miles wide on its western side), where the "horses and chariots" could be brought into action, Joshua again coming suddenly upon them and chasing them towards their several territories —towards great Sidon northwest through plain, gorge, and ford, towards Misrephoth (perhaps Musheirifeh),[10] near the coast on the way to Dor, and unto the valley of Mispeh eastward, that is (as Dr. Thomson thinks), by the great Wady et Theim or over the ridge of Hermon.

The brief description of the solemn reading of the law and of the blessings and the curses at Mount Ebal and Gerizim in the valley of Shechem, shows distinctly not only the arrangement of the people, with their officers, divided in two halves with the priests before them and the ark between them, but the scene is made complete by the presence of the women, the little ones and the strangers in the audience. And while it is not necessary to suppose the two responsive groups to be upon the mountains, yet if they had been actually spread not only up the sides, but to the top, the question which has been raised as to the voice being heard at that distance has been settled by experiment. "In the early morning," says Tristram, "we could not only see from Gerizim a man driving his ass down a path on

---

[10] Grove's objection to this identification, that "it is far from Sidon," overlooks the fact that it was on a different (third) line of flight and need not be near Sidon.

Mount Ebal, but we could hear every word he uttered; and on a subsequent occasion, in order to test the matter more thoroughly, two of our party stationed themselves on opposite sides of the valley, and with perfect ease recited the commandments antiphonally."[11] Bonar and other travelers have done the same thing with the same result. The writer of "Joshua" knew what he narrated.

A noteworthy indication of the presence of Israel on the east of the Jordan, when the arrangements were made for crossing it, is found in the explanation of the phrase "beyond Jordan" in ch. i. 15. As the people were then on the east side of the river, King James's translators changed the text by wrongly rendering "this side of Jordan"; whereas the phrase was the usual geographical term for the east side of the river. To avoid any misunderstanding the writer, being on that east side and having used the term in verse 14 in its usual sense, repeats it in verse 15 with the added explanation, "toward the sunrising." In the mouth of the Gibeonites, permanent residents of Palestine (ix. 10), it needed no such explanation. But in three instances (v. 1; xii. 7; xxii. 7) the writer uses the phrase in its untechnical s nse, namely, the other side of the river from his position (as also in Deut. xi. 30), but in each instance carefully adds "westward". The twofold and unsettled usage, with explanation, indicates the presence of the new-comer.

The same fact perhaps appears in so slight a

---

[11] Tristram, The Land of Israel, p. 152.

matter as the spelling of the name Jericho. In the Pentateuch it occurs eleven times, invariably spelled in the same way; in Joshua it occurs fourteen times, as invariably spelled in a slightly different way, implying also a slightly different pronunciation. What does it signify? "The natural reply," in the words of Canon Girdlestone, "is that they picked up a new pronunciation after they came to the place."[12] All these things, greater and smaller, point to personal knowledge, contact and participation.

4. The commemoration of some of the prominent events by memorial names and landmarks, already mentioned, deserves distinct attention as a venerable and national testimony.

5. Another mark of authenticity is found in the minute and well-nigh exhaustive description of the land in the conquest, and more especially in the assignment to the tribes. It makes the reasonable impression of being the contemporaneous record of a governmental transaction, and has gained for the book of Joshua the name of the "Domesday Book" of Palestine. So full is the record that we have first the definite list of thirty-one kings or local chiefs who were conquered and dispossessed (xii. 7-24), then a statement of the regions at the time still unconquered (xiii. 1-7), followed by the assignment of their respective territories to the several tribes, with a description of their boundaries from point to point, by cities, natural landmarks, and

---
[12] Girdlestone, Lex Mosaica, p. 119. In the Pentateuch יְרִחוֹ; in Joshua יְרִיחוֹ. The Massoretes punctuate with different vowels.

main points of compass, completed by an enumeration of the towns thus included. That this was an official anticipatory allotment in Joshua's time is supported by two considerations: (1) that, as we are informed, the tribes did not then succeed in taking possession of the allotted territory, and (2) that it cannot be shown that at any subsequent period, whether in the times of the judges or kings, much less after the exile, did the several tribes actually occupy these precise territories.

But although the lines could not then be run by the surveyor's compass, the boundaries are described in a thoroughly business-like way, with the distinctness of a title deed, very different from the loose grants first made by England and France in America, and much more exact and definite than for a long time were the boundary lines of portions of the United States. In truth, owing to the smallness of the territory and the irregularity of its surface (and the lack of the compass), the reference to natural landmarks is extraordinarily abundant. One has but to read the description of Judah's territory (ch. xv. 1-12) to appreciate the fact.[13]

No less striking is the list of towns and cities. Some three hundred are mentioned by name, often "with their villages." Now by a process of careful exploration and interrogation, inaugurated mainly by Dr. Robinson and elaborated by the Palestine Exploration Fund, a large part of these places have been definitely located. Many of them were un-

---

1) See Appendix, note iv.

known to scholars for ages, often wrongly identified by mediæval or monkish traditions, but now found with the true names clinging to them as handed down in the native tongue of that country of unchanging customs, frequently disguised by phonetic changes, but recoverable on analysis, and confirmed by geographical and local facts. For it is noteworthy how largely the lists of Joshua have guided in the investigation. The author took special pains to make his description clear. Sometimes he did it by adding a second name, perhaps a newer one to the older, as in the case of Hebron, Hazor, Debir, Kirjath-jearim, Jerusalem; even more frequently by giving its situation, as Aroer, Michmethah, Geliloth, Bezer, Ataroth, Adar, "Kedesh in Galilee" (there being another in the south of Judah), and "Gilgal that is over against the ascent of Adummim, which is on the south side of the river" —there being other Gilgals.

A notable instance is that of the Gilgal of Joshua's first encampment, distinct from two or three other places of the same name, but till recently undiscovered. Even Dr. Robinson had said in 1841, "No trace of its name or site remains;" and Tristram, in 1865, "Nor does any trace remain, either in stone or tradition, of Gilgal." But in the same year it was found, and the finding has been confirmed, in the site called Jiljulieh, marked by about a dozen small mounds (some ten feet in diameter and four feet high), and a large oblong tank lined with rubble, and near it a Bedawin graveyard. It corresponds well with the requirements of the narrative, being nearly three miles from the ancient Jericho and four and a half from the Jordan."

So Debir on the border line of Judah does not appear to have been recognized since the Christian Era till within a few years; but has now been identified with Dahariyeh, situated among ancient tombs and quarries, with a valley, a short distance to the north, full of springs, some on the hill-side and some in the bed of the valley, corresponding to the "upper and nether" springs which Achsah asked and gained from her father Caleb (xv. 19).

Perhaps more interesting still was the discovery of the long-lost Gezer. It was in Joshua's time and long afterwards an important place, prominent (under the name of Gazara) also in the time of the Maccabees. It ceased to be inhabited or its site to be known, and, owing partly to an erroneous statement in the "Onomasticon," its identification had been virtually given up as a hopeless problem. But in 1870 M. Clermont-Ganneau, led by geographical and historical considerations, fixed upon Tell Jezer, about four miles W. N. W. of Amwas. On revisiting the place three years later, the sagacity of his former decision was rewarded by the discovery of three inscriptions, "boundary of Gezer," in Hebrew letters, supposed by him to belong to the second century B. C. There was also discovered there about the same time a rude terra cotta

---
14 Conder regards "the recovery of Gilgal as one of the most important successes of the Survey work." (Tent Work, ii, p. 6.) It is accepted by Grove and Wilson. Clermont-Ganneau casts some doubt on it. (Archæological Researches, 1896, p. 37.)

female figure, which from its characteristics he inclines to regard as a possible sample of Canaanite art.[15]

An incidental and therefore significant mark of the early date of the enumeration is the retention of the (Hebrew) article in connection with many of the local names derived from natural objects. Thus in Josh. xviii. 12-27 there are seven such instances, such as the Ramah (height), but simply Ramah in Neh. xi. 33, Jer. xxxi. 15; and the Chephirah (village), but Chephirah in Ezek. ii. 25 and Neh. vii. 29. So also in the case of Mizpeh.[16] It is like the change in the New Testament from the descriptive term "the Christ" of the gospels to the proper name "Christ" of the epistles. It is a point too minute for recognition in the Revised Version, but none the less noteworthy on that account.

We mention in this connection but one other incidental mark of antiquity, namely, the allusions to Tyre and Sidon, and the relative prominence of the latter city. Tyre is once mentioned, merely as a fenced city (R.V. xix. 29); the other city is twice mentioned as "great Zidon" (xi. 8; xix. 28), or, as Gesenius would have it, "Zidon the metropolis"; and the whole region in which Sidon was situated, from Misrephoth unto Lebanon, is described (xiii. 6) as that of the Zidonians. This is not only in accordance with the admitted fact that Sidon is the oldest Phenician settlement and Tyre its offspring,

---

[15] Ib., pp. 224-275.
[16] But the form Mispah, occurring elsewhere, retains the article.

but with the additional fact that for a long period it was the chief city. Thus in Homer we find it mentioned four times, and Tyre not once, except by allusion to Tyrian purple."

Now this description and distribution of territory alone occupies some six chapters, and a large part of it is ascribed by German analysts to post-exilic priests and a later compiler (redactor), part of it to the later times of the monarchy; and although some portions are referred to two writers (JE) living less than four hundred years after Joshua, they are supposed to have been so worked over that, as stated by Dr. B. W. Bacon, there has been, "in the opinion of all, such an obliteration of the characteristics of J and E by Rd, or so thorough an incorporation of them into P^2, that they are only traceable with difficulty and in a few passages." But any one who can believe that in the troublous times of the later monarchy or in the revolutionary condition after the exile any man or body of men would sit down to the wearisome task of composing these obsolete descriptions, or that in so doing they could avoid the grossest antiquarian errors as to the state of things from six hundred to a thousand years before their time, or that they could have persuaded their contemporaries that these new assignments of territory had come down to them from the days of Joshua —any one who can believe all this is endowed with a German rather than an Anglo-Saxon faith.

5. The consistency and candor of the narrative

---

[17] Iliad, vi., 289; xxiii., 743 Odyssey, xv., 418; xvii., 424.

mark its truthfulness. As an account of a remarkably skillful military campaign it is, with whatever minor difficulties attended, on the whole clear and satisfactory. It frankly recounts the errors and defeats as well as the successes of the invading host. The writer does not claim a short and easy subjugation, but a long and hard struggle, a seven years' war attended with reverses and failing of absolute completeness.

The mode of entrance was wisely planned. No attempt was made to force the way directly north from Kadesh-barnea against the "hill" strongholds (Deut. i. 43) where the Israelites had once rashly ventured, against the warning of Moses, and had been disastrously routed to Hormah (Num. iv. 40-45); but the same Hormah was taken in this campaign in the course of victory from the north (Josh. xii. 13; xv. 30; xix. 4). And it is noteworthy that this place, under its alternate name Zephath (Judg. i. 17), has apparently been found after thirty-five hundred years, with the name Sebaita still clinging to it.[18]

Instead of this fool-hardy attempt, the Israelites were led circuitously through Edom and Moab, by a course where their line of march and some of their halting places can now be traced, till they appeared unexpectedly east of the Jordan at the northern end of the Dead Sea. Here was the key of Palestine, and the entrance was by the same flank

---
[18] The map of the Palestine Exploration Fund, revised by Conder and Wilson, so recognizes it, after Palmer, Rowland, Seetzen. Strack accepts it. Dillmann thinks the location suitable, though he is doubtful about the phonetic correspondence with Zephath.

movement by which the Arabs invaded the country in the seventh century. It was a direct push for the heart of the land, cutting its tribes in two. Spies, secretly sent over the Jordan, report a panic already begun. The leader at once crosses the river, invests and captures Jericho, a walled town, where, in the deserted mound twelve hundred feet long and from fifty to ninety feet high, the mud-brick wall at the base has within the last three years yielded fragments of the most ancient type of Palestinian pottery.

It is not necessary here to discuss the method of crossing, nor the question whether, as some think, the place Adam (mentioned in connection with it) is the modern Damieh, some twenty miles above Jericho. It is perhaps worth mentioning that M. Clermont-Ganneau has brought to light a remarkable account, by the Arab chronicler Nowairi, of a complete obstruction and arrest of the flow of the Jordan, when the waters were high during the rainy month of December, A. D. 1267. He is persuaded that the account is thoroughly historical, and that it casts light on the Bible narrative. A lofty mound (kabar) on the west bank—so reads the story—was undermined, fell into the river channel and formed a dam about twenty-five miles above Damieh, which lasted several hours, the waters meanwhile spreading over the valley above the dam. This account, if authentic, having respect only to a natural occurrence without any pre-arrangement or prevision, would illustrate the Scripture account only as showing the conformation of the river bed and adjacent region to the requirements of the Scripture account. The movements of the great leader were rapid and vigorous. It was but three days from the report of the spies to the crossing of the Jordan. After the brief pause at Gilgal, Jericho was besieged and taken in seven days. Spies were sent to Ai, followed at once by an expedition which was a failure, and by another with greater forces and better tactics, which was a victory. By this rapid stroke he had gained a strategic point midway in the country, and the opportunity to strike further in either direction. It would be interesting, were it practicable, to follow his campaign in detail. The narrative, though brief, is almost as distinct an account of the making of Palestine as is Freeman's of the making of England, and explains the condition of the country as it became known in later times. But vigorous and skillful as were his movements, the writer is careful to say that Joshua "made war a long time with those kings."

For the candor of the history is as marked as is its consistency. It narrates the failures and what might be regarded as the discreditable things as frankly as the honors and the successes. The lodging of the spies at the harlot's house; the defeat in the first attack on Ai; the successful imposture of the Gibeonites, deceiving not only the princes of the congregation but Joshua himself; the murmuring of the congregation against the princes for not breaking their oath; the fraud of Achan; the inability to expel the Geshurites, the Maachathites, the inhabitants of Jerusalem and of the cities around Megiddo; the misunderstanding and threatened war between the tribes on account of the altar beyond Jordan; and that series of transactions, namely, the systematic destruction of the cities and all therein, so severely criticised and condemned by those who do not grasp the whole situation in three respects, (1) the issue at stake for all time on the destiny of Israel, (2) the deep and poisonous corruption of the native tribes, whose worship even was a compound of "blood and lust," and (3) the right of God, who gave life, to take it, whether by natural decay or catastrophe, government penalty, or, should he so choose, by direct appointment—all these things, whatever men may think of them, are there without reserve or apology. Surely one who accepts the statement of Cæsar or of Xenophon, sufficiently favorable to themselves, and refuses credence to this frank, fearless and consistent history, accounting, as it does, for the subsequent course of events, exhibits an incredulity only less surprising than the positive credulity of believing that such a minutely circumstantial narrative was gratuitously fabricated many hundreds of years after the alleged time of the transaction. It imagines a piling up of invention upon invention to an unparalleled extent and with a success equally unparalleled—a success that has imposed on the wise and great minds of the world for more than two thousand years, and that has been discredited in recent times only on speculative grounds, without the basis of one known external fact.

6. Equally indicative of reality and truth is the portraiture of Joshua himself. It shows us the natuarl development of the early promise—of the clearheaded, prompt, undaunted young man whom Moses appointed leader in the battle with Amalek (Ex. xvii. 9), who accompanied Moses up the mountain of the law-giving and at his descent (xxxii. 17), who remained in the tabernacle when Moses went to plead for rebellious Israel (xxxiii. 11), and who stood unshaken with Caleb when the other ten spies and all Israel were panic-stricken and mutinous; thus becoming the trained "minister" of Moses, and the one man endowed with the calmness, firmness, sagacity, energy and faith needed in the leader of the great and new enterprise. In its strength and symmetry, his character was as much beyond the invention of later Judaism as it was above the level of his own time. Without one word of comment, he stands out in fact not only a great leader "without fear or reproach," but a majestic presence, so controlling his countrymen by the force of his example, influence and parting counsels, that Israel served the Lord all the days of Joshua and all the days of the elders that overlived Joshua. Fact only explains the record.

7. Special confirmation comes from recently discovered ancient documents, namely, the tablet found at Tell el Hesy in Palestine and the numerous similar ones (320) found at Tell Amarna in

Egypt. The addresses of the letters fix their date in the reign of Amenophis IV., about 1480 B. C., and therefore a considerable time before Joshua's conquest. The confirmation as to the state of Palestine in general, and largely in detail, is recognized as something remarkable. Lieutenant Conder well says of them, "These letters are the most important documents ever discovered in connection with the Bible, and they most fully confirm the historical statements of the book of Joshua, and prove the antiquity of civilization in Syria and Palestine."[19]

Before specifying some of these details it may be well to say that the list of towns mentioned in the inscription of Thothmes III., as conquered by him at an earlier date (near 1600 B. C.), contains more than fifty towns in Galilee, Bashan and Philistia confidently identified with those in the book of Joshua, besides some eighteen others conjecturally recognized. The list of Thothmes is important in several respects. It proves the great antiquity of the towns; and as the same names continued in the Tell Amarna tablets a century or more later, as well as in the Biblical records, it shows the tenacity with which names of towns cling to their sites in that country. But since most of even the important towns long ago so completely disappeared as to leave only the slight ruins known in the native tongue as "tells," it shows the insurmountable peril of any late writer who should attempt to portray the conditions and events of those times.

---
[19] Tell Amarna Tablets, p. 6.

First of all, these discoveries settle—not the possibility and fact of writing in the time of Moses and Joshua, for that was settled long ago against the doubts and denials of some scholars early in this century—but they show the probability of its use by them. It had long been found that in the land from which their ancestor Abraham came, writing and libraries were abundant before his migration; also that in Egypt the Israelites had been surrounded on every hand by writing, as conspicuous in the farm records of sheep, oxen and the like as on the monuments of the kings; and quite recently that in Arabia also the arts of civilization (including that of writing) existed apparently as early as the conquest. And now it is absolutely settled that in the land to which the Israelites were journeying, the art of writing, and that in a very elaborate form, was widespread and long established. There are letters from Tennib, Gebal, Beirut, Tyre, Accho (Acre), Hazor, Joppa, Askelon, Makkedah, Lachish, Gezer, Jerusalem, and other cities not named, east and west, north and south. Among the other places mentioned in the letters are Rabbah, Keilah, Sarepta, Edrei, Ashtaroth, Gaza, Gath, Zemar, Zorah, Beth-shemesh, and others of less note, in all 130 towns. It is the Palestine of Joshua.

Again, the language of the letters is noteworthy. They are written in the cuneiform (wedge-shaped) script, thus of themselves proving what was once disputed but already settled by the monuments—the earlier influence and control of Babylonia in Palestine. But the language itself, says Conder, "is very like the Aramaic of the Talmud, and is like the Arabic in many particulars rather than like Hebrew. It is the same language, in an archaic condition, which is now spoken in Palestine."[20] Sayce also maintains that the disclosures of the letters prove that "long before the Israelitish invasion the language of Canaan was in all respects the same as that of the Old Testament,"[21]—meaning, as his illustrations show, in its fundamental character rather than in all its details. But the fact that the language, if Aramaic, was in an archaic condition, has an important bearing upon attempts at minute analysis; and assignments to certain definite constituents must be gravely affected by the possibility, if not the probability, of a revision of the whole early history having taken place, to make it intelligible in later times; if not so thorough a revision as would be necessary to make the Anglo-Saxon version of the Gospels of A. D. 955 intelligible to a reader of the present time, yet perhaps quite as much as would be requisite for Wickliffe's Gospels of 1384. The consideration will bear more emphasis than it has received.

Again, these documents disclose a condition of the tribes in Palestine such as is described in Joshua. The enemies encountered by Joshua are specified in the narrative as the Hittites, the Amorites, the Canaanites, the Perizzites, the Hivites, the Jebu-

---

20 Tell Amarna Tablets, p. 3.
21 The Higher Critics and the Monuments, p. 357.

sites. Of these the first two appear most prominent. In one instance (i. 4) the whole territory is summarily described as the land of the Hittites; the Hittites appear in every general enumeration of the tribes (iii. 10; ix. 1; xi. 3; xii. 8), and the Hittites and the Amorites usually appear first in each enumeration—in three of these instances. They are mentioned, not as occupants of only single cities, but widespread tribes; we read of "all the cities of Sihon, king of the Amorites" (xiii. 10), and of five kings of the Amorites (x. 5), and the Hittites are mentioned without any restricted locality.

Now it is but forty years since an Oxford Fellow[22] ventured to pronounce the Bible references to the Hittites "unhistorical," and still later (1883) another Oxford Fellow (now professor)[23] in the Encyclopædia Britannica said substantially the same thing. But meanwhile the records of Rameses II. have exhibited the Hittites as in his day (the supposed era of the oppression) a powerful nation on the north, with whom his battles were apparently a drawn game, and with whom he was glad to form a treaty; while, curiously enough, he speaks in the very words of Joshua (i. 3) of "the land of the Hittites" (except that he calls it "the great land"); and quite notably the Tell Amarna letters, a century earlier, speak of the "kings of the land of the Hittites" and "the land of the Amorites," these two being then the formidable foes of the then Egyptian

---

[22] F. W. Newman.   [23] T. K. Cheyne.

governors in Palestine. In the letters published by Conder mention is made of the Hittites at least twenty times, and eleven times of the land of the Hittites; and the nation appears pressing down from the north upon Palestine, the terror of all the northern cities. The Amorites are mentioned at least eleven times, and, next to the Hittites, appear to be the most formidable foe. Here also are the Canaanites, the king, and once the kings, of the land of Canaan. Six letters are from the king of Jerusalem, the city bearing then the name applied to it in Joshua (xv. 63; xvi. 28). The king of Hazor, who is described in Joshua as the "head of the kingdoms" (xviii. 10) that fought the battle of Merom, has two letters speaking of the city and "her fortresses"; and his name is rendered "Jabin" by Conder. The ancient rivalry of Tyre and Sidon is also indicated in the letters. We thus find ourselves in the midst of the tribes mentioned in our book not long subsequent to this time.

Again, these letters show the weakening power of Egypt in Palestine, and an evident tendency towards the complete withdrawal of the troops, which must have preceded the conquest by Israel. Thothmes III. had conquered Palestine, and Rameses II. had twice overrun the country and subdued its chief cities.[24] But his own inscriptions show that his hold was weakening, from the fact that he was obliged to make the second invasion, besieging its cities (e. g. Askelon), and from the fact that after

---

[24] Brugsch, History of Egypt, II., pp. 68, 69.

his boasted but doubtful victory over the Hittites on the Orontes he was constrained to make with them a treaty of alliance.[25] In view of the previous known control of the country, it might have seemed strange that Joshua never encounters Egyptian troops there. The explanation is found in these tablets: the troops had been recently withdrawn. A large part of the letters consists of urgent appeals to the king of Egypt for troops, without any indication of their arrival. Indeed one of the writers from Phenicia says, "If you grant us no Egyptian soldiers no city in the plains will be zealous for thee," and he adds, "The chain of Egyptian soldiers has quitted all the lands; they have disappeared to the king."[26] The king of Jerusalem writes in the same strain: "The Abiri chiefs plunder all the lands. Since the chiefs of the soldiers have gone away, quitting the lands this year, O king, my lord, and since there is no chief of Egyptian soldiers, there is ruin to the lands of the king, my lord."[27] The letters, says Sayce, show "that all parts of Palestine were in that disturbed condition which usually precedes the fall of the central authority. Enemies were attacking it from without, and the petty princes were fighting among themselves within." This weakened state of affairs was the condition in which Joshua found the land, and was the preparation for the success of his invasion.

---

25 Ib., II., pp. 71-76.
26 Conder's Tell Amarna Letters, p. 63.
27 Winkler's collection of 296 of these letters, most of them from Phenician and Canaanite princes, gives a still more striking exhibition of the disorder and alarm pervading the country.

It deserves mention in this connection also that the inscriptions at Wady Maghara and Sarabit el Khadim in the Sinaitic peninsula show records of monarchs before and after the supposed time of the passage of the Israelites, but none of that date, accounting for the fact that they met no Egyptian troops on the way.

No less remarkable is the correspondence and confirmation afforded by these letters in minor details. In Joshua we read that the cities of the Anakim were "great and fenced" (xiv. 12), and that the survivors of the battle of Gibeon entered into "fenced cities" (xii. 20). Jericho and Ai were walled, and the implication is that it was so with Lachish (x. 31). In the letters we read in as many as six places of a fortress, three times of fortresses, with specifications. It was at the base of the mound of ancient Jericho (es Sultan), as previously mentioned, that Mr. Bliss in 1894 found traces of the mud-brick wall containing specimens of the most ancient pottery; and at Tell el Hesy (supposed to be Lachish) the same explorer in 1890 excavated a series of ruined walls overlying each other, and preceding the Greek occupation, apparently corresponding well to the Scripture notices of the place in the times of Manasseh, Hezekiah, Ahaz, Jehoshaphat, Rehoboam, the Judges, attended with a corresponding change of pottery, till he reached in the lower stratum that kind which is regarded as Amorite.[28]

---

28 Petrie's Tell el Hesy, p. 41. Bliss' Mound of Many Cities, pp. 40, 41.

Except on the basis of actual knowledge, it was a most unsafe thing to ascribe chariots to the people of Palestine at that remote period. But the writer of Joshua mentions them both in the north at Lake Merom (xi. 4, 6), and in the valley of Jezreel, in Beth-shan and vicinity, that is, in the center and in the eastern part of Palestine. The tablets fully verify his statements. Not only are Egyptian chariots spoken of and called for not less than a dozen times, but the Hittites are coming to Tennib with chariots; we read of chariots at Khazi, at Irkata, chariots sent to Gebal in Phenicia, the horses and chariots of the chief of Beirut, chariots at Makkedah, and the chariots and horses of the chief of Naziba. The numerous horses and chariots of the Hittites are also mentioned in connection with the battle of Rameses II. on the Orontes, as described in the poem of the Pentaur.

The wedge of gold of fifty shekels weight secreted by Achan is accounted for by the abundant Babylonish intercourse involved in the general use of the Babylonish writing; and by the frequent mention of gold in these letters, once even a throne of gold for the king (of Egypt), once a bag full of gold, as a present.

The trumpets at Jericho find an echo in the letters where the chief of Pabaha "made the trumpets to be blown." The introductory salutation in almost every letter in which the writer addresses the king of Egypt contains the phrase, "I bow myself seven times at the feet of my lord," occasionally "seven times seven times"; thus reminding us in general of the peculiarity of the number seven both in Canaan and in Egypt, and especially how a few miles east of the Jordan, and at an earlier date, Jacob had "bowed himself seven times to the ground until he came to his brother." (Gen. xiii. 3).

As Joshua found horses already in the country (xi. 6, 9), and sheep and oxen at Jericho (vi. 21), the tablets contain seven letters from Yadaya, captain of the horse at Ascalon, and the king of Naziba goes with his horses and chariots; while sheep and oxen are sent from Ascalon to meet the soldiers, and a thousand oxen belonging to Yasdata of Makkedah are slain by his enemy.[29]

As Joshua informs the tribes (xxiv. 13), "The vineyards and oliveyards which ye planted not, ye do eat," so we find the captain of the horse, in the letters, sending "oil and drink" to meet the soldiers of the king.

The low stage of civilization, or barbarism, which some modern writers choose to find prevailing in and around Palestine, is disproved by these facts, as well as the following: Ships of Sidon (p. 107), ships of the land of the Amorites (p. 46), Beirut and Sidon sending ships (p. 51), wheat, herbs and trees of the garden at Gebal (p. 80), gardens and mulberries at Beirut (p. 98), tin at Tennib (p. 31) and a chain of bronze (p. 42), copper and agate at Tyre (p. 106), silver that is pure (p. 154), plenty of silver and gold in the temple of the gods (p. 92), male

---

[29] It was not thought best to encumber the text or the notes with the pages of these references, although contained in the author's manuscript.

and female slaves (p. 90), even the cultivation of the papyrus (p. 90), and apparently its use for writing (p. 126). The degradation was in morals.

The phraseology of the tablets occasionally and unexpectedly illustrates that of the Scriptures. The word Elohim (God), which in Joshua, as throughout the Old Testament, is a plural with a singular meaning, is found as a plural in addressing the king of Egypt as "a god and a sun in my sight" (p. 18). The writer's "countenance is towards the servants of the king" (p. 35), he is "the footstool at the feet of the king," his enemy is a "dog" (p. 65), and sometimes "the rebel son of a dog" (p. 34); and it is quite striking to find the phrase with which Shimei cursed David, "Thou man of blood" (2 Sam. xvi. 7), occurring more than a dozen times in these letters. Other instances might be mentioned, as, for example, the name of Abimelec at Tyre.

8. A memorable event, significant alike for the history of Egypt and of Palestine, was the burial of Joseph, thus recorded (xxiv. 32): "And the bones of Joseph, which the children of Israel brought up out of Egypt, buried they in Shechem in a parcel of ground which Jacob bought of Hamor the father of Shechem for a hundred pieces of silver; and it became the inheritance of the children of Joseph."[30]

This statement is confirmed as strongly as the cir-

---

[30] We do not care to include in these references Conder's name, Adonizebek, for the king of Jerusalem, inasmuch as Dr. Winkler and Dr. Sayce render otherwise. Nor can we, for a similar reason, accept the translation of "Habiri" as Hebrew (with Conder) or Confederates (with Sayce); nor is the rendering of Sayce, "without father or mother" (as applied to the king of Jerusalem), sufficiently established.

cumstances admit by both Palestinian and Egyptian sources. In that land where names cling to places, the supposed tomb of Joseph is still revered by Jews, Samaritans, Mohammedans and Christians. Although we can trace this tradition only to the early part of the fourth century, intrinsically there is no more reason for supposing that the burial place of Joseph would have been forgotten than that of Charlemagne, who was buried at Aix-la-Chapelle more than a thousand years ago. The destruction of the original chapel which Charlemagne built for his burial place did not obliterate the memory of it, and the exploration of the vault beneath the present cathedral proved the truth of the belief; but though fear of the population of Nablous is said to have prevented a similar examination of the tomb of Joseph, it would be difficult to render a valid reason for doubting the ancient tradition.[31]

But recently a corroboration has been acutely observed in an Egyptian source. It is found in the well-known statements preserved by Josephus from the great Egyptian historian Manetho (about 300 B. C.) and the later Chaeremon, who, though a Greek, lived and wrote in Alexandria. Although these accounts are confused and contain many manifest mistakes as to names, dates and numbers (some of them attributed to errors and corrections by scribes), it is conceded by sober judges, like Koenig, Brugsch, Bunsen, and Ewald,[32] that Manetho was a

---

[31] Tristram's Land of Israel, p. 149.
[32] Koenig, History of the Hebrews, Eng. Trans., pp. 257-9. Brugsch, History of Egypt, Vol. I., pp. 42-3. Bunsen's Egypt's Place, I., 89; III., 196-7. Ewald's History of Israel, I., p. 502 ff.

learned and able historian, and under his account of the Jews and their exit there was, in the words of Koenig, "a core of historical truth" with Egyptian coloring. Now from the midst of statements not concerning the present question there emerges the following: that the mixed multitude (described by him as leprous) made war upon the king of Egypt, having chosen as their ruler a priest of Heliopolis (On) whose name was Osarsiph; that the king at first retreated before them, but afterwards conquered them and drove them to Syria; and that Osarsiph changed his name and was called Moses. Chaeremon (also quoted by Josephus) mentions Joseph and Moses as scribes who led an assault upon the Egyptian king; he fled before the attack, but his son, born at the time, when grown to man's estate pursued the Jews into Syria.

Now here, in this partially disguised form, appears the extraordinary and unforgotten fact that when Moses led Israel up out of Egypt to Palestine, the other great leader and head of Israel in Egypt went up with Moses to his last resting-place in the promised land—the dead with the living.

9. The chief events related in the book of Joshua are referred to in the subsequent books of the Old Testament as unquestionable facts in the history of the times of Joshua. The five most striking single transactions there narrated are the crossing of the Jordan, the taking of Jericho, the trouble with Achan and its effects, the dealings with the Gibeonites, and the Divine interposition at Beth-horon,

described by a quotation from the book of Jasher. The crossing of the Jordan is referred to in Psalm cxiv. 3, 5; the doom of Jericho as pronounced by Joshua, in 1 Kings xvi. 34; the case of Achan was commemorated in the name then given to the valley of Achor, which became permanent (Hosea ii. 15; Is. lxv. 10), and the words of Joshua are virtually cited (1 Kings xviii. 17, 18); the treaty with the Gibeonites, accompanied with an oath, is mentioned (2 Sam. xxi. 2); the quotation from Jasher in Hab. iii. 11.

In addition to these may be mentioned "the oak of the pillar that was in Shechem" (Judg. ix. 6, R. V.), a reference to the pillar set up under an oak in Shechem in connection with his farewell address and the covenant made with Israel (Josh. xxiv. 20). Solomon's prayer (1 Kings viii. 56, 57) contains a quotation from Josh. xxiii. 14, and a statement in the words of Josh. i. 5; and a vital incorporation of a chief transaction recorded in this book into the permanent life of the nation is found in the fact contained in the genealogical table of Matthew (i. 5), that Rahab[33] became mother of Boaz, the husband of Ruth, and thus the ancestress of Christ. These verifications thus pervading the subsequent history of the nation are all the more satisfactory that they are casual and incidental; and they are the more striking, as allusions to a narrative of only twenty-

---

[33] "The Rahab" in Matthew designating, as Bengel remarks, the Rahab of Jericho. Though some objections have been raised, such writers as Meyer, Alford, Lord Hervey, agree that no other Rahab can be understood here. And the validity of the record would be evident from the fact that nothing but its admitted truth would admit the name into the ancestry of David against Jewish pride and prejudice.

four chapters and their contents, when we observe the common absence of such allusions and confirmations in connection with many other thoroughly accepted writings and persons and events. For example, the great history of Thucydides, it is stated, is not mentioned by Xenophon nor in Aristotle's Politics, nor indeed till Polybius, between two and three hundred years later;[34] Thucydides himself nowhere mentions his contemporary Socrates; and "neither Herodotus nor Thucydides ever mentions Rome, though the conquests of the Roman people were, in the times of those historians, extended far and wide."[35]

In view, then, of all these considerations, negative and positive, inasmuch as on the negative side not one known historic fact has been or can be adduced to invalidate this history, and, on the positive side, the convergence of all these various indications—all the indications and confirmations which the case admits—it is hardly too much to say that one who refuses to accept the narrative as veritable history in all its main features, is hardly susceptible to fair historic proof of remote events.

---
[34] Waco, The Inspiration of the Old Testament, Preface, p. xviii.
[35] Gregory's Evidences of Christianity, p. 220.

CHAPTER III

FROM THE EXODUS TO THE CONQUEST

Having found that the book of Joshua is essentially a narrative of facts, it is in order to examine its testimony upon the transactions preceding the conquest. We find here that from beginning to end its statements and allusions are inseparably interlocked with the previous history.

The testimony thus given is by incidental and natural allusion, and therefore of special weight, and is a résumé of the chief events of the previous history. It is found mostly in scattered references, except when Joshua near the close of his career (xxiv.) prefaces the solemn covenant of the people with a brief sketch of the past dealings of God with them and their ancestors. Beginning with the mention of the original home of their ancestor, Abraham, and the idolatry of their fathers, he proceeds with the call of Abraham, the journey to Canaan, the birth of Isaac, Jacob and Esau, Jacob's descent into Egypt, the plagues, the leadership of Moses and Aaron, the pursuit by the Egyptians and their destruction in the Red Sea, the long season in the wilderness, the conflict with the Amorites and the victory, the war with Moab and the career of Balaam, closing with the crossing of the Jordan and the possession of the land. All this is the fitting introduction to the solemn covenant and the warning in regard to the future.

But besides this connected retrospect, there are scattered throughout the book, and interwoven with it from beginning to end, still more numerous and minute references to previous history. They occur not chiefly as formal statements, but more in the conferences and addresses, as matters mostly of recent occurrence, assumed to be well-known and unquestioned. All is done with such an air of honesty and perfect reality that one who impugns their verity must ascribe to some unknown deceiver a marvelous mania and ingenuity for fabrication, and an equally marvelous patience of needless invention.

Among these assumed and asserted facts are such as these: The assignment of the territorial boundaries by Moses (i. 3, 4); the giving of the law by him (i. 7), in a written form (i. 8; viii. 34); the passage of the Red Sea (iv. 23); the conquest of Sihon and Og (ii. 10; ix. 10); the iniquity of Peor (xxii. 17); the ark of the covenant and the attendance of the priests (iii. 3, seq.); the established arrangement of elders (vii. 6; viii. 10, 33); Moses' written command to build an altar (viii. 31); the blessings and curses and the command of Moses to read them to Israel (viii. 33-35); his command to destroy the inhabitants of Canaan (ix. 24; xi. 12); the commands specially given to Joshua (xi. 15); the previous separation of the tribe of Levi (xiii. 33; xviii. 7); the command of the Lord to distribute the land to the tribes by lot (xiv. 1, 2); the spies sent from Kadesh-barnea, their cowardice, the faithfulness of Caleb and the promise made to him by Moses (xiv. 6-10); the direction to appoint cities of refuge (xx. 1), and cities for the priests (xxi. 2).

It will be perceived that the book of Joshua thus repeats and verifies the chief facts of the Exodus, as more fully narrated in the Pentateuch. Let us then look directly at the narrative of that event, in order to see how far it bears the impress of truth, both in its inherent consistency, and in its conformity to known facts and circumstances, many of them of recent discovery.

It is evident that the man who by all traditions, Egyptian, Hebrew and classic, led the movement, was a remarkable man. The indisputable proof is that he founded institutions and consolidated a people more thoroughly and permanently than any other man in all history. This cannot be gainsaid.

The leader knew the route over which he led the host; for, according to the account, he had twice been over a large part of it, going to and from Midian; and in the forty years' interval he certainly had opportunity to explore or learn of the whole territory of the wandering, now traversed by Arabs. Furthermore, on leaving Sinai by a route which he might not have traversed on his way between Egypt and Midian, we find him urgently requesting Hobab, a resident Midianite, to be to him "instead of eyes" in the wilderness before him (Num. x. 31), and the ark, apparently accompanied by Moses himself, preceded the march to search out a resting place or camping ground.

Again, it is made clear by incidental hints and allusions that the whole expedition was maturely arranged and completely organized. Neither the ordinary reader nor, apparently, the ordinary commentator has sufficiently observed the long and careful preparation. Moses was summoned to it while still in Midian, and therefore had opportunity in returning to Egypt to examine the route which he afterwards took. On the way he opened the matter to Aaron, and, on his arrival in Egypt, to the elders. Moses and Aaron visited Pharaoh, requesting permission to go to the wilderness to sacrifice, and were refused. Then the officers remonstrated with Pharaoh for the severity of their tasks. Moses and Aaron appear again to have visited the king in vain (Ex. vi. 13). The length of these negotiations does not appear, but must have consumed some time. Then came the series of plagues, the first of which continued seven days; and the entire series, with the intervals, as has been inferred from casual indications, such as the slight touches of reality concerning the barley, flax, wheat and rye (Ex. ix. 31, 32), and ending with the full moon of the month Nisan, must have occupied several months, perhaps nearly a year.[1]

The immediate notice for the departure, which followed on the fourteenth of the month, was given before the tenth of the month (Ex. xii. 3). The

---
[1] See note vi., Appendix.

only mark of haste was at the last moment, when Pharaoh's urgency hurried them forth before the bread was leavened (xii. 34). But they seem to have had time then or before to *ask* (Hebrew and R. V., not "borrow") "jewels of silver and jewels of gold and raiment," gladly given (ver. 36), to hasten their departure, and justly due them for all the stationary property left behind, to say nothing of their unrequited toil.

It appears, also, that they did not go forth as a disorderly crowd, but with orderly arrangement (Ex. xiii. 18),[2] "all their hosts" (xii. 41), "by their hosts" (xii. 51). We are even told the names of the men who were "over the hosts" of the several tribes as they moved onward from Sinai (Num. x. 14-28). This division would have enabled the great company to spread, if necessary, over a wide territory on the way, as Sherman on his march to the sea separated his army into divisions moving on somewhat parallel lines. They took with them their flocks and herds, needful for sustenance, but apparently reduced on the way. It is to be noted that the ark with its attendants could and sometimes did proceed by itself.

The reason for the abandonment of the direct northern route is given, namely, the prospect of a war with the Philistines in their southern strongholds, an obstacle which the rash people afterwards found to be insuperable (Num. xiv. 40-45). The

---

[2] See note vii., Appendix.

change of direction and abrupt turn to the south,³ when they had already reached the edge of the wilderness, gave Pharaoh's army opportunity to overtake them before they had left his territory.

Equally in accordance with known facts and circumstances was the line of march, so far as it can be traced. Their original territory in Egypt is conceded to have comprised the wady Tumilat, and probably, as their numbers increased, the eastern part of the Delta from the Tanitic branch of the Nile to the desert and the Red Sea, corresponding somewhat to the modern province of Sharkieh. The first rendezvous was Rameses, and the next station Succoth. The line of march was thus at first along this valley Tumilat, through which in the time of Seti I., and before the Exodus, there ran, as now, a sweet water canal, thus facilitating and explaining the movement. For by the excavations of Naville in 1883 inscriptions were found at Tell el Maskutah, which prove that place to be the site of the ancient Pithom (of which more hereafter),⁴ and the region in which it lies to be Succoth, some ten miles west of Lake Timseh in an air line. The identification is now generally accepted by Egyptologists. Rameses is not yet known, but by M. Naville is conjecturally found at Saft el Henneh,⁵ about twenty-five miles further west; although it is generally understood that the name represented a

---
3 The stronger rendering, "turn back," of the R. V., with Dillmann and Strack, is undoubtedly better than the "turn" of the A. V., though supported by Knobel and DeWette.
4 Naville's The Store-city of Pithom, Egypt Exploration Fund.
5 Naville's Goshen and the Shrine of Saft el Henneh, Egypt Exploration Fund.

region as well as a town, while the rendezvous of such a host could hardly have been confined to a single city. There is nothing to determine exactly the next station, Etham, on the edge of the wilderness. The line of the modern Suez Canal would in general mark the edge of the desert, and the course was eastward and perhaps somewhat northerly on the great traveled route to Palestine. But here they were directed to "turn back" (or about) and encamp between Migdol and the sea, that is, west of the Red Sea. The abrupt turn to the south, and the delay thus caused, gave time for the news to reach Pharaoh and for him to overtake them (xiv. 5).

Pharaoh's equipment with chariots for the pursuit rests on a sure historic basis. For in the poem of the Pentaur, celebrating the exploits of Rameses II., the more commonly supposed monarch of the oppression, his chariots and charioteers are mentioned a dozen times;[6] and the monuments show both him and his son in their chariots.[7] Even the number of the chariots, "six hundred," is less than a fourth part of the number of chariots which the same poem asserts to have been encountered by him in the great battle with the Hittites on the Orontes, namely "twenty-five hundred," and "as numerous as the sand."[8] If these numbers of the poet be regarded as an exaggeration, the statement still goes to

---

6 Brugsch, History of Egypt, II., p. 56 seq.

7 Erman, Life in Ancient Egypt, p. 492. Wilkinson's Ancient Egyptians (Birch's ed.), III., p. 224.

8 Brugsch, II., pp. 56, 59, 60.

show that the chariot force of the times was a strong arm of war.

From the halt on the edge of the wilderness the march was southward to the place of crossing. Here the correspondence of the narrative to the localities is such that at least three different places have been selected by judicious observers as feasible and as conforming more or less closely to the requirements of the narrative. The difficulty of deciding absolutely between them arises from the difficulty of identifying with certainty the localities specified, Pi-hahiroth, Migdol, Baal-zephon; and that difficulty arises largely from the fact that on the eastern and desert border of Egypt there has not been any continuous occupancy and settlement from ancient times, as in Palestine, to hand down the names in unbroken succession. The three points suggested are these: One south of Lake Timsah near Serapeum, advocated by Naville, Ebers, Poole, de Lesseps and others; the one advocated by Dr. Dawson and others, between the Bitter Lakes and the Gulf of Suez, not far from Geneffe at the terrace of Chaloof; and that maintained by Robinson and held until recently by many, if not most, scholars, which finds it near Suez.[9] The theory of a northern passage, not through the Red Sea, but by the Serbonian Bog, advocated by Schleiden and Brugsch (for a time), was extinguished by the discovery of Pithom.

It is not necessary for the present purpose to dis-

---
9 See note viii., Appendix.

cuss the respective merits of these different views, inasmuch as each of them claims to furnish an explanation of the transaction. Since, however, the first two views assume that the Gulf of Suez extended then continuously to Lake Timsah, whereas at the terrace of Chaloof the land rises twenty-seven feet above the sea level, and thirty feet at Serapeum, and these views suppose a different state of things from the present, namely an elevation of these localities since the exodus, and thus rest on a basis of speculation, however weighty the opinion, we will simply show how the crossing at Suez would accord with the facts of the present situation.

It is not important to insist upon the identification, proposed formerly by many scholars, of Pi-hahiroth (or Hahiroth, Numbers xxxiii. 8) with Ajroud, four hours northwest of Suez, where there is a plain, a deep well (though of bitter water) and a fortress; nor of Migdol with Bir Suweis, two miles from Suez, where are now two wells of brackish water and a stone building of the seventh century; nor of Baal-zephon with Jebel Atakah, although a mountain 3,200 feet in height is a conspicuous landmark. Still it is a fact that whereas the Israelites were to encamp before Baal-zephon by the sea, here is a large plain for encampment, about ten by eleven miles in extent, having the sea or gulf on the east, and Jebel Atakah obstructing the march southward. In the gulf at this point are (or were before the dredging of it for the Suez Canal) two fords, one north of Suez, the other just south of it, both passable at low tide, and now also, except where the canal channel has to be crossed by boats. The northern one was where Napoleon crossed in 1799, and would have been drowned on his return but for his presence of mind; where Russeger, Niebuhr's guides, and Tischendorf's Arabs crossed. The southern one always has been accounted safer. Extensive shoals extend far out in a southeasterly direction, and a long, narrow sand-bank reaches towards them from the eastern shore, leaving at low tide a small channel some 780 feet wide and from three and a half to five and a half feet deep. But at high tide the width is about three miles,[10] and the elaborate map of the Suez Canal Company gives the difference between the highest and lowest known seas as *ten feet and seven inches*. Here are the conditions for the safe crossing of the Israelites and the drowning of the Egyptians.[11] The statement of the Scripture narrative that the Lord "caused the sea to go back by a strong east wind all night" conforms to the fact mentioned by the travelers Wellsted, Schubert and Tischendorf, namely, the great effect produced on the height of the waters by a long-continued northeast or southeast wind in connection with the tide. Now as the gulf was made "dry land" by the all-night blowing of the "east (or northeast) wind," so also when the Israelites "saw the Egyptians dead upon the sea-

---

[10] These figures were given to the author by M. Mauriac, engineer of the Suez Canal.

[11] One recent writer (Professor H. A. Harper) inquires, "Why should it be thought necessary that Pharaoh and his host descended a 'steep bank into a fearful chasm?'" If he had visited the spot, he would have seen no steep bank nor fearful chasm.

shore," that is, the eastern shore, where they then were, we have a casual hint of a change in the direction of the wind which had forced the waters back and lined the eastern shore with the dead. A variation of less than ten feet and seven inches would explain the transaction as described in the narrative.

Dr. Robinson makes a computation[12] to show the feasibility of the passage of two millions, moving at the rate of only two miles an hour, within the allotted time: a dry space of half a mile or more would admit a thousand persons abreast, and a column two thousand in depth, two miles or more from front to rear; this would require an hour for the entire column to enter the channel, and two hours more to move over the distance of three or four miles, or an hour and a half for the present distance of three miles, making, on this last supposition, two hours and a half in all. It may be added that if, on account of the flocks and herds, we suppose the time to be doubled, the interval between sunset and sunrise in April, being about twelve hours, would still allow ample time for the safe passage of Israel, and, when the waters were driven back in full volume, for the destruction of the pursuing host. It would undoubtedly be a difficult movement to arrange and execute with such a great company as the Israelites, but a Moses or a Napoleon would be capable of effecting it. The circumstances conform to the narrative; and similar rea-

---
[12] Biblical Researches, I., p. 84.

soning would apply if the event took place at either of the other places advocated, under the state of things supposed. "Whatever may have been the exact course of this event," says Ewald, "its historical certainty is well established."[13] The remarkable event is celebrated in two commemoration odes, as they may be called, the song of Moses and the song of Miriam; in regard to the second of which Dillmann, though considering the first in its present form as a subsequent expansion of a shorter song coming down from Moses' time, says there can be little doubt of the high and highest antiquity of these very lines,[14] and Kittel in his recent history remarks, "It would be groundless skepticism to maintain that the song is an artificial echo of the later legends concerning the passage of the Red Sea."[15]

After the crossing of the sea there is little liability to mistake in tracing, in the main, their journey as far as Sinai. By whatever place the sea or gulf was passed, whether at Serapeum, Chaloof or Suez, the springs now bearing the Arabic name Wells (or fountains) of Moses, a few miles southeast of Suez, could not have failed to be an important place on the march. Some of those who favor the more northerly crossing suppose them to be Elim. Here the water which flows down the sloping strata from Er Rahah is obstructed by the work of countless infusoria cementing the sand, comes to the surface in a copious spring of disagreeable taste, and can

---
13 Geschichte, I., p. 109.
14 Comment *in loco*.
15 History of the Hebrews (translation), I., p. 226.

be reached along a considerable distance by digging. The present writer noticed eight wells of various depths, and another traveler counted nineteen. Also about four miles north is another very considerable fountain, Ain Naba, though also of brackish water. The Wells of Moses were important as a water supply for Suez before the construction of the sweet water canal, and in conjunction with the other fountain must have been equally important to the Israelite host.[16] From this point the line of march is for a long distance unmistakable, since it must lie between the sea on the west and the high, unbroken and impassable range of Er Rahah, eight or ten miles to the east.

It is doubtful whether, with Robinson and others, we should identify the bitter fountain of Marah with the present Ain Hawwarah, although this is a very brackish but scanty fountain always avoided by the Arabs (says Mr. Holland), and the distance would correspond well with three days' journey of some twelve miles each, leisurely taken because free from danger and pressure. It is also true that in all that distance no water is to be found, except at Ain Berwad, six miles from the traveled route, and that a small brackish pool or fountain lying seven feet below the surface, about nine feet in diameter and two and a half feet in depth, so obscure that travelers do not know of it.[17]

---

[16] Prof. H. A. Harper finds here the bitter Marah—somewhat singularly, inasmuch as while he calls the water somewhat brackish, he mentions that formerly Suez depended chiefly for its supply of sweet water upon Ayun Musa.

[17] The writer learned of it through his Arabs, and visited it.

The next station was Elim, where were three score and ten palm trees and twelve fountains of water. This station is now almost universally recognized as Wady Gharandel, about five miles beyond Hawwarah. Here are springs which form a running stream, and at length considerable pools, frequented by wild ducks and other birds, in which also Palmer found a bathing place. Randall saw marks of freshets several feet high, as indicated on the tamarisk shrubs. Water is found here through the year, and, though varying in quality, so good that the traveler's water supply is here replenished. It was so on the journey of the present writer. He also counted in 1874 thirty palm trees and about ten old stumps, several of which showed marks of the fires kindled by the reckless Arabs, who are rapidly destroying the trees of the Sinaitic peninsula. In 1855 Bonar found more than eighty palm trees. The soil is damp among them, and apparently water could be found by digging.

They removed from Elim and encamped by the sea. This encampment is unmistakable and is therefore almost universally agreed upon. A short day's journey ending with a turn to the right, through Wady Tayibeh, the only passable road to the sea, would bring them to a sandy plain extending four or five miles along the shore, shut in by a high promontory on the north, a range of cliffs on the east, and a rocky wall approaching quite close to the shore on the south. It affords room for a great camp, and is the only place for many miles that does so.

From thence they proceeded to the wilderness of Sin, where the people became rebellious under their hardships. Next along the shore after passing the rock-wall already mentioned is the arid and heated plain of El Murkha, where on the 11th of February, 1874, the thermometer registered 96 degrees Fahrenheit.[18] If here is the wilderness of Sin, it accounts for the murmuring. It was here also that the supply of manna commenced; and here occurs (Ex. xvi. 13) the first mention of quails in the camp. Here W. H. Bartlett saw "numerous quails."[19]

Before reaching Sinai four other stations are mentioned which, with the exception of Rephidim, there are no means of identifying with confidence, although there have been conjectures. There were no permanent settlements to fix the names. It would not have been difficult for them to accomplish in those five days what the modern traveler, moving at the rate of two and three-quarter miles an hour, does in three days. Their distress for water after leaving the wilderness of Sin, requiring a special interposition to furnish it, accords with the fact that no water is to be found to-day on that route till the oasis in Feiran is reached. We will not insist on the tradition which Palmer found among the Arabs, that a certain huge rock (Hesy el Khattatin), not far from the entrance to the

---

18 This was the writer's experience.
19 Bartlett's Forty Days in the Desert, p. 40.

oasis, and surrounded by heaps of pebbles, is the scene of miraculous supply. But the oasis itself, far the finest in the peninsula, several miles in length and watered a part of the distance by a copious stream, is not only too remarkable a spot to have been neglected on the march, but the struggle for its possession would fully account for the battle with the Amalekites. One of the high hills (Tahuneh) on the north side of the western entrance of the oasis, on which the ruins of a church and of several chapels bear witness to an ancient notion of special sanctity, and which has a (late) tradition that it was the scene of Moses' prayer, would at all events be in accordance with the narrative, since it overlooks the valley. The objection that this supposed Rephidim is too far from Sinai for a day's march of the great host by the easier of two routes, is met by Professor Palmer with the suggestion that Moses and his chief elders may have taken the shorter and harder route (over Nagb Hawa), leaving the host to come by the longer and easier way.

It should also be said that when the host left the encampment (or before arriving there), it was practicable for them to divide, part of them taking the northern route by Wady Hamr, and the remainder this southern route; and that the latter allows a diversion through a part of the route by Wady Shellal; but the wagons (Num. vii. 3, 7, 8) could have been drawn only down along the coast of the sea, then up nearly at right angles through Wady Feiran.

There the way is perfectly practicable through the whole distance, as the narrative requires.[20]

According to the record about eleven months were spent at Sinai, the place of the law-giving.[21] The vicinity of Jebel Musa (the Mount of Moses) singularly corresponds to all the requirements of the narrative. The long plain of Er Rahah, two miles long and half a mile broad, slopes gradually towards the northern peak, Sufsafeh, yielding space enough for two million persons,[22] each having a square yard to stand upon in sight of the mountain, besides additional room in the side valleys, Leja and Ed Deir. The mountain rises abruptly like a wall from the foot of this plain, so that it "might be touched" (Heb. xii. 18), and bounds could be "set about" it (Ex. xix. 23). The water supply for the encampment is also noticeable, there being running streams in four of the neighboring valleys, one of them near the very foot of Sufsafeh, into which the relics of the golden calf could have been cast; not to mention some five wells now existing, indicating the abundance of water in the vicinity. In the neighboring valleys (e. g. Mukalifeh and Nukhf) vegetation is still to be found,[23] which there

---

[20] These several routes were explored by the writer, the northern, the southern with its divisions, besides following Wady Hibrau, which some have suggested without good reason. At the entrance of Wady Feiran from the coast he had the surprise of seeing the tracks of a wagon, probably on the way to Tor.

[21] See note ix., Appendix.

[22] By actual measurements by Capt. Palmer of the Ordnance Survey, Palmer's Desert of the Exodus, p. 117.

[23] The writer saw a large flock of goats in Wady Sebaijeh. In Wady Nukhf, three hours distant, and about five miles long and between one and two miles broad where we crossed it—there was there, as estimated by one of the company, who was a farmer's son, vegetation enough for a thousand

is good reason to believe may have been more abundant for the cattle then than for the flocks of the Arabs now. A remarkable correspondence is found here to the statement that as Moses descended from the mountain he heard the noise of the shouting worshipers of the golden calf before seeing them (Ex. xiii. 18). Now there is a steep, almost perpendicular, descent on the north side through the ravine of Sikket Shoeib, where the traveler is so shut in that he can hear the sound from a camp at the traditional "Hill of Aaron" some time before he comes in sight of it. Professor Palmer mentions having frequently had this experience.[24]

Beyond Sinai, by reason of the loss of names in an uninhabited region, and the absence of specified landmarks, the station before reaching Kadesh-barnea cannot be confidently located. Kadesh-barnea is now generally considered to be at Ain Gadiz, as discovered by Rowland and Williams, partly verified by Palmer, and confirmed by H. C. Trumbull, though still requiring more deliberate examination and more exact description.[25] A general correspondence even here, at least as to the distances traveled, can be indicated. Whereas in Deut. i. 2 we read that "there are eleven days' journey from Horeb by way of Mount Seir unto Kadesh-barnea," Professor Palmer thinks that this notice

---

cattle three months. (From Egypt to Palestine, pp. 285, 286.) We also saw goats among the rocks, as it seemed, though really in small wadies, before reaching Sinai.

[24] The author descended through the ravine, but his camp was at a distance, near the Convent.

[25] See Appendix, note x.

in connection with other indications "brings us into the region of absolute certainty," inasmuch as a comparison of the list of stations given in Numbers xxxiii., and the hints in regard to it, together with the places and distances of the Peutinger tables, will show very closely that number of moderate days' marches. Whether or not his suggested identifications are valid, the general correspondence is sufficient for our purpose.[26]

From Kadesh-barnea the rebellious portion of the host made their ill-fated expedition to the hill region and were routed unto Zephath or Hormah, which may perhaps be found in Sebaita (though not certainly), where are now extensive ruins, and about three miles and a half to the north traces of a ruined fort on a hill El Meshrifeh.

From this time, as has been suggested by several writers, we may reasonably suppose the people have to spread themselves out over the more fertile portions of the peninsula, and more especially the southern parts of the Negeb or south country, and wherever the modern Arabs find their livelihood. One thing, however, is conspicuously noticeable and consistent, that although interpositions for the supply of water are mentioned but in a few instances, the food supply of the manna was constant to the end. For while it is evident to every intelligent observer that the fertility of the Sinaitic peninsula has been and is continually diminished through the wanton destruction of its trees by the modern Arabs,

---
[26] See note xi., Appendix.

all the more rapidly since the construction of the modern canal and railway has furnished a market for their charcoal,[27] it is equally evident that no large body of people could be wholly supplied with food for any great length of time by the natural resources of the country; and it must be frankly said that the supernatural interposition is indispensable to the history. But water is found not only at intervals in the peninsula, but in numerous places around the edges of the desert of Et Tih,[28] and in the south country, besides the pools that remain or may be created in the wadies after the rains, and possible reservoirs and wells, as now at Nakhl in the heart of the desert. In these regions the Arabs of seven tribes now sustain their sheep, goats and camels.

In the final departure from Kadesh, which appears to have been their headquarters, their march was not directly north through the strongholds of the Amorite country, but by way of the Red Sea, east of the Arabah (or Ghor), through Edom and Moab. Here, after passing Jebel Harun (Mount Aaron), 4,000 feet high, and held sacred by the native as the supposed scene of Aaron's death, we confidently strike their line of march at Ar (now Rabba) of Moab, Aroer (Arair), Dibon (Diban), Heshbon (Hesban), not to mention conjectural sites. This part of the way would undoubtedly correspond to what is now the great caravan route from Da-

---

[27] It is a common experience of travelers, as of the author, to encounter companies of Arabs, their camels loaded with charcoal.

[28] Nearly thirty places can be specified on or around this desert where water can be found, in springs, streams, pools, wells, or just beneath the surface. See Bartlett's From Egypt to Palestine, p. 318 seq.

mascus to Mecca. From the commanding peak above Ain Minyeh, Balaam could see "Israel dwelling according to their tribes" (Num. xiv. 2), "in the plains of Moab on this side Jordan by Jericho" (Num. xxii. 1); and from Pisgah (Ras Siaghah), west of Nebo (Jebel Neba) or that vicinity, Moses could do as he was directed (Deut. iii. 27), and see "all the land of Gilead and Dan, and all Naphtali, and all the land of Ephraim and Manasseh, and all the land of Judah unto the utmost sea, and the south, and the plain of Jericho, the city of palm trees, unto Zoar"—as Tristram testifies from his personal experience.[29] Conder also suggests that in the weird and almost inaccessible gorge, Zerka Main, 1,700 feet deep, may be recognized the valley in the land of Moab where Moses was buried (Num. xxxiv. 6), and "no man knoweth of his sepulchre."[30]

Thus the account of this march of Israel, which is also summarized in Deuteronomy, bears every mark of a veritable narrative by a participant, and is not reasonably supposable to have been so accurately invented in all these details by some hypothetical writer many hundred years later.

Here comes in another confirmation and check, as it might be called. It is found (Num. xxxiii.) in the separate enumeration of forty-two encampments written down, as the text declares, by Moses at command of God. It is a bald enumeration without comment, except in three instances where there

---
[29] Tristram, Land of Israel, pp. 540-3; Conder, Heth and Moab, p. 133 seq. Conder suggests to read "towards" Dan and the utmost sea, instead of "unto."
[30] Heth and Moab, p. 151.

is a reference to some attendant fact, of which Aaron's death is the most prominent. It carries the aspect both of elaborate care and of antiquity. For while it includes the stations described in the narrative (as far as Moab), it contains others that not only cannot now be identified, but that do not appear elsewhere in the Hexateuch, apparently lost out of knowledge. Now even if this list of stations stood unsupported by the narrative, what conceivable inducement could a writer a thousand years later[31] have to take the pains and run the risk of manufacturing such a barren catalogue, and especially to introduce these aimless additions to the existing account? The question staggers even the audacity and credulity of Wellhausen, who admits that "it is less easy to account on the theory of pure fiction for the numerous names somewhat arranged like a catalogue," and that "the forty places really existed in the region." But he calmly inquires, "Was it such a difficult matter to find out forty definite stations in the wilderness for the forty years' wandering?" And he carefully changes the forty-two to the round number "forty."[32] This style of argument is quite worthy of Wellhausen. But it was hardly to be expected from a writer like Dr. Driver to dismiss the great and impressive mass of this kind of evidence, now becoming fully recognized by all sober and judicious investigators, with the cool remark, "It is an error to suppose, as seems sometimes to be done, that topographical explora-

---
31 It is ascribed in Kautzsch to P.
32 History of Israel, p. 350.

tion, or the *testimony of inscriptions*, supplies a refutation of critical conclusions concerning the Old Testament.'"[33]

And here the analysts multiply the number of witnesses to the truth of the list. For while carefully going through the narrative itself to justify the ascriptions of the list to a late ("priest") writer, by excluding from it here and there a sentence (those which mention the several removals), yet in most instances the adjacent portion confirms the statement in regard to the place, and that too by passages ascribed by the same analysts to two or three other older writers;[34] so that according to their own standard we have an accumulation of testimonies.

If still additional corroborations of this plain narrative were needed, they may be found in many allusions to attendant circumstances of the journey. The shittim wood (acacia, seyal), of which the tabernacle was constructed, is the only timber wood of any size in the Sinaitic peninsula, although even in very early times almost extinct in Egypt[35] proper, and not common in Palestine. It may be called characteristic of the Sinaitic peninsula, and is a hard, close-grained wood of an orange-brown color, fitted for fine cabinet work. Rev. D. A. Randall in his book of travels, however, mentions that he saw no acacia of sufficient size for the boards of the tabernacle, namely, ten cubits long by one and

---

[33] Introduction to the Old Testament, p. xiii.
[34] J, E, JE, R.
[35] Erman's Life in Ancient Egypt, p. 451.

a half wide.[36] But notwithstanding the destruction of these trees (and the retem) for many years by the Arabs for charcoal, which they transport to Suez, the present writer in 1874 saw in Wady Saal acacias two feet in diameter; and Mr. Holland found specimens that were nine feet in circumference. If, as Tristram suggests, the burning bush (Hebrew "seneh") was a smaller species of acacia, that also is occasionally found The palm is once mentioned, at Elim. It is also found at the oasis of Feiran, and usually only at places where there is or can be found some sign of water. The station "Rithmah," it is suggested by Robinson, Stanley, Tristram and others, may derive its name from the abundance of the retem, another desert tree of frequent occurrence. These, or three of them, are the trees most peculiar to their line of march. The tamarisk or tarfa, with its slender roots running sometimes thirty feet along under the barren surface (as the writer saw), is occasionally met with, but not mentioned. The monks of Sinai gather a honey-like substance from its branches, which they sell to the traveler at the rate of two francs for about three ounces, and which even Ritter ventured to suppose might be the manna of the Israelites. The impossibility of the supposition is proved, among other reasons, by the fact that, as Stanley[37] mentions, the quantity at present produced would be sufficient only to support one man six months; and Schubert declares that the entire amount col-

---

[36] P. 274.   [37] Sinai and Palestine, p. 28,

lected in most productive years is hardly six hundred-weight, and in other years scarcely one-third of that amount; and that the price it brought in Cairo when he wrote was sixty Spanish dollars for less than five pounds.[38] The narrative makes no mention of it.

Of the fauna of the desert actually encountered, the narrative mentions only quails and fiery serpents. The account of the quails (Num. xi. 31,32) is in singular accordance with facts known concerning the region.[39] The bird is encountered by travelers in the peninsula (e. g. Randall and W. H. Bartlett). It is abundant in north Africa,[40] flies thence in great flocks over the Arabian desert. holding its way, especially when fatigued, just above the ground and within reach, and when the flock alights, they are so exhausted that they may easily be captured or killed. They usually arrive at night, helpless till they are rested, sometimes two days, and then fly on. In this particular case they would seem to have come by night; for the people gathered them all day, all night, and all the next day. And their flight[41] (not their accumulation) was two cubits above the ground, or breast high. It was at Kibroth Hattaavah,[42] opposite to a narrow part of the Gulf of Suez, these birds being accustomed, on account of

---

[38] Schubert, Reise, Vol. II., p. 347.
[39] Tristram gives a full statement, Natural History of the Bible, pp. 231, 232.
[40] McCoan's Egypt, p. 326.
[41] So Knobel, Dillmann, Strack, Speaker's Commentary.
[42] Near this place both Schubert and Stanley saw immense flocks of birds flying over. "The sky was literally darkened," says Stanley, "by innumerable birds." But in this case they were cranes.

their weak flight, to seek the shortest passage and halt where they can. It was in the spring also, when they take their northward flight from Africa. The people spread them all abroad about the camp (verse 32) to dry, as Herodotus says the Egyptians were in the habit of doing.[43] Here all is exactly true to the life, and is a description made upon the spot.

The only reference to the serpent is after leaving Mount Hor (Num xxi. 6, 8), to the fiery serpent, or possibly burning serpent, that is, producing burning heat in the body.[44] Tristram found four species of venomous serpents in and around Palestine; Palmer speaks of them in the Peninsula;[45] and Schubert saw between Akabah and Sinai a poisonous serpent with fiery spots.

From the list of clean and unclean animals (Lev. xi.) nothing can be certainly inferred in this connection, although many if not all the animals are to be seen in the region traversed. According to Tristram, however, at least five or six of these species never lived in the Nile valley nor in wooded and hilly Palestine.[46] If he is correct, this would be a special mark of the desert journey. He also has called attention to the fact that all the different antelopes are mentioned in Deuteronomy among the clean beasts, but not in Leviticus; and suggests as an explanation that when the laws were announced

---

43 Herodotus, ii., 77. See also Rawlinson's Herodotus, Vol. II., p. 109, note.
44 Knobel, Dillmann, Strack.
45 The Desert of the Exodus, p. 99.
46 Cited by Driver, Deuteronomy, p. 160, note.

immediately after the exodus they would be strange to the Israelites, but after thirty-nine years had been passed in their haunts they would be familiar to them all."[47]

Again, the singular collection of brief and unrelated facts of legislation in the Mosaic code, such as is found in Leviticus xix., strongly mark them as commands and prohibitions growing out of the occasions and the time, and not the fabrication of late system-makers. This chapter is part of what is designated by German scholars "the Code of Holiness," and is ascribed by them to the priests during the exile. But the priests, being then free from the duties of the temple and the altar, had abundant leisure to frame a systematic code, arranged in an orderly manner. But Dr. Henry Hayman has minutely shown not only the lack of coherence in this one chapter, but much of the same characteristic pervading the whole so-called Code (Lev. xvii.-xxv.). "To call it the Priests' *Code* was not a happy thought of the critics, codification being precisely the element which it does *not* present." Nor is this quality confined to the Priests' Code, but extends more or less to the whole legislation; "the treatment by repetitions, digressions, dismemberment and insertions, being not so much the exception as the rule, gives the Mosaic legislation the interspersed and fragmentary character of a painted window."[48] The only reasonable explanation is,

---

[47] The City and the Land, p. 80.
[48] The Independent, April 28, 1892. See note xii.

not that this was the deliberate composition of system-makers, but that the legislation sprang from the occasions, and perhaps was sometimes diverted by them; and that its sacred authority was so fully recognized by the scribes of the law in later times that they did not presume to change the order for a better arrangement. Sometimes we can seem to recognize the occasion. Blunt called attention to an ancient tradition that the prohibition of wine and strong drink to the priests when they went into the tabernacle, immediately following the offense of the priests Nadab and Abihu, may naturally explain the cause of that offense. It has also been noticed that the direction to make themselves fringes to cause them to remember the commandments of the Lord (Num. xv. 38, 39) immediately follows the punishment of the man who violated the great law to "remember the Sabbath Day to keep it holy."

During the thirty-eight years' wandering but two events are recorded. This fact, sometimes alleged as incompatible with so long a lapse of time, is in harmony with the plan of the narrative: "The host of Israel," says Edersheim, "being doomed to judgment, ceased to be the subject of sacred history, while the rising generation, in whom the life and hope of Israel now centered, had as yet no history of their own."[49] The two events which are recorded were so momentous in their bearing on the maintenance of the decalogue and the divinely

---
[49] Edersheim's The Exodus and the Wandering, p. 173.

established polity as to be specially made a permanent warning. They are records of the summary punishments for daring disobedience, namely, the violation of the Sabbath, and the rebellion of Korah and his associates (Num. xvi). And it is recorded that Korah, Dathan and Abiram were joined by two sons of Reuben, and that 250 men of renown were led away by them. The fact that sons of Reuben should have united with Korah and his associates (of the family of Kohath) has been naturally and shrewdly accounted for by Blunt,[50] by the proximity of their encampment to that of the Reubenites, both being on the south side of the tabernacle (Num. iii. 29; ii. 10); to which Edersheim adds that Reuben, being the first-born, naturally had a grievance against the exaltation of Aaron and Moses of the tribe of Levi above all the congregation (xvi. 3).

In the same line of indications of contemporaneous facts and reality are the exhaustively (some would say wearisomely) minute directions for the construction, furnishing, care and conveyance of the tabernacle. It occupies not far from 150 verses in the original instructions (Ex. xxv., seq.) Then comes a briefer recapitulation by Moses to the congregation, in thirty verses, preceded by a caution that no work shall be done, not even the kindling of a fire, on the Sabbath, and followed by four and a half chapters (xxxvi., seq.) of an equally minute and business-like statement of the accomplishment of

---

[50] Blunt's Undesigned Coincidences, p. 84.

the work. This last gives the names of the two master workmen, Bezaleel and Aholiab, their parentage and tribe, the facts of their being aided by every wise-hearted man and supplied with certain specified contributions of the congregation, the spinning of fine linen and goats' hair by the women, and the special gift of precious stones by the rulers. Where in classic literature is there to be found anything like it in fullness of detail and reality of appearance? Cæsar's bridge over the Rhine is described by him in twenty lines. It is paralleled only by the plans and specifications of a modern architect, and, but for the inability to interpret all the ancient technical terms, might be very closely reconstructed. Indeed the doubt hanging over the meaning of some of the terms long before the Christian Era, as obsolete terms, indicates the antiquity of the directions; as where the Septuagint and the two other Greek versions unquestionably mistranslate the words wrongly rendered "badgers' skins" in the English version; and modern expositors are in doubt, the revised version giving the alternative of seal skins or porpoise skins. Still further, the time occupied in the work, some nine months, is in keeping with its elaborateness.

Now as an actual record of a transaction of the times, a transaction of sacred and central significance to the chosen people, this singular minuteness and voluminousness of detail is perfectly accounted for; but as an alleged fabrication of after ages in regard to a fictitious affair a thousand years obsolete, it involves the supposition of a stolid and aimless industry and a laborious and superfluous trifling not credible in priest or layman.

This is not all. Such a specification of details involves an amount of accurate knowledge of historic facts not supposable, yes, not possible, in any late writer of fiction. In fact, in the earlier part of the present century such scholars, not merely as Von Bohlen and Vater, but even De Wette, could declare that the construction of the tabernacle and the priests' garments implied a cultivation of the arts and an abundance of costly materials which we could not expect of the Israelites when they left Egypt, and that the whole description of the tabernacle therefore belongs, not to history, but to fiction. This bold statement now shows the impossibility of its being a fiction. It was in their day necessary even to argue the case with the most learned men that the art of writing was practiced so early as the exodus. It is undoubtedly safe to say that from before the time of Ezra the priest till well on in the present century no human being could have ventured on such a detailed account of the materials and processes without blundering at every turn. For, as the reader will find by referring to the narrative, we are told there of men and women bringing for the structure brooches and ear-rings and signet-rings and armlets (or necklaces, R. V.), of gold, and blue and purple and scarlet and fine twined linen, and the women spinning it with their hands, the men offering silver and brass (bronze or copper), and the rulers bringing precious stones of several varieties (twelve) for the ephod and the breastplate; of rings and chains and wreathen work of pure gold, engraving on the stones and on the plate of gold, casting and overlaying, "beaten" (or carved) work, and the like.

It remained for explorers *of the present century* to find ample evidence of all this skill prevailing in Egypt, at and long before the time of the exodus. The very finest of fine linen has been found there. Spinning and weaving by hand is delineated in the paintings, and bright colors were employed. The whole process of working gold is delineated in the tombs at Beni Hassan as early as the twelfth dynasty; goldsmiths are often mentioned, and even "the chief goldsmith to the king."[51] In addition to other specimens of their work, we have the remarkable collection found in the tomb of Queen Ahhotep of the eighth dynasty (before the exodus), which no visitor to the former Boulak Museum will forget, and the equally beautiful and "wonderful jewelry"[52] of the twelfth dynasty discovered at Dashur in 1894.[53] These trinkets were often interlaced with precious stones or enamel, and sometimes false stones made of glass and skillfully colored. Of these stones Wilkinson mentions lapis-lazuli, cornelian, amethyst, agate, pearls, hæmatite, serpentine, root of emerald, adding that "the sole Museum of Leyden possesses an infinite variety of these objects which were once the pride of the ladies of

---

51 Erman, p. 460.   52 Ib., p. 461.   53 See note xiii., Appendix.

Thebes."[54] Engraving was done on stones of all kinds, and in one instance a name was found neatly cut on a glass bead about 1500 B. C.[55]

"The domain of the lapidary," says Maspero, "included the amethyst, the emerald, the garnet, the aquamarine, the chrysoprase, the innumerable varieties of agate and jasper, lapis-lazuli, feldspath, obsidian; also various rocks, such as granite, serpentine and porphyry; certain fossils, as yellow amber and some kinds of turquoise; organic remains, as coral, mother-of-pearl and pearls; metallic oxides, such as hæmatite, the oriental turquoise, and malachite."[56]

Bronze also was sufficiently abundant, as, for example, a bronze statuette of Rameses II., cast hollow, and beautifully chased.[57]

Two significant circumstances are to be noted in the construction of the tabernacle: First, silver is less abundantly used than gold. In Egypt silver appears to have been much less used for jewelry than gold. Wilkinson (so far as we find) mentions one silver ring, while he gives representations of some score of golden trinkets, before the discovery of the Ahhotep or the Dashur collections. Erman accounts for it by the fact that there were no silver mines in Egypt. He also affirms that "in the oldest empire silver was regarded as the most valuable metal"; whether that be so or not, he states that as a matter of fact "in the tombs silver objects are much rarer than gold ones."[58] Thus the use of sil-

---

[54] Wilkinson, ii., 343-345.   [55] Ibid., 141.
[56] Egypt. Archæology, p. 240-1.   [57] Erman, p. 461.   [58] Ib., p. 461.

ver in the tabernacle corresponds to the circumstances of the land from which their supplies were drawn.

Still more noteworthy is the case in regard to iron. In the abundant accounts of metals and metal-working in the wilderness, as well as of the carpentry, there is not an allusion to any use of iron, in forms greater or smaller. Here is a striking correspondence to the fact of the scanty use of iron in early Egypt. Wilkinson, in 1836, left the question of its use in uncertainty. Birch, in 1883, cited but four instances of it as early as the Ramessids, though not doubting its use in later times; and only in 1894 does Erman venture to say that its use for tools under the old empire "can scarcely be considered doubtful."[59] This correspondence shows convincingly not only the accuracy of the statements of the narrative, but its virtual contemporaneousness with the transaction, as will immediately appear.

For when Israel had reached the plains of Moab by Jordan (Num. xxxv. 1; Deut. i. 19), we find at length two laws mentioning "an instrument of iron." How comes this? They had now arrived in the region east of the Mediterranean, where the use of iron was well known and comparatively common. Iron vessels were brought from Syria and Phenicia as tributes to Thothmes III.[60] Also farther

---

[59] A piece of slag brought by the writer from the Egyptian mines at Wady Maghara showed that all the copper but eight-tenths per cent had been smelted out; but the more infusible iron, amounting to twenty-three per cent, remained.

[60] Birch in Wilkinson's Egypt, ii., 251. See also Records of the Past, ii., 52. Brugsch (i., 368) gives the full list of the tribute, among which are found two suits of iron armor (p. 373), an iron suit of armor decorated with gold (p. 375), vessels of iron (p. 376), iron (p. 380).

east, in Mesopotamia (Naharain), iron was to be found, it being now the most abundant metal in the mountains four days from Mosul,[61] and in the northwest palace at Nimrud Layard found several iron helmets and scales of iron armor, all ready to drop in pieces with rust.[62] He found also at Nimrud iron spear heads, arrow heads, and the head of a hatchet, and even specimens of bronze cast over iron.[63] And while it does not appear from the surroundings how early was the date, the inscription of Thothmes, already mentioned, comes to our aid, and informs us that among the spoils carried away "from the river-land of the miserable Naharain" were "iron suits of armor and weapons." Here, then, is the clue to the absence of all mention of iron till the arrival in Moab; there was practically no iron behind them, it was then around them. In the book of Judges and the later books it is often mentioned —thirty times or more.

Now for any writer in after ages, eight hundred or a thousand years later, to pass safely through all these liabilities to mistake, snares and pitfalls at every step, maintaining his accuracy even in the minutest points of difference between the lands and the ages and the circumstances, and with no collection of antiquarian books or museum to guide him, there can be no hesitation in saying is absolutely out of the question. Yet, as may be seen in Kautzsch's recent work, modern critics have the courage to

---

[61] Layard's Nineveh, ii., 315,316.   [62] Ib. i., 278.
[63] Layard's Babylon and Nineveh, pp. 191, 194, 557, 596.

assign the whole narrative of the structure of the tabernacle to P, during the exile in Babylonia, with revisions later.[64] In this light we can understand the wisdom which permanently incorporated in the narrative such an amount of dry and, to posterity, otherwise seemingly useless details.

But this matter of the tabernacle and its concomitants is but one portion of the case as it has been brought forward in this chapter. The argument is cumulative. And when we take into account all the correspondences to geographic and historic fact in the narrative of the exodus and the wandering, it would seem as though the evidences of virtually contemporaneous writing and personal knowledge were insuperable. It is a question level to the apprehension of all ordinary intelligence. It is a somewhat perilous thing for a writer to declare it "an error to suppose that topographical exploration, or the testimony of inscriptions, supplies a refutation of critical conclusions respecting the books of the Old Testament." And for the author of such an assertion to say of another scholar that he[65] "is singularly unable to distinguish between a good argument and a bad one" is still more perilous.

---

[64] Kautzsch says about 500 B. C. in Babylonia was the composition of the proper priest codex. (Supplement, p. 129.) More fully stated (p. 188): "The priestly book of history and law in the Pentateuch and Joshua originated as the product of Babylonia and subsequent Jerusalem schools of priests from about 500 to 400 B. C." Some critics speak of a P1, P2 P3, and Cornill even P4. Kautzsch covers virtually the same ground.

[65] Driver's Introduction, p. 149, of Prof. Bissell. So too, Mr. Girdlestone "employs himself largely in beating the air" (p. xiv.)

CHAPTER IV

THE RESIDENCE IN EGYPT

The Biblical account of the residence of the Israelites in Egypt exhibits the same minutely accurate knowledge of Egyptian facts, and circumstantial correctness of statement; the former showing the close proximity of the narrative to the times of the exodus, and both standing voucher for the general truthfulness of the narrative. In the great company of German speculators there have been found some two or three writers (Stade, Meyer and Juste) who have expressed their doubts that the Israelites ever made a settlement in Egpyt. This was to be expected, but is too preposterous to have found a respectable following even in Germany. As Kittel remarks, "There is no event in the entire history of Israel that has more deeply impressed itself on the memory of later generations of this people than the abode in Egypt and the exodus form the land of the Nile. Samuel, Saul, Solomon, almost even David himself, stand in the background, compared with the Egyptian house of bondage and the glorious delivery therefrom. Evidently we have here no mere creation of the legends of the patriarchs, but a fact which lived deep down in the consciousness of the people in quite early times, from Hosea and the book of Samuel onwards, a fact graven deep in their memory. It would betoken a high and more than normal deficiency of historical sense in the Israelite national character, if a purely mythical occurrence gave the key-note of the whole national life, and formed the starting point of the entire circle of religious thought as early as the days of the first literary prophets.'"

This is a mild statement of the case. The appeal can be made not merely to the historic sense, but to the convergence of historic facts, settled beyond contradiction after three thousand years. During the present century early Egyptian life has been disclosed by the monuments and documents with extraordinary fullness, far more complete than the knowledge we have of the course of life at the early Plymouth colony in this country. It covers public, private and social life in all their forms. Now any man who should attempt a delineation of life in the early Plymouth colony, writing in England, or even in New England, without access to full contemporary records and documents, would be certain to blunder at almost every step. And even if there were placed in his hands the surviving contemporary documents, such as Bradford's History, Morton's Memorial, Winslow's Narrative, De Rassière's letter, and he were granted a visit to the collection of antiquities at Plymouth, there is not a man now living who, with all those helps, can fill up a year's or a month's daily life there during Bradford's whole lifetime with such an amount of minute and accurate detail as is contained in the

---
1 History of the Hebrews, I., p. 185, English translation. He gives references which it is not necessary to quote.

Pentateuch concerning the Egypt of three thousand years ago. But by what possibility could an Israelite in Palestine or Babylonia, hundreds of years later, obtain that surprising amount of exact information?

Yet through all these difficulties and perils the sacred writer walks boldly on, with a certainty of direct statement and casual allusion which it was left to the present century to discover. He touches on public and private matters, personal habits, customs of society, modes of living, the products, resources and seasons of the country, the condition, occupations, food and drink of the inhabitants, to some degree their language, and other miscellaneous matters and implications.

The futile attempt to impeach the accuracy of this delineation, made in 1835 by Peter von Bohlen, professor of oriental languages at Koenigsberg, though now an old story, is worth recalling. Some of the points on which he alleged "mistakes and inaccuracies" (thereby betraying, as was remarked at the time, that he lived out of Egypt and long after Moses), were these things in Genesis: The brick-making; the animals, namely sheep and asses; the use of animal food; the cultivation of the vine, which at present is very scanty, and not very successful except for raisins,[2] whereas under both the Old and New Empires we find vineyards and the whole process of wine-making, six different kinds of wine enumerated, and in one instance 1,500 jars

---

[2] McCoan's Egypt, p. 332.

of it sealed by one head-gardener; and other matters.³

On these points Hengstenberg not only completely refuted his denial, but he went further and showed positively the correspondence of the narrative to the then known facts in the following particulars: The existence of eunuchs in Egypt; the morals and manners of Egyptian women, as seen in the temptation of Joseph; the functions of the baker and the carrying of baskets on the head; the shaving of the beard on coming from the prison; the signet-ring;⁴ the fine linen; the gold chain; the sitting posture at meals (Gen. xliii .33),⁵ whereas among the Hebrews from at least the time of Amos (and perhaps in the time of the patriarchs) reclining was the custom; the embalming of the dead (Gen. l. 11); the coffin, apparently of wood (Gen. l. 26), a common material, and fitted for the transportation better than those of stone, which were also used; the grievous mourning of the Egyptians (l. 11); even its duration, seventy days (l. 3);⁶ the use of papyrus (Ex. ii. 3, R. V., margin) for an ark or basket, with the pitch to cement it together and the bitumen to make it water-tight; the beating by the taskmasters, the bastinado (Ex. v. 14); the hard bondage in building (Ex. i. 14); the bricks com-

---

3 Erman, p. 110.
4 On Gen. xii. 42, Von Bohlen said, "It is scarcely necessary to mention that these objects of luxury, especially polished stones, belong to a later time."
5 Dillmann so understands Gen. xxviii. 4, Strack and some others dissenting. Sitting is indicated Gen. xxvii.19, Judg. xix 6, 1 Sam. xx. 5, 24, 1 Kings xiii. 20; but reclining Am. vi. 4, Ezek. xxiii. 41, and among the Babylonians, Esther i. 6, vii. 8; also in Palestine in the time of Christ.
6 So apparently Herodotus, ii., 86. Diodorus says seventy-two, i., 72.

pacted by straw; the freedom enjoyed by Egyptian women, and their occasional failings, even to intoxication at feasts, unsparingly delineated on the monuments.

Most of the above-mentioned correspondences have been known for half a century, and if they were all, they are enough to show the boldness and certainty with which the writer moves among all the conditions of ancient Egyptian life.

But time and further discovery only increase the strength of the evidence of personal knowledge, and in some lines in a very extraordinary manner. In Ex. v. 8 we read of "a tale of bricks" being required of the Hebrews by their taskmasters; and it is a late discovery by Chabas that in the forced labor of foreigners in making bricks "a daily tale was required."[7] A still more noteworthy fact has come to light in the excavations made in 1883 by Petrie at Pithom, to be mentioned later. The narrative tells how the straw ordinarily supplied to be mixed with the clay for the sun-dried bricks, was withholden, and the people were scattered abroad to "gather stubble instead of straw." Miss Amelia B. Edwards writes thus: "It is a curious and interesting fact that the Pithom bricks are of three qualities. In the lower courses of these massive walls they are mixed with chopped straw; higher up, when the straw may be supposed to have run short, the clay is found to be mixed with reeds— the same kind of reeds which grow to-day in the

---

[7] R. S. Poole, Cont. Review, March, 1879, p. 755.

bed of the old Pharaonic Nile, and which are translated as 'stubble' in the Bible. Finally, when the reeds were used up, the bricks of the upper courses consist of mere Nile mud, with no binding substance whatever."[8]

It was one of the charges made by Von Bohlen (and repeated by some others) that the writer of Genesis betrayed "ignorance of the natural condition of Egypt" in describing a seven years' famine, or indeed any famine at all, Egypt being alleged to be so regularly watered by the Nile as to have no such experiences. Unquestionably famines are rare in Egypt, especially protracted ones; and this makes the narrative the more remarkable. For Brugsch finds an Egyptian record belonging to the Hyksos period (the supposed period of Joseph's residence in Egypt), of "a famine lasting many years."[9] No other such famine is recorded in later Egyptian history till that of A. D. 1064-1071, remarkable for having lasted seven years, like that of Joseph. Dr. Brugsch is quite confident that in this ancient record of the time of Rasekenen III. we have an account of the very famine of Joseph; and Kittel is inclined, though with hesitation, to agree with him. That is not important.

---

8 Pharaohs, Fellahs and Explorers, p. 50.

9 Hist. Eg., I., p. 304. In the tomb of one Baba at El Kab. In his Stein-inschrift und Bibelwort (1891), pp. 90 seq., Brugsch gives still another record found by him later in a rock in the island Sehel, between the first cataract and Elephantine. This speaks definitely of a famine of seven years. Though the famine is ascribed to the times of King Tozer, more than a thousand years before Joseph, Brugsch maintains from the language and style that the inscription belongs to the centuries not long B. C., and that it records a tradition of the ancient famine, that was still handed down (p. 96).

The main point is the fact of a protracted famine in Egypt.

The temptation of Joseph by Potiphar's wife has seemed to some quite improbable in its details. But the freedom with which the Egyptian women moved about has long been proved by the monuments; while the Egyptian story of the Two Brothers, brought to light not many years ago, sets forth a series of transactions so singularly like the narrative in the main facts of the temptation, the resistance and the accusation, as almost to suggest a common origin, though against all probability.[10]

In reference to the whole history of Joseph, Kittel makes a statement of profound significance to those who, like himself, accept the literary decomposition of the Pentateuch into several narratives: "It was comparatively easy to maintain that an author who knew Egypt, and perhaps had lived there for a time, composed the story of Joseph and clothed it in an Egyptian garb. This account of the matter is *almost impossible now* that two distinct sources for the history of Joseph, J and E, are universally recognized. The sources vary so widely from each other that they must have been written at different times and places. They contain many differences of no small importance, so that they can hardly be traced back to a common literary original, yet they agree completely in bearing the genuine Egyptian stamp. It must also be admitted

---

10 Now to be found in various volumes, e. g. Ebers' Egypt, pp. 311-314; Brugsch's Hist. I., pp. 309-311; Records of the Past, II., 137.

that the Egyptian element in the narrative cannot be mere literary coloring. It must belong to the core of the narrative. This points to a comparatively high antiquity, and testifies to the existence of an ancient tradition, dating as far back as the Egyptian period itself.'"[11] The argument is of great weight from his point of view; although we do not admit it to be "comparatively easy" for any one writer four or five hundred years later to have so perfectly clothed the narrative "in an Egyptian garb."

But these things are but a small part of the marks of intimate and personal knowledge of the condition of Egypt, and in its different phases, in the times of Abraham, Joseph and the exodus respectively.

The series of plagues shows the strongest local coloring, the supernatural elements standing in close relation to the natural, as has been pointed out by various commentators from Hengstenberg to the present time. Among these things are the red color of the Nile at a certain season, the frogs, the swarms of tormenting insects, the murrain, the locusts; and in connection with the locusts and the hail we have (Ex. ix. 31, 32) an incidental allusion to the order of the ripening of the flax, barley, wheat and rye or spelt. Hail is very rare in Egypt; but on the 19th of December, 1873, the present writer experienced in Alexandria a storm of wind and rain, mingled with hail, so severe as to confine at home those who were not compelled to be abroad;

---

[11] History of the Hebrews, i., p. 188.

and as evidence of the destructive power of hail in extraordinary cases, he has before him as he writes a dispatch dated May 25, 1896, from Minot, North Dakota, informing the Associated Press in Boston of a hail storm on the day before, in which the "stones were of enormous size and fell with terrific force," and that "cattle on the ranges suffered severely, many being pounded to death by the hail." Indeed, so minutely close is this local coloring that in Ex. vii. 19 the several words translated rivers, streams, ponds and pools of water are recognized by Knobel, Dillmann and others as designating (in the Hebrew) the Nile itself and its arms, the canals, the lakes or ponds, and "all other collections of water, as cisterns, wells, pools and reservoirs" (Dillmann). But while the natural basis, so to call it, appears in all the plagues, the narrative, which does not ignore it, also steadily rises above it, so that, in the words of Kalisch, "we cannot but acknowledge the *miraculous character* with which all without exception are stamped." He specifies their taking place at unusual times; the rapid succession of very rare occurrences; the aggravation of their character; their occurrence as predicted; their cessation at the prayer of Moses; their limitation to the Egyptians.[12]

When we turn to the time of Abraham, we find in the list of presents made to him by Pharaoh, oxen, sheep and asses, all of which are found abundantly delineated on the monuments of the earlier

---
[12] Comment on Ex. vii., pp. 117, 118.

times; yet no mention of horses, although horses and chariots occur in the narrative of the Exodus. The explanation is to be found in the now well settled fact that horses were not introduced into Egypt, certainly not mentioned, till the eighteenth dynasty —that is, after the time of Abraham.[13]

The mention of camels among the gifts to Abraham, however, has been cited as an anachronism, inasmuch as no inscription and no painting shows the animal in Egypt before Grecian times. But although Birch and Erman concede the point, and Dillmann suggests that the two words may be the addition of a copyist or an editor (in itself a very possible supposition), yet neither the concession nor the explanation are called for. As matter of fact, in the borings made by the sagacious Hekekian Bey between the years 1851 and 1854 in the Nile valley (some ninety-five in number, and penetrating in some instances to the depth of sixty feet), "bones of the ox, hog, dog, *dromedary* and ass were not uncommon."[14] Furthermore, the Egyptian traveler, or Mohar, about the fourteenth century B. C., calls for camel to eat in Palestine, evidently indicating thereby a knowledge of the animal.[15] Wiedemann, in 1891, remarks also that "the presence of the animal in the Nile valley is attested by the classics, and that therefore the non-mention of it cannot be due to its being unknown in the land, but if not simply accidental, must rest on other,

---
13 Erman, p. 493; Wilkinson, II., p. 101.
14 Lyell's Antiquity of Man, p. 35.
15 Records of the Past, II., p. 112.

perhaps religious, grounds.'"[16] Both Wilkinson and Ebers[17] have called attention to the similar fact that poultry, although known from other sources to have been abundant in ancient Egypt, as in modern times, do not appear on the monuments. The suggestion of Ebers that the camel was in ancient times confined to northern Egypt would explain its absence from the drawings, which are most abundant in southern Egypt. Whatever the explanation, the fact appears to have been settled by Hekekian Bey.

The freshness and immediateness of the writer's knowledge is indicated by the Egyptian words and phrases clinging to his narrative. Ebers cites the reed-grass (R. V. Gen. xl. 2), where the word *achu* is borrowed from the Egyptian, and the phrase "brink of the river" (ver. 3), literally "lip of the river," is an Egyptian phrase (though not exclusively so), and throughout the chapter "the river" is the Nile, after the Egyptian conception. Mr. Poole (after Chabas) finds the oath "by the life of Pharaoh" (Gen. xlii. 1, 15, 16) to be traceable in Egyptian official proceedings, as well as the bowing on the staff (Gen. xliii. 29-31, Septuagint). The phrase "ark of bulrushes," or chest of papyrus (ii. 3), contains a word, *tevah*, which has an Egyptian equivalent, *tba*, as old as the twelfth dynasty,[18] meaning chest; *gome*, papyrus, has its equivalent in the Coptic *kam;* the pitch, *zepheth* (Hebrew), is found in the Egyptian *sft;* and the traveler can still

---

16 Cited by Strack in his Comment on Gen. xii. 16.
17 Egypt, p. 268.
18 Birch in Bunsen's Egypt, I. p. 482.

see "flags" growing by the borders of the Nile, where the current is sluggish enough to permit. The *hin* reproduces the Egpytian *han*,[19] a vase or measure, and the *ephah* is also an Egyptian measure. The stubble and straw of Ex. v. 12 are in the Hebrew close transcripts of Egyptian words meaning straw and chaff. The pot in which the manna was to be deposited (Ex. xvi. 33) is expressed by a term not found elsewhere in the Bible, which in the inscriptions, according to Brugsch, means a casket or vase for oblations. The timbrel of Miriam bore an Egyptian name.[20] The "chariots" of the triumphal song of the Israelites, *markeboth*, is the monumental word *markabatu* for the same thing. Many other words in this part of the narrative, words of common life, such as are wont to cling to a speech, offer no Hebrew derivations, and are ascribed with more or less confidence to an Egyptian origin, such as the words for enchantment, sorcerers, frogs, boils, blains, flax, and others. Any uncertainty in regard to these, however, does not detract from the significance of the cases that are clear.

Dr. Ebers confidently finds two of the spices, such as the Ishmaelites were carrying down to Egypt (Gen. xxxvii. 25), among the ingredients of the celebrated incense Kyphi, as mentioned in a papyrus at the laboratory of the Edfu temple: the "incense," probably tragacanth, is in Hebrew *nekoth*, in modern Arabic *naka'at* (tragacanth), and in the

---
19 Ib., p. 462.
20 The last five instances are on the authority of Brugsch's Dictionary of Hieroglyphics, as cited by Canon Cook in The Speaker's Commentary.

papyrus *nekpat;* the "balm," in Hebrew *tsori*, in the papyrus *tsara*.[21] Mr. Tomkins accepts the identification.[22]

This point admits of further illustration. We add only a remark of Mr. Poole: "It is chiefly in proper names that we recognize the Egyptian influence on the Hebrews. That of Moses has been admitted to be Egyptian. There is no Hebrew derivation of Aaron and Miriam." He mentions also Phinehas.[23]

On no question of the veracity of the Scripture narrative have its assailants been more absolutely routed than in regard to the Hittites. They are mentioned at intervals through a period of about a thousand years. First Abraham deals with members of the race at Hebron. Just before the entrance into Palestine we find them apparently consolidated, localized farther north, and become a great power so that Canaan is even described summarily as "the land of the Hittites." They are among the most formidable foes encountered by Joshua. They appear in the times of David and Solomon, both of whom took Hittite wives, the former having two Hittites, Uriah and Ahimelech, among his most faithful captains. In the time of Jehoram the army of Benhadad were panic-struck and fled from the siege of Samaria because, as they said, "the king of Israel hath hired against us the kings of the Egyptians and the kings of the Hittites to come

---
21 Ebers' Egypt, p. 290.
22 Tompkins' Life and Times of Joseph, p. 37.
23 Contemporary Review, 1879, p. 755.

upon us"—where, it will be seen, the Hittites are placed in the same category with the Egyptians of that period. Now with the cool assurance which assails any scriptural statement which is not supposed capable of outside corroboration, Professors Cheyne and W. F. Newman pronounced this representation of Hittite power to be unworthy of credence. The former declared that the Bible statements concerning the Hittites "cannot be taken as of equal authority with Egyptian and Assyrian inscriptions," also that "the Hittites seem to have been included among the Canaanites by mistake." He little thought that both Egyptian and Assyrian inscriptions were ready to silence him. Professor Newman went so far as to say of the panic of the Syrian army, "The unhistorical tone is too manifest," "the particular ground of alarm attributed to them does not exhibit the writer's acquaintance with the times in very favorable light," "no Hittite kings can be compared with the king of Judah, the real and near ally who is not named at all," "nor is there a single mark of acquaintance with the contemporaneous history."

These bold assertions are now annihilated. The early, long-continued and steadily growing power of this nation till it became an equal foe of the Egyptians, the fact of its steady pressure southward into Palestine, its protracted contact and conflict with the Assyrian kings from the time of Sargon I. till Sargon II., more than a thousand years,[24]

---

[24] Wright's The Empire of the Hittites, pp. 37, 123.

are now thoroughly proved by inscriptions and documents from Egypt, Assyria and Palestine. They appear to be first mentioned in the time of Usertesen I. in Egypt;[25] were known in connection with other allied nations in the times of Thothmes III., are designated in the inscriptions as "the great people," whom, however, that great warrior conquered, subjecting them to a heavy tribute which he records in its details (about B. C. 1600).[26] But in the time of Rameses II. this nation had become so powerful that after a doubtful victory at Kadesh on the Orontes, claimed by the Egyptian monarch, "the great ruler of Egypt" was constrained to make a covenant on equal terms with "the great Prince of the Kheta" (Hittites), to "be at peace with him forever."[27]

The Assyrian inscriptions show constant warfare going on between the Hittites and the several Assyrian monarchs, Tiglath-pileser (1120 B. C.), Assurnazirpal (about 870 B. C.), Shalmaneser, and Sargon II., till, in 717 B. C., they were finally overthrown by the last named monarch, and disappeared from the Assyrian inscriptions.[28] Meanwhile another side-light is cast on the nation by recently discovered inscriptions of the Vannic king Menuas, one of which, discovered at Van, speaks of war with the Hittites, and the capture of 2,113 soldiers, indicating also the Hittite border upon the

---

25 Brugsch's Hist., II., p. 405.
26 Ib., I., 379 seq.
27 Ib., II., p. 71 seq.
28 Wright's Empire of the Hittites, p. 122, 123.

Euphrates near Palu;[29] and another inscription at Palu some fifty miles from Harpoot, very recently copied by Rev. J. L. Barton and translated by Professor Sayce. The latter inscription, carved at a considerable height on the castle rock, written in the Vannic language with the Assyrian characters by the same Menuas, records his making war with the Hittite king of Malatia, about 800 B. C.

And now since the year 1887, and the discovery of the Tell Amarna contemporary documents of about the date 1480 B. C.,[30] we are able to trace the southward progress of this powerful race as they carry conquest and terror from the region of Aleppo some three hundred miles to the south of Damascus, and towards Phenicia. No less than eight of the letters published by Conder mention the Hittites as an advancing foe, and despairingly appeal to Egypt for help, while others of them evidently refer to the same formidable enemy, "men of blood."[31] And thus at last the Biblical representation of this people is fully sustained, and the unfounded cavils made to recoil upon their authors. Moreover the helplessness of Egypt to protect her tributaries, and the internal conflicts of the native tribes of Palestine, indicate a state of affairs ready for, and explanatory of, the Israelite invasion and conquest.

---

29 Records of the Past, New Series Vol. I pp. 164-167. The facts concerning the second inscription were communicated to the author by Mr. Barton.

30 The date is determined by that of Amenophis IV., to whom the letters were written.

31 Conder's Tell Amarna Letters, 1893. These letters show the Amorites threatening the Egyptian possessions in southern Palestine, while the Hittites are doing so in the north. The larger collection of Winckler exhibits these facts much more abundantly.

We mention but one other fact in connection with Egypt, the discovery of Pithom, one of the two store cities (R. V.) which Pharaoh compelled the Israelites to build (Ex. i. 11). This remarkable discovery was reserved for the year 1883, and the explorations of M. Naville, and is now accepted by Egyptologists. The name of the place (Pi Tum) is given five times in the inscription; the name of the god Tum is repeated many times. Rameses II. is represented, in a carving on a monolith, seated between the gods Ra and Tum; his oval is on a fragment of a temple, and on a black granite hawk, and the ruins correspond to the uses of a store city. Within an enclosure of enormously thick walls, comprising a space of 55,000 square yards, are the remains of a temple, and some "very strange buildings" having smooth walls from two to three yards in thickness. These form a great number of rectangular compartments having no communication with one another, but opening only upwards, and about two yards from the bottom are provided with rectangular holes for timbers. Naville believes them to have been built for no other purpose than that of store houses or granaries into which the Pharaohs gathered the provisions necessary for armies about to cross the desert, or even for caravans which were on the road to Syria.[32] The place is about twelve miles west of Ismalieh, in Wady Tumilat (included in Goshen), and in what the inscriptions seem to indicate as the territory of Suc-

---

[32] The Store City of Pithom, by Edward Naville (1885), pp. 13 seq.

coth, in which was one of the stations of the Israelites on the exodus. It was also upon the sweet water canal, which was as old as the time of Rameses, and would have been on the natural line of the march. The peculiarity as to the structure of the bricks has been mentioned on a previous page.[33]

Now without further enumerating the tokens of minute accuracy in these accounts concerning Egypt and its affairs from the time of Abraham to that of Moses, it becomes clear that here is a narrative which, when subjected to the closest scrutiny by every known test and by tests unknown for ages, is shown to be thoroughly trustworthy; and not only so, but to manifest such a knowledge of the facts and circumstances of those times and places as was impossible—we use the word deliberately—to any writer living a thousand or five hundred years after the time, as well as far away from the scenes, and without any records on which to draw. And by the very postulate of modern hostile critics, the writer or writers had no contemporary authorities.

Scho.arly writers who have given most attention to the *facts* of modern discovery are most emphatic in their verdict on these matters. Conder does not hesitate to say that the Tell Amarna letters "most fully confirm the historical statements of the book of Joshua."[34] Dr. W. Wright, speaking of the references to the Hittites in the Bible, says: "We have examined the contemporary records of Baby-

---

[33] See page 88.   [34] The Tell Amarna Tablets, p. 6.

lon, Assyria and Egypt, and we find not only collateral evidence which creates a probability in favor of the sacred narratives, but side-lights which shine so clearly on the incidents that unbelief is impossible."[135] Canon Tristram, a skillful naturalist, thinks the special "mention of the desert animals is one of the strongest pieces of evidence in favor of the authenticity of the book of Deuteronomy."[136] Sir Walter Besant, so many years secretary of the Palestine Exploration Fund, and perfectly conversant with its results, in a careful and continuous answer (too long to quote in full) to the inquiry whether these researches actually prove the historical part of the Old Testament, reaches the conclusion: "To my mind, absolute truth in local details—a thing which cannot possibly be invented, when it is spread over a history covering many centuries—is proof almost absolute as to the truth of the things related."[137]

In the same strain, and still more decisive as to not only the truthfulness but the substantial contemporaneousness of the closing part of Genesis and the first third of Exodus, are the words of so eminent a judge as the late R. S. Poole, written before some of the very latest discoveries: "It is now certain that the narrative of the history of Joseph and the sojourn and Exodus of the Israelites, that is to say, the portion from Genesis xxxix. to Exodus xv., so far as it relates to Egypt, is sub-

---
35 The Empire of the Hittites, p. 123.
36 The City and the Land, p. 80.
37 Ib., p. 123.

stantially not much later than B. C. 1300; in other words, was written when the memory of the events was fresh. The minute accuracy of the text is inconsistent with any later date. It is not merely that it shows knowledge of Egypt, but knowledge of Egpyt under the Ramessides, and yet earlier. The condition of the country, the chief cities of the frontier, the composition of the army, are true of the age of the Ramessides and not true of the age of the Pharaohs contemporary with Solomon and his successors." After alluding to many details which sustain his position, he mentions the significant fact that "foreign Egyptologists who have no theological bias, as independent scholars appear uniformly to accept its text (that of the Pentateuch) as an authority to be cited side by side with the Egyptian monuments." He specifies Lepsius, Brugsch and Chabas, adding that "it is impossible that they can, for instance, hold Kuenen's theories as to the date of the Pentateuch as far as the part relating to Egypt is concerned. They have taken the two sets of documents, Hebrew and Egyptian, side by side, and in the working of elaborate problems found everything consistent with accuracy on both sides; and of course accuracy would not be maintained in a tradition handed down through several centuries. If the large portion of the Pentateuch relating to the Egyptian period of Hebrew history, including as it does Elohistic as well as Jehovistic sections, is of the remote antiquity here claimed for it, no one can doubt that the first four books of Moses are of the same antiquity."[38] Such facts and testimonies are apprehensible to all fair-minded men.

In this same connection should be borne in mind the national commemorative observances of the Hebrew nation, existing as great central landmarks in their history, and explained only by the truthfulness of the narrative—the passover, perpetuating the hurried departure; the feast of the tabernacles, commemorating the dwelling in booths in the wilderness (Lev. xxiii. 43); the consecration of the first-born in commemoration of their deliverance when the first-born of Egypt perished. These things stand somewhat like our Fourth of July and Washington's birthday, telling their own story through the history of the nation, with the important differences that they were enjoined as religious observances, and as transmitted from contemporaneous times. How they could have been imposed upon the nation at any later date as transmitted observances has never yet been shown.

Now in the presence of such an array of indisputable facts as can thus be gathered up at every point where a test can be applied, theories, however ingenious, resting upon the introduction of supposed but absolutely unknown writers, compilers and editors, upon skillful dissections of the text into parts and often into comminuted fragments, transpositions *ad libitum*, rejections and assumed omissions, need not count for much with men who are

---

[38] Contemp. Rev., 1879, pp. 758, 759. See note xiv., Appendix.

governed by evidence and not by speculations.

It has sometimes been objected that the Hebrews are not mentioned on the Egyptian monuments. But Kittel speaks with emphasis on this point: "This is not to be wondered at, considering how many such foreign immigrations took place, especially during the middle kingdom. There is not a single statement in the old Egyptian monuments which can be unhesitatingly explained as referring to the immigration of the so-called Hyksos. Yet this was of far more significance to Egypt than that of the Hebrews. To determine when and whence the Hyksos came we have to depend on late and inadequate information. The monuments do not even give their name. This being so, it is simply marvelous how the silence of the monuments with respect to the Hebrews could have been adduced as a weighty argument against their having stayed in Egypt."[39] He also suggests how Egyptian pride would have prevented the mention of their immigration and exodus; and how almost incredible that a nation with the national sentiment and almost arrogance of the Jews would have invented the fiction of a "long-continued and shameful bondage" of their forefathers. To this it is to be added that the monuments in their reference to foreign nations always commemorate the alleged victories and conquests of the Egyptian monarchs, and never their humiliations. This was the state of the case when Kittel wrote in 1887.

---

39 History, I., p. 185.

But it is not proper to close the present chapter without allusion to the recent unquestionable finding of Israel on the Egyptian monuments, and that too in an inscription of Menephtah, the commonly supposed monarch of the exodus. It is dated in the fifth year of that monarch, the same year in which another inscription of his (previously known) had mentioned his conquest of the Libyans. The earlier part of the recent find (December, 1895) glorifies his defeat of the same Libyan invasion, and the passage immediately connected with the mention of Israel is translated by Mr. Griffith for M. Petrie as follows: "For the sun of Egypt has wrought this change; he was born as the fated means of revenging it, the king Menephtah. Chiefs bend down, saying, 'Peace to thee'; not one of the nine raises the head. Vanquished are the Tahennu (N. Africans); the Kheta (Hittites) are quieted; ravaged is Pa-kannu (Kanan) with all violence; taken is Ascadni (Askelon?); seized is Kazmel; Yenu (Yanoh) of the Syrians is made as though it had not existed; the people of Israel is spoiled, it hath no seed; Syria has become as widows in the land of Egypt; all lands together are in peace. Every one that was a marauder hath been subdued by the king Menephtah, who gives life like the sun every day."[40]

Professor Hommel's translation agrees substantially with this in the sentence relating to Israel, explaining, however, that the word rendered

---

[40] Petrie in the Contemporary Review, May, 1896, p. 622. Note xxxiii.

"spoiled" (*fckt*) does not occur elsewhere, but has a determinative meaning "evil things," and is possibly connected with another (*fk*), meaning "overrun an enemy"; and he renders the phrase, "it has no fruit."[41] Sayce translates "the Israelites are minished (?) so that they have no seed."[42] All three writers agree that the word expresses some serious damage done to Israel, and that the word "seed" is used in the Egyptian, as in our own language, of offspring or posterity. This last circumstance has been regarded as a striking coincidence with the Scripture account of the measures adopted by Pharaoh to exterminate the Israelites.

A collateral difficulty, not affecting the main point, the mention of Israel by Menephtah, has been raised, Petrie thinking the whole paragraph to narrate a succession of conquests, and, from the mention of the Hittites and localities in Syria and Palestine in the connection, that the damage to Israel must have been in Palestine and not in Egypt; while Sayce, Hommel and Dr. Selin (and others) understand it to refer to the suppression of Israel in Egypt. While we may wait for further light, several considerations are urged, strongly pointing to the latter view: (1) it does not appear that Menephtah ever was in Asia, or made any actual conquests except over the Libyans; (2) his defeat of the Libyans was but the repelling of an invasion; (3) the phraseology ("is spoiled, it hath no seed"), in which it is difficult not to see a refer-

---
41 In the Independent, Sept. 24, 1896.
42 Ib., July 11, 1896.

ence to the measures of Pharaoh, as recorded in Exodus i.; (4) the absence of the determinative meaning country or city, which is attached to the other names but wanting here, while the sign denoting simply man or woman (or persons) follows the name Israel; (5) the natural apprehension of the whole paragraph, not as a record of conquests which this monarch does not appear to have made, but, in connection with a boastful outburst immediately following his defeat of the Libyan invasion, a glorification of the relations of the empire or its ruler to its former enemies, among which is mentioned the movement, for a time successful, to suppress the Israelites.

Whatever ultimate decision, if any, may be reached on this collateral point, we may say, in the words of Professor Hommel, "However dark the reference of Menephtah may be to Israel, nevertheless the fact that mention is made of them, and that too in the connection to which I have referred (as having participated in the Egyptian troubles of previous years), is itself a matter of great importance, in so far as it confirms what has been before surmised, namely, Menephtah is the Pharaoh of the exodus." At all events it has furnished the only wanting link in the historic chain, namely, the Pharaoh's own statement of his severities upon Israel.

CHAPTER V

THE PATRIARCHAL HISTORY

IT has become customary with a certain class of modern writers to deny more or less completely the Scripture narratives of the patriarchs. They are resolved into names of clans, or they are legends, or traditions with a possible historic core, or they are ideas clothed in a personal form. The denial is conducted with much diversity of treatment, from the supercilious doggedness of Wellhausen to the patronizing courtesy of an Oxford Fellow, who informs us thus: "Even the noble narrative of the Jahvist is not sober history. Yet in another and a very real sense the Hexateuch becomes in the hands of scholars a history of unique interest. It is not indeed the history of Abraham and Jacob, of Moses and Joshua. It is the history—a history which cannot deceive any more than the history deciphered by geologists on the rocks can deceive—of religious ideas.'"[1] It seems that it had to fall into the "hands of scholars" to divest it of its personal life before it acquired this "unique interest" to mankind. With the personality of the men goes also, of course, the reality of the transactions.

The narratives take us into times otherwise prehistoric. The denier certainly has this advantage,

---
[1] Addis, The Documents of the Hexateuch, p. xcv.

which he is not slow to use, that he can deny indiscriminately their statements without being confronted with parallel accounts, except in the impregnable case of Abraham's time. Nevertheless the whole series of biographies admits of the most satisfactory indications of being veritable history.

We have (1) the weighty fact of the incorporation of these personages, with varying distinctness, into all the history, or, if one prefer, traditions of the Hebrew nation; (2) accounts of the environments of these personages, proved to be minutely accurate; (3) a series of portraitures, not only lifelike in the greatest diversity, as well as in the traits and inconsistencies of the characters, but not to be accounted for except as delineations of real life.

On the first of these points, perhaps no more needs to be said. But it carries a weight best appreciated by historians. As to the second, take but a specimen of the indubitable surroundings in which the biography of Joseph is embodied: a petted and therefore hated brother, finding his way to a pasture-ground, still fertile; rescued from death by being hidden in a pit where rock-hewn pits are yet numerous, near the great caravan road to Egypt; conveyed thither by a band of itinerants carrying to that country well-known articles of traffic; gradually rising to power in a mode not rare in despotism, whether ancient Rome, France of the middle ages, or modern Turkey, all the while in contact with local customs, which it requires of Ebers twenty closely-printed columns to point out;[2]

---
[2] Smith's Dict. of the Bible, 2nd ed., article "Joseph."

embalmed at his death, and in after years carried by the great host to be buried in the place which his father had bought for an hundred pieces of silver, where his tomb is held in reverence to the present day;—what is there in this simple and consistent story, even if it stood alone, to awaken an instant's doubt or suspicion? The other lives also are enveloped, though less abundantly, in the atmosphere of contemporary fact.

Take an instance so incidental as to attract no notice. When Jacob and Laban made a covenant and raised a stone heap, Laban named it Jegar-sahadutha, but Jacob called it Galeed, both names meaning "heap of witness," the first in Aramean, the second in Hebrew (Gen. xxxi. 47, 48). Not only do the diverse vernaculars of the two men thus appear, but, as Knobel and Dillmann remark, "the situation of the place at the boundary seems to have occasioned the double naming. For north of Gilead dwelt in part Aramean-speaking races (xxii. 14), but in the southern part of the land east of the Jordan such races cannot be shown till a later date." Also in corroboration of the fact that Hebrew was the early tongue of Palestine, the Tell Amarna letters from Phenicia give here and there a Canaanitish word by the side of its Assyrian equivalent. These (as well as certain Hebrew inflections occurring in the letters) afford fresh indications that Hebrew was originally "the language of Canaan."[3]

---
[3] Records of the Past, New Series, vi., p. 47. An instance occurs on p. 75 of a Hebrew explanatory word. Similar instances are found in Vol. v., pp. 75, 76, 81, and elsewhere.

When we pass from the environments to the characters themselves, the impression of reality and truth has been made upon the race down to the present time. The world has accepted and admired these life-like portraits, and pronounced them genuine, and will not give them up; simple, candid, direct, unsparing, delicate in their shadings, striking in their variety and their contrasts, and human in every aspect, even in their inconsistencies. The romancer has not drawn such characters. They are Shakespearean in their variety, but some of them are beyond what Shakespeare has portrayed.

The narrative contains never a word of admiraiton or depreciation. It casts over all a pure, "dry light." It records events in their histories without comment. It supports no theories and takes no sides, except always for the right. It has no men whose faults it is bound to hide, nor any whose virtues it is bound to conceal. Thus in the dealings of Abraham and Abimelech, the latter appears to advantage. By nature Esau is a more attractive character in some respects than Jacob. In the difficulty between Sarah and Hagar, Sarah's magnanimity is not forthcoming. In the arrangements between the sons of Jacob and the Shechemites, the comparative honor of the latter and the infamy of the former are plainly told. Rachel, the favorite wife of Jacob, obtains no special favoritism at the historian's hands. The beloved Joseph, though occupying so large a space in the lifetime of his family, loses his prominence in the subsequent history of the nation, and Benjamin still more, while Levi is marked for his cruelty in the affair of Shechem; and Judah's profligacy in the case of Tamar, ancestor of Christ though he was, is fully recorded.

Noah, so great and strong as to stand out against the corruption of the whole world, and for long years to hold on his work of obedience to God and of preparation for a catastrophe of which no sign had appeared, yet afterwards falls a victim to the intoxicating cup he himself had prepared, and disgraces himself before his children. But he recovers himself, and utters a prophecy of remarkable fulfillment.

What a magnificent character is presented in Abraham, "the friend of God"!—the man who at the call of God "went out, not knowing whither he went," a model of faith to the end of the world; the associate of princes; the man of peace and concession, and for once only the fighting hero; the conciliatory husband and careful father; moving among the tribes and nations with dignity and power; by migration from Ur to Canaan changing the destiny of the world; yet not so immaculate but that twice at least he gave way to fear and equivocation, though even then under the strain of his conjugal affections. And what a thoroughly and touchingly human episode is that of Sarah, Hagar and Ishmael! And what a startling and well-nigh incomprehensible side-narrative is that of Lot! Who ever invented such a story? And where in all literature or history a more telling stroke in one word than the portraiture of Ishmael and his race in Genesis xvi. 12, "He shall be a wild ass of a man"?[4]—a picture which has held good for more than three thousand years, of which we may well ask, Is it not something more than history narrated, even history anticipated?

In marked but life-like contrast is Abraham's son Isaac; a simple, peace-loving shepherd, meditative and devout, leaving his father to manage his affairs; imitative of his father's faults; mourning for his mother; captivated by his dashing Esau; planning for the family succession, but baffled by his scheming wife; astounded at his mistake, then quietly accepting the plain will of God.

The character and career of Jacob is equally unique: versatile, unfaltering and successful, timid but resolute, dreading yet meeting responsibilities; shrinking from open fraud, yet yielding to his imperious mother; seemingly absorbed in selfish schemes, yet terribly intense in his attachments; ever a man of peace, but steadily embroiled in troubles; beginning life laden with Jewish craft, and maturing and mellowing at last into a venerable presence as he stands before Pharaoh, and a saint and prophet at the close of life. Can anything be more realistic than many of the incidents of this history, such as the fraudulent procurement of the blessing, the flight from Padan-aram and interview with Laban when overtaken, and the en-

---

4 So Ewald, Kalisch, Knobel, Dillmann, Strack. Rosennueller had rendered still more closely, "onager homo," a wild-ass man. The Revisers render, a wild ass among men.

counter with Esau on the way? So also the diverse traits and conduct of his several children would invite careful study were they found in some old secular story.

What an unmistakable verity is the picture of Jacob and Esau, in their strong contrast of character and destiny! The one draws and holds our sympathy by his very impulsiveness, frankness and heedlessness; and we pity and lament his folly and his failures. But he is fitful and passionate and void of principle and of purpose, as bitter in his hate as in his grief, as hasty to threaten death as to forgive and to forget.

Still more striking in its diversity from the other lives, and we might say from all other lives, is the history of Joseph. Here is a colorless account of a beautiful character, without a tinge of insipidity; a child-like boy, petted but not spoiled; a manly man, trusted and always true; a loving son, a cautious and forgiving brother; a kidnapped youth making his way by force of character to the stewardship of a great house; a prisoner on false charges, emerging ultimately by the favor of Providence to be the virtual head of the kingdom, and a statesman equal to unequaled emergencies; the savior of his father's family and race; the old man with his great-grandchildren at his knees; the patriot claiming a burial in his native land. Interspersed in the narrative are transactions simply related, such as the grief of the father, and the interview with the brethren, which have long been recognized as among the most pathetic and life-like in the whole circle of literature. And the entire history, as already remarked, is embedded in a solid basis of Egyptian history impervious to the minutest hostile criticism, so that nothing is wanting to the entire verisimilitude.[5]

Waiving now all consideration of the exact details of custom and environment, and fixing our attention on these several characters in their wide variety and striking qualities, we may well ask for the production of any known, probable or conjectural individual, living from five hundred to a thousand years later—or at any other period of Jewish history—who was capable of inventing such personages, or of describing them except as he drew from real life. The matter appeals to the tribunals of letters and of sound judgment alike.

But in regard to the period of history in which Abraham, the earliest of these patriarchs (except Noah), bears a part, as contained in the fourteenth chapter of Genesis, a good Providence has within the last few years brought extraordinary confirmations, though the great and independent scholar, Ewald, more than fifty years ago had the sagacity to recognize its "inestimable value to the historian," and to regard the whole piece as "written prior to Moses."[6] Such Germans as Noeldeke, Hitzig and Hilgenfeld ventured to pronounce it an invention

---

[5] Yet in Kautzsch's German translation the story of Joseph is referred to J, E, JE, R, and P, extending from the 9th to the 5th century B. C. or later. It is dissected into some ninety fragments, twenty-two of which, if we have counted rightly, occur in one chapter (xxxvii.) of 35 verses.

[6] History of Israel, I., pp. 301, 52, Eng. Trans.

for the glorification of Abraham; and Kuenen, not to be outdone, asserts it to be "of very recent date," with three names and places changed into men, the previous inhabitants of the trans-Jordan district "adopted" from Deuteronomy, and verses 18-20 "intended to glorify the priesthood and to justify their claiming of tithes.'"[7] These airy dogmatisms appear now to be effectually extinguished beneath the weight of rock-cut inscriptions. Doubt was formerly expressed that at so early a period the monarchs of the Euphrates region had pushed west as far as Palestine. These doubts have been set at rest. Not only do the Tell Amarna letters, written in the Babylonian-Assyrian script, from Tyre, Sidon, Beirut, Jerusalem, Askelon, Hazor, Makkedah, Lachish, Accho, and numerous other places throughout and around Palestine about 1450 B. C., prove the already long established influence of the oriental monarchies in the region of the Mediterranean, but Ammisatana, king of Babylon (from about 2115 to 2090 B. C.),[8] proclaimed himself as king also of Martu (the west-land or Mediterranean coast);[9] and quite recently discovered inscriptions show that Sargon I. (assigned to about 3800 B. C.) made several expeditions not only to the Mediterranean coast but to the island of Cyprus, where seals bearing the name of his son Naramsin have been found. According to Mr. Boscawen, the son

---

[7] The Hexateuch, p. 324.
[8] Sayce gives the date 2241-2216 B. C. (The Higher Criticism, etc., p. 163).
[9] Records of the Past, New Series, V., p. 103. Schrader (Keilinschriften, p. 136) says that Kudur Mabag took the same title; so also say Sayce, Strack und Fried. Delitzsch.

and successor even pushed his way till he took possession of the mines in the Sinaitic peninsula, whence he was driven out by Snefru of Egypt,[10] whose name may be still seen carved above the entrance of the old mine in Wady Maghara, some 3,700 years before Christ, as commonly reckoned. The localities of the eastern kings are satisfactorily ascertained, in three instances at least. Shinar is Sumer, the region of Babylonia, including Babylon; Elam the mountainous region to the east of Babylon; Ellasar probably Larsa, represented now by the ruins of Senkereh. The word "nations" (Goiim, R. V.) is now commonly regarded as a proper name designating the Guti or Kuti of the inscriptions, situated to the northeast of Babylon.[11]

Light has been steadily cast upon the personnel and relations of these kings, growing clearer to the present time. Some years ago Schrader pronounced Arioch to be unquestionably the same as Iriarku, king of Larsa, and son of Kurdur-mabug, king of Sumer and Akkad,[12] and the identification has been accepted. Arioch and two others appear to be the allies and subordinates of Chedorlaomer, the head of the expedition. Now an inscription of Assur-

---

[10] Boscawen's The Bible and the Monuments, pp. 24, 25. Sayce says four expeditions, which appears to be Boscawen's account.

[11] It may be added that three such oriental experts as Schrader, Halevy and Friedrich Delitzsch since 1887 have held to the identity of Amraphel with the great Khammurabi, or Ammurabi (about 2100 B. C.). The suggestion supposes a change having taken place in the final l. Dillmann and Strack cite the opinion without protest, and Friedrich Delitzsch says (Delitzsch's Genesis, p. 525) it "rests on no feeble foot." Prof. Lyon (Bib. World, June, 1896, p. 431) remarks that the form is in its first syllables in keeping with that of Ammisatana and Ammisaduga of the same dynasty, while no subsequent ruler for 368 years has a name beginning thus. He calls attention to the fact that the difference between the Hebrew Amraphel and the Assyrian Ammurabi is not greater than between Nebuchadrezzar and Nabium-Kuduri-uzur.

[12] Keilinschriften, p. 135.

banipal, king of Assyria, records a conquest of Babylonia by the Elamites about 2280 B. C., that is, before the time of the expedition.[13] The names of three of the kings until quite recently had not been found. An approximation or analogy to the name Chedorlaomer was found in three royal names beginning with Chedor (*Kudur* in the Assyrian). But in January, 1896, Mr. Pinches, of the British Museum, read to the Victoria Institute a paper in which he mentions having found on some mutilated cuneiform tablets in that museum the names Kudurlachgumal, Eriakua, and Tudchula, which he identifies with Chedorlaomer, Arioch and Tidal, the first of them being called "king of Elam," as is Chedorlaomer.[14] The names of the Canaanite kings there are, of course, no inscriptions to verify; but the narrative conforms to what appears in the Tell Amarna letters, in that each was sovereign of a city.

We can follow the course of the invasion in general and to some degree in detail. Crossing the Euphrates probably by the customary northern route, they moved southward, east of the Jordan, to Ashteroth Karnaim (Tell Ashtarah), which Thothmes III. had already found and taken,[15] Kiriathaim (Kureyat), past Mount Seir, to "El Paran by the wilderness" (the border of the desert of et Tih), and most likely to Elath (or Ailah), at the head of the Gulf of Akaba. On the return they are found

---
[13] Tomkins' Life and Times of Abraham, p. 176.
[14] Cited by Prof. Lyon, Biblical World, June, 1896, p. 431. Mentioned also by Sayce, London Academy, September 7, 1895.
[15] Records of the Past, V., p. 45.

at Kadesh (Ain Gadis), next at Engedi, on the west side of the Dead Sea. Having surrounded and isolated the five native kings, the battle is joined in a region of "bitumen pits"—bitumen having abounded both in ancient and in modern times on the shores and at times on the waters of the Dead Sea. After plundering the wealthy cities that lay near the great north and south caravan road, they took the west side route to the neighborhood of Dan. While they lay here in the fancied security of old oriental armies after a victory, but visible from the southern headlands,[16] Abraham attacks them with his smaller band, not in open fight, but by a night surprise, and pursues them towards, but not to, Damascus. He is met on his return by the king of Salem. This part of the narrative has been questioned. But since the year 1887 not less than six letters have been given to the world written by the king of "Urusalim," showing that before the conquest of Palestine by the Israelites Jerusalem was governed by a king (as we read in Joshua), that it bore the name of which Salem is a part, and that the usual explanation, "city of peace," is a probable one.[17]

In the historic facts incorporated into this narrative it thus stands thoroughly confirmed, as far as tests can be applied, while the movements described are in entire consistency with each other and with the known conditions. So minute is this corre-

---

16 Thomson's The Land and the Book, ii., p. 553.
17 Conder's Tell Amarna Letters, p. 147 It is not safe to follow Conder in identifying the *Khabiri* with Hebrews, nor Sayce in thinking them "confederates." The striking views expressed by the latter concerning the king of Jerusalem appear to need confirmation.

spondence that Mr. Tomkins has shown with much probability that at the first invasion by Chedorlaomer, fourteen years before the second, Abraham "must have been dwelling at Haran when this great motley array of the four eastern kings drew its march through Haran on its way to conquest; and again returning with spoils and captives to Chaldea and to Elam. So that Abraham had very probably set eyes on Chedorlaomer some fourteen years before he found himself in arms against him."[18] And the very words used in the Hebrew for "bitumen pits" Dr. Thompson found in use to designate the numerous wells of bitumen in the chalky marl at Ed Daher south of Lebanon, namely, *biaret hummar* in the cognate Arabic tongue.[19]

It is worthy of mention that the narrative exhibits some unobtrusive tokens of antiquity; giving in connection with old names (in one instance, of a perished city) equivalent names, apparently older: "Bela, the same is Zoar" (twice); "the vale of Siddim, which is the Salt Sea"; "En Mishpat, the same is Kadesh." In one instance only the older name is given, namely Hazezon Tamar, as though the narrative might be older than the name Engedi. Other peculiarities are noticeable, such as the term Hebrew applied to Abraham, and the word for "trained men," which is not found elsewhere.[20]

---

[18] Life and Times of Abraham, p. 184.
[19] The Land and the Book, ii., p. 527.
[20] The name "Dan" in the narrative is easily accounted for, as a name so noted that it took the place of Laish, the latter being entirely dropped in the copying, as unnecessary, even if originally added as a synonym: just as "the Fork" and "Duquesne" were merged in Pittsburg, and the Indian name

But whatever may be the age of this part of the narrative, it shows a contemporaneous knowledge of historic persons, facts and situations that cannot be shaken, and proves it to be a trustworthy statement.

Here we have reached a point nearly two thousand years before Christ, in a test question, vigorously disputed, where our narrative rests on an impregnable historic basis. The narrative deals too, with actual personages throughout, as well as historic events; and by these tokens, together with its inherent consistency and its conformity to all local requirements, takes away the last shadow of excuse for dismissing Abraham as "a free creation of unconscious art,"[21] or resolving him into "an epoch, a race or order of men or a roving social environment,"[22] or for viewing him as other than he is described in the simplest mode, a magnificent personage, in close communion with God, thus moving majestically among his contemporaries, setting an example of faith for all time, and leading off an undying movement in the world's history.

In ascending the line of the Scripture narrative, we recede farther and farther from the domain of secular chronicles, and can test the accounts, aside from their aspect of honesty and candor, only by their conformity, general or special, to such fragments of outside knowledge and such traditions as can be brought into the comparison.

Shawmut and the English name Trimountain were lost from the 7th of September, 1630, when the Court of Assistants "ordered that Trimountain be called Boston."

21 Wellhausen, History of Israel, Eng. Trans., p. 320.

22 There is an appearance of yielding to this unsupported view in McCurdy's History, Prophecy and the Monuments, ii., pp. 89, 90, although somewhat indistinct and possibly not intended.

That Abraham was buried in Hebron, and that his remains were deposited in a cave beneath the present strange edifice, the Haram with its enclosed mosque, is the united tradition of Jews, Christians and Mohammedans, the latter of whom hold the place in such reverence that only royal authority or influence has secured admission within the building. The present edifice is assigned (from its style of masonry) to the Herodian age at least, and it is known that there is a cave beneath it; and travelers from Robinson to Conder have been satisfied of the truth of the tradition. The present structure may very well be the successor of former ones, inasmuch as Josephus relates that the sepulchers of Abraham and his descendants were built in Hebron, and that their monuments of excellent marble were to be seen in his day in Hebron.[23] It is a curious fact, however it may be accounted for, that whereas Abraham came originally from Ur of the Chaldees, there is an old temple in the ruins of that ancient city (now Mugheir) the length of which, as given by Loftus, is 198 feet,[24] while the length of the Haram in Hebron, as given by Conder, is 198 feet.[25] The width, however, is not the same; that of the former being 133, of the latter 112 feet.

When the Speaker's Commenary on Genesis was published (1871), opinion was divided whether to find Ur, the early home of Abraham, at Mugheir in southern Babylonia, or at Urfa, about 600 miles

---

23 Jewish Wars, iv., 9, 7.
24 Travels in Caldea, p. 129.
25 Tent Work in Palestine, ii., p. 81.

northwest of it. The former is now accepted by nearly all Assyriologists and most expositors—with an occasional dissent, as that of Strack. Here are ruins of a very ancient city, among which the most noteworthy things are a great temple of the moon-god, and the immense number of tombs in and around the extensive ruins. It is one of the greatest burial places known; and it is thought that, perhaps for its supposed sanctity, the dead were for many centuries brought there for burial. It is proved to have had as early as Abraham's time a varied and extensive literature.[26] The annals of Assurbanipal show that Babylonia had been overrun by the Elamites in 2280 B. C., and most of the inscriptions of Kudur-mabuk and Eriarku of Larsa have been found at Mugheir. Whether or not there is weight in the suggestion of Mr. Tomkins that the conquest may have been adverse to the house of Terah, and that "when Abraham assailed the eastern forces to rescue Lot, he was probably encountering an old enemy of his house and people,"[27] it is not difficult to discover a reason for the selection of Haran as the place of migration. It was not only the crossing-point of the Syrian, Assyrian and Babylonian trade routes, but, like Mugheir, it had a great temple of the moon-god, indicating a close alliance between the two places, and thus the most natural and home-like resort. In this connection, also, it is not to be overlooked that Abraham left Haran

---

26 See Smith's Caldean Genesis, p. 25, and Sayce's Ancient Empires of the East, p 167 seq.

27 Tomkins' Life and Times, p. 200, and Boscawen's Bible and Monuments, p. 25.

for Palestine with gathered "substance" and "souls" or persons, and that in Palestine he was able to muster three hundred and eighteen trained men, or fighting retainers, implying a wealth and standing on which the hand of the conqueror might have lain heavily. Yet even if such a secular motive might have influenced Terah, a far higher motive impelled Abraham.

He went from a land where they "served other gods" (Gen. xxxi. 30; Josh. xxiv. 2), as is abundantly shown by the temples and inscriptions of Chaldea from the earliest times. Assurbanipal records how the early monarch Kudur-nankundi worshiped "the great gods"; Urukh founded a temple of the sun at Larsa, a temple to Ishtar at Erech, a temple to Bel and another to Beltis at Nippur, and at Zirgulla a temple to Sarili, the "king of the gods." At Mugheir and at Haran, as already mentioned, there were great temples to the moon-god.[28]

The early civilization and culture in and around Ur in Abraham's time are proved to have been such as would explain such a development as his. As a specimen even of business methods Boscawen quotes a mortgage deed which reads thus: "Concerning the loan of his silver (money) he places for security a house, field, garden, man-servant and maid-servant;" and he inquires, "With such carefully drawn deeds in use before he (Abraham) left his Chaldean home, is it any wonder that the trans-

---

[28] Records of the Past, iii., pp. 8, 9.

action of the purchase of the cave of Machpelah is carried out with such commercial accuracy?"[129] His Scripture environments are found to be true to the times.

It is not necessary to follow him, as may be done easily in the main, on his way through Canaan, except to suggest that crossing the Euphrates at the usual place or places nearly west of Haran, his journey would be by the neighborhood of Damascus, and thus perhaps account for his having later as a steward of his house Eliezer of Damascus (Gen. xv. 2). The historic correspondence of the condition of Egypt at the time with the implications and statements of the narrative, has been sufficiently indicated already.

Ascending still higher, we find the same congruity with all ascertained facts; as in connection with Babel and the dispersion. The land Shinar is found in the ancient Sumer, lower Mesopotamia. The building material is not the stone and mortar of Egypt nor its sun-dried bricks, but burnt brick cemented with bitumen. Now while it might easily be said that a later writer in Babylonia would have been aware that bitumen occurs in that region, as at Hit or Is, and at Nimrud (near Mosul), and that Birs Nimrud and the temple at Mugheir are in part built of burnt brick and bitumen, the sacred writer is also aware that in Egypt they built with "stone and mortar" (Gen. xi. 3). He has definite knowledge, and makes no mistakes. The Hebrew nar-

---

[129] The Bible and the Monuments, p. 25.

rative contains verbal reminders of the region. The words "brick" and "make brick" are the same in the Hebrew as in the Assyrian and Babylonian;[30] but the process of "burning them thoroughly" is a process almost never practiced in Egypt until Roman times. As to the tower itself, it is hardly worth while to look for traces of a building that was not finished, although the story is started from time to time that such traces have been found. There is, however, a tradition in the classic writers, thus stated by Ovid: "They say that the giants aspired to the celestial kingdom, and that they heaped up the lofty mountains to the stars. Then the omnipotent father hurled his thunderbolt, crashing through Olympus, and struck down Ossa piled on Pelion."[31] There is also cited a distinct Babylonish tradition, one form of which (as given by Abydenus, probably from Berosus) reads that "the early men, having become puffed up and having despised the gods, undertook a lofty tower where Babylon now is. It was already near heaven when the winds came to the aid of the gods and overthrew the work upon the builders. The ruins of it are said to be at Babylon. Hitherto men had been of one tongue, but now discordant speech was upon them from the gods." In another form (given by Alexander Polyhistor as from "the Sybil") it says, "When all men spoke the same language, some of them built an exceeding high tower in order to ascend into heaven. God, however, having made winds to blow, thwarted

---

[30] Schrader, K. A. T., p. 121.
[31] Ovid, Metamorphoses, i., 152.

them and gave to each a language of his own; wherefore the city was called Babylon." The independence of this tradition is seen, as has been remarked, in the statement that the winds were employed in the work of destruction. Professor Davis of Princeton inclines to insist on this as representing a genuine Babylonian tradition, and that "its kinship with the Hebrew narrative is unmistakable."[32] Dillmann, who thinks it not proved that such a tradition was circulated in Babylonia, still remarks that "dark historical reminiscences lie at the foundation of the narrative" as a whole.[33] Schrader also thinks it cannot well be doubted that "the saga here encountered has rested upon a building once actually existing, and that it may naturally have been only one of two, either the ruins called Babil on the east bank of the Euphrates or the remarkable ruined tower on the west bank, called Birs Nimrud, still rising 154 feet above the level of the plain."[34] But though Delitzsch thinks it not impossible that ruins of the building or at least traces of its site should have been preserved;[35] and while it is not impossible, as some have suggested, that one of these ruins may commemorate the site, the only confirmation to be claimed for the tower and its significance is the tradition of the battle with the gods.[36]

---
[32] For full details the reader is referred to his Genesis and Semetic traditions (1894).
[33] Commentary *in loco*.
[34] Keilinschriften, pp. 121-123.
[35] New Commentary, Eng. trans., i., p. 353.
[36] George Smith's belief of a reference to the building in a Babylonian tablet, though at first approved by Sayce, must be given up as not well founded (Chaldean Genesis, pp. 163,164). Nor can Nebuchadnezzar's inscription that he had restored a damaged tower built by a former king (Records of the Past, vii., p. 71) be well appealed to in evidence.

But the narrative speaks also of a dispersion, and names Shinar or Sumer as the radiating center. That this general region was the point of departure for the race in its dispersion appears to be now the somewhat concurrent opinion of various classes of scientific men. It is quite remarkable what a variety of indications all point in that direction. Thus from his special point of view Guyot lays great stress on a consideration generally overlooked, which, in his own words, "has not been sufficiently insisted on, and to which has not been attributed the importance it deserves. The fact is the following: While all the types of animals and of plants go on decreasing in perfection, from the equatorial to the polar regions, in proportion to the temperatures, man presents to our view his purest, his most perfect type at the very center of Asia-Europe, in the regions of Iran, of Armenia, and of the Caucasus; and, departing from this geographical center in the three grand directions of the lands, the types gradually lose the beauty of their forms in proportion to their distance, even to the extreme points of the southern continents, where we find the most deformed and degenerate races, and the lowest in the scale of humanity." After unfolding the fact in several pages of detail, he inquires, "Does not this surprising coincidence seem to designate those Caucasian regions as the cradle of man, the point of departure for the races of the earth?"[37] St. Hilaire called attention to the fact that of the domesticated animals

---

[37] Guyot, The Earth and Man, pp. 254, 262.

that have accompanied man, thirty-five in number, thirty-one appear to have originated in Central Asia or Northern Africa. Others have noted the fact that most of the cereals which are used by man have had their earliest and most congenial, if not their native home, in this general region.[38] "Wheat is found only where man is found," and while its precise origin is an open question, yet according to Berosus wheat, barley and sesame grew wild in the region of Babylonia; and it is stated that wheat still does so in the neighborhood of Anah.[39] Other considerations, linguistic, historic and archæological, point in the same direction. The field is too broad even for an outline sketch of the whole argument. But after a protracted discussion of its various branches, Ebrard reaches the conclusion that "resting on purely physiological, ethnographical, historical and linguistic investigations is the scientifically certain fact that the population of all parts of the earth has gone forth from the west of inner Asia, the Euphrates region."[40] So also Zoeckler, as the result of similar investigations: "That this original seat (of the human race) was situated eastward of the home-land of the book of Revelation, somewhere in southern Asia, is established by the most weighty indications of ethnography and natural science. Neither South Africa nor America, neither a mythical Atlantis nor a tertiary Lemuria, have half so good claims to be the starting point of both

---

38 Cited in Southall's Recent Origin of Man, p. 43.
39 Sayce, Ancient Empires of the East, p. 96.
40 Ebrard, Christian Apologetics, iii., p. 312.

together, our race and its attendant domestic animals and cereals, as the territory limited by the Euphrates on the west and the Indus and Ganges on the east."[41] Quatrefages, while inclined, though not with entire positiveness, to find the center of radiation somewhat farther east, at the great central plateau, concludes his statement by saying that no facts have yet been discovered which authorize us to place the cradle of the human race elsewhere than in Asia.[42] It is also quite interesting to observe how such a writer as Lefèvre, who avowedly discarded the guidance of "the Hebrew Bible" in this matter, yet approximates to its position. For he concludes that the American races came from Asia; dwells on the fundamental identity between the languages of rival nations, separated by manners, aspirations and distance; emphasizes the fact that the Aryan races, spread from Iceland to the mouth of the Ganges and from Sweden to Crete, without including the two Americas and Australia, "owe to a single definite group, and not to their own initiative, their languages, their institutions and the germ of their destiny." He avoids naming a definite center of radiation for the various nations, but he reaches a stage where, "from the eastern slope of the great Asiatic plateaus, the ancestors of the Chinese descended their rivers, the Blue and the Yellow, and two centers of civilization arose, on the banks of the Nile and at the mouth of the Eu-

---

41 Urstand des Menschen, p. 241. His primary reference is to the garden of Eden, but of course it applies here.
42 The Human Species, p. 178.

phrates."[43] His subsequent and detailed account of the dispersion from the latter region is in close conformity to the Scripture account."[44] This account does unquestionably explain most naturally a divergent movement of the nations to the east and southeast, northwest, west and southwest. It would conform to the fact that in general the farther the departure from the center, the greater the growing degradation, except so far as some higher influence penetrated the seclusion.

The exact process of the confusion of tongues, recorded in this narrative, is obscure in the absence of detailed information. It has been perhaps wisely viewed as a precipitation of what would otherwise have taken place in the course of events, whereby in their isolation from each other the races have formed nearly a thousand languages. On the broad question of one original speech there are as yet no means of reaching an absolute decision outside of this narrative. Two great families of languages are now universally recognized, namely, the Semitic and the Aryan or Indo-European; and certain relationships found to exist between them. There are still wanting further investigations, if they can ever be made satisfactorily, which may decide the question of other relationships. Meanwhile it is sufficient, perhaps, to quote the conclusion reached by one of the most noted comparative philologists of this generation. Max Müller writes thus: "We

---
43 Lefevre, Race and Language, p. 260.
44 See note xv., Appendix.

have examined all possible forms which language can assume, and we have now to ask, can we reconcile with these three distinct forms, the radical, the terminational, the inflectional, the admission of one common origin of human speech? I answer decidedly, Yes."[45] Bunsen, with his multifarious learning, had already said: "Comparative philology would have been compelled to set forth as a postulate some such division of languages in Asia if the Bible had not preserved to us this great, true, historic event."[46] And still earlier Alexander von Humboldt, who had no reference to the Bible, at the close of his long life had made the suggestion that the comparative study of the languages "may lead to a generalization of views regarding the affinity of the races, and their conjectural extension *from one common point of radiation.*"[47] While therefore we can appeal to no contemporary history, for the reason that there is none, the results of the most careful modern research tend strongly to corroborate the narrative.

When we ascend one step further, to the history of Noah after the departure from the ark, we are on similarly firm ground. The mountains of Ararat, where the ark rested, are in the Armenian territory. Noah was intoxicated with the wine which he had made. In that region the vine is now, and through all historic times has been, abundant, thriving in some instances at a height of 4,000 feet

---
45 Mueller, Science of Language, First Series, p. 329.
46 Bunsen, Bibelwerk, i., p. 30.
47 Cosmos, ii., pp. 111, 112.

above the sea level. Here Xenophon with the ten thousand found old and excellent wine,[48] and here Justin Perkins, in 1843, found wine, and intoxication too, in abundance. It is to be observed also that the narrative does not spare the weakness and the shame of Noah. But it records as well his utterances when he "awoke from his wine," that is, recovered from his intoxication.

Though not indispensable to this discussion, it is quite appropriate to call attention to the remarkable anticipation of history in those utterances concerning Shem, Ham and Japheth. In regard to the first, it takes the form of a burst of praise: "Blessed be Jehovah, God of Shem." That was to be the blessing of the Shemite race—God revealed as Jehovah to Abraham and his descendants, and through them to the world. Shem was to be the depositary of the revelation. The declaration concerning Japheth, "God shall make wide room for Japheth," has been fulfilled partly in the Persian, Greek and Roman expansion, and still more remarkably even in later times, when the great historic races of the world have been and are Japhetic races. The additional promise, "He (Japheth)[49] shall dwell in the tents of Shem," easily means, shall share in his privileges. Dillmann would find here the reception of the Japhetic nations into the alliance of the old Semitic nations, which may be valid as far as it extends, without exhausting the fullness of the

---

[48] Anabasis, iv., 4, 9.

[49] Whatever the grammatical antecedent in this clause, the actual subject is clearly Japheth, whose destiny is declared. So now the best expositors.

blessing imparted to Shem. Delitzsch adds well, that it involves "the entrance of Japheth into the kingdom of God, which is with Japheth"; an assurance which has been signally fulfilled. The announcement that Canaan (i. e., his descendants) should be a servant of servants both to Shem and to Japheth was fulfilled in connection with Shem when the Canaanites were extirpated or reduced to be hewers of wood and drawers of water by the Israelites; and in connection with Japheth, as Delitzsch remarks, "when the Greeks and Romans overthrew Tyre and Carthage, after the Phenician coast and colonial power had already been broken by the Assyrians, Chaldeans and Persians. Hannibal came to feel this curse when he beheld the head of Asdrubal thrown over the Punic entrenchments by the Romans, and exclaimed, '*Agnosco fortunam Carthaginis.*' The third Punic War (149-146) ended in the total demolition of Carthage, and the infliction of the curse upon its site"—an event which changed the destinies of modern civilization.

The quality both of the narrative and the utterance appears in the fact that these announcements were not arbitrary but had their foundation and justification in the qualities of the posterity, already foreshadowed in their ancestors. The reason expressly involved in the subjugation of the Canaanites (in Gen. xv. 16) is their "iniquity"; in regard to which Lenormant has said that no other nation has rivaled them in the mixture of blood and debauchery with which they thought to honor the Deity.[50]

---
[50] Lenormant, Manual of the Ancient History of the East, ii., 219.

The overthrow of Carthage is conceded to have been the deliverance of the world from its most threatening danger.

Dillmann speaks thus of these prophecies: "Deeply moved by the transaction, and thoroughly discerning the nature of his sons, Noah, as one controlled by a higher spirit, by virtue of his paternal dignity, solemnly and in lofty strains pronounces upon them the blessing and the curse."

CHAPTER VI

THE TABLE OF THE NATIONS

NOT the least important portion of the Hexateuch for the present purpose is the table of the nations, contained in the tenth chapter of Genesis. Although easily passed over as a bald and uninteresting catalogue of names, it stands like a solid rock foundation and proof of the historic character of the book. The chief difficulty in the use of it springs from the extreme remoteness of its facts, and the scantiness of our modern knowledge to make connection with it. No other consecutive history extends back half-way towards its starting point. The migrations and minglings of the nations, the changes and interchanges of languages, and often the difficulty of identifying a name when transferred from one tongue to another, largely embarrass the interpretation. But to whatever extent, with our present and increasing resources, we can put it to the test, it stands the test as far as we can go, and constantly passes beyond our reach. It constitutes the one central and continuous line with which the fragmentary historic allusions from other sources are wont to be compared.

1. Lest it should be thought that the value of this record is exaggerated, the concurrent testimony of some of the ablest, most learned and respected

modern scholars is subjoined. Bunsen wrote in 1860: "The table of the nations in Genesis is the most learned of all ancient documents and the most ancient of all learned ones. It is altogether the most astonishing and admirable monument of the tradition."[1] Knobel, in 1860, pronounced it "a historical monument," declared that "the peoples mentioned in it are historical, that in the time of the author the Hebrews knew well the most noted of the nations within the region designated, and that there can be no doubt that continued research will ever more confirm the trustworthiness of this our oldest ethnography."[2] Again, in 1875, he emphasized the breadth of its survey, and the remarkable peculiarity that whereas other ancient nations commonly did not concern themselves about foreign communities unless in matters of state or commerce, and often despised them as barbarians, here a multitude of races is passed in review, to whom the Israelites stood in no relations of life.[3] The statement is repeated almost literally by Dillmann in 1892.[4] Brugsch says, in 1891: "It has the highest significance for scientific investigation."[5] George Rawlinson concludes his detailed examination of the contents of the chapter thus: "The record, rightly interpreted, completely harmonizes with the science (ethnology), and not only so, but anticipates many of the most curious and remarkable discover-

---

[1] Bibelwerk, Erster Theil, p. 63.
[2] Exegetisches Handbuch, Genesis, p. 107.
[3] Kommentar, 3rd ed., p. 176.
[4] Die Genesis, p. 162.
[5] Steininschrift, p. 49.

ies which ethnology has made in comparatively recent times. The thorough harmony which exists between ethnological science and this unique record is a strong argument for the truth of both."[6] Delitzsch says in the last edition of his commentary: "Nowhere is found a survey of the connection of nations that can be compared with the ethnological table of the Bible; nowhere one so universal in proportion to its horizon, and so all-comprising, at least with regard to its purpose."[7] To Kalisch it is "an unparalleled list, the combined result of deep reflection and research, and no less valuable as a historical document than as a lasting proof of the brilliant capacity of the Hebrew mind."[8] Ebers wrote, in 1868, that "in the presence of the great genealogical tree of Genesis we stand on firmer ground" (than as to the locality of paradise), and that his own effort was directed only to ascertaining what lands or nations the author intended by his names, and finding their geographical position.[9] Sir J. W. Dawson, in 1894, terms it "a scrap of pre-historic lore of the most intensely interesting character," speaks of the "sure scientific instinct" of the author, and after some explanatory remarks he proceeds: "These points being premised, we can clear away the fogs which have been gathered around this luminous spot in the early history of the world, and can trace at least the principal ethnic lines which have radiated from it."[10]

---

[6] Origin of Nations., p. 252.
[7] New Commentary, Eng. trans., i., p. 300.
[8] Commentary on Genesis, p. 287. [9] Egypt, etc., pp. 36, 37.
[10] The Meeting Place of Geology and History, pp. 183, 184, 188.

Strack, in his commentary published in the same year, says: "The statements of the table have rendered manifold services to scientific inquiry, as connecting links and guides. Many of them that were formerly doubted or pronounced erroneous have been proved by farther investigation to be correct. It is to be observed that everything mythical or monstrous is strictly avoided. The authors speak only of what they know, what they hold to be true on the basis of the knowledge of their time; they make no inventions, so that Herder judiciously observes 'the poverty of this list and of its information is its guaranty.'"[11]

We have thus gathered up some of the testimonies of the foremost modern scholars in regard to the historic character and value of a part of the sacred narrative which far antedates all other consecutive history, in order to show by this remarkable test how little is to be feared in the long run from arbitrary and precipitate flings at the Hexateuch, whether pronounced "unhistorical," "saga" "legend" or "myth."

2. Still more remarkable, indeed unparalleled, is the underlying principle of the enumeration. Knobel and subsequent commentators (e. g. Dillmann, Delitzsch, Strack) have pointedly called attention to its characteristic basis, the family relationship of the nations. While other lists of countries, as those of the Babylonians and Egyptians, treat only of conquered or tributary nations, and the

---

[11] Kommentar, Die Genesis, p. 35.

Hellenes spoke of οἱ βάρβαροι, the barbarians, and the Chinese of outside barbarians and foreign devils, "Israel is here," as Knobel remarks, "only a member of collective humanity. All men are of the same race, the same worth, and the same designation—brethren and relatives of each other. This biblical view proceeds from the greatness and entireness of humanity." It is the same view so earnestly and constantly set forth by the illustrious Hungarian patriot, Kossuth, when in 1851-2 he journeyed through this country, everywhere dwelling on "the solidarity of the nations." Without insisting on the suggestion of some respectable interpreters (e. g. Delitzsch and Strack), the implication of a common hope in store for all these races as branches and twigs of one common stock, descendants of one pious ancestor, we may well emphasize the moral elevation involved in this underlying principle of enumeration, not only as unique and deserving of profound respect, but as worthy of a place in a revelation from God.

3. The evident antiquity of the document, in its substance. The precise period from which the composition of the table dates has been a matter of much discussion and diversity of opinion. Some have gone to the extreme of calling it post-exilic; a view which it has been well said is precluded alike by what it contains and what it does not contain. Its historic character is clearly incompatible with any such supposition; it might as well be attributed to the nineteenth century. Ewald, Ebers

and others advocate the time of the early kings. Delitzsch thinks that, for reasons which he gives, it cannot be later than that, and speaks of its "hoary antiquity." Ebrard makes a strong showing for the view of a pre-Abrahamic text, transmitted orally and with some additions indicative of the time of Moses, written out in the time of Moses, and previous to the departure from Egypt.[12] It is, however, by no means necessary to suppose it to have been an unwritten tradition till the time of Moses; for we now know that for ages previous to that time writing was abundant both in Egypt, where Moses had his home, and in Babylonia, from which Abraham came.

Among the indications that carry the table far back into the past are the following: While Elam is mentioned, Persia, which was unimportant and unknown till the sixth century B. C., is not recognized; Nineveh (verses 11, 12) was as yet but one of four distinct settlements, and not, as it became from the time of Sennacherib (705-681 B. C.), the collective name of them all, while the northernmost town, Khorsabad, built by Sargon (721-705 B. C.), is not alluded to; the Arabian name, which occurs in Isaiah, Ezekiel and Jeremiah, does not appear, nor does Minni, mentioned in Jer. i. 27, in connection with Ashkenaz of ch. x. 3, and in the Assyrian inscriptions (716 B. C.); Sidon, the older Phenician city, is introduced, but not Tyre, which after the time of David and Solomon became so much

---

[12] Ebrard, Christian Apologetics, ii., 296 seq.

more important, and which even before the conquest of Palestine is shown by the Tell Amarna letters to have been in rivalry with Sidon;[13] and further still, verse 19 of the chapter carries us back very distinctly to a time before the destruction of the cities of the plain, that is, before the times of Abraham; for it is difficult to comprehend otherwise the incidental allusion, "as thou goest unto Sodom and Gomorrah and Admah and Zeboim." The German critics are constrained to recognize the great antiquity of the allusion, it being assigned, in Kautzsch's translation, as well as in Holzinger's[14] and Koenig's[15] introductions, to J, their oldest narrator; and even such an extremist as Wellhausen has to admit that the table (which he guesses had originally but seven generations instead of ten) "cannot have been wanting in JE," the combination of the two oldest.[16] But the allusion to the destroyed cities as apparently existent and known to the traveler, speaks for itself. The limitations of the list are in favor of its antiquity. The designation of many of the races by a personal name, as it is commonly understood, would naturally indicate a tradition handed down so long as to have identified a race with an ancestor.

4. The historic value of this table, as has been remarked by more than one writer, can hardly be overestimated. It forms the central and continuous

---

13 Conder's Tell Amarna Letters, p. 100 seq.
14 Holzinger, Einleitung, p. 149.
15 Koenig, Einleitung, p. 190.
16 History of Israel, p. 313.

thread of early history, so far as its range extends, and a standard with which modern discoveries are compared to bring them into coherence and unity. The chief difficulty in the explanation of the table consists in the poverty of our other sources of knowledge of those early times, and the impracticability of tracing the nations as made known to later history, back through their migrations and mutations and the linguistic changes, to their ancestry. This difficulty has given rise to many differences of identification in details, while there is a somewhat general and growing agreement in regard to main facts.

The table has its obvious limitations. It presents ethnological groups of peoples traced to their ancestry or their early home, and relates to their primary distribution from one common center, the land of Shinar. It follows them in that dispersion to different stages: Shem, naturally, to the sixth generation; Ham partly to the third or fourth; Japheth only to the first division of the main lines. It has nothing to do with their subsequent migrations and changes or interchanges. The Japhethites are dismissed mainly along two lines; one southwest along the Mediterranean, the other northwest beyond the Black Sea. The Hamitic tribes are traced to the region of the Euphrates, Arabia, Egypt and Ethiopia, as well as Phenicia. The Semitic races are located, speaking generally, between these northern and southern peoples.

Various obscurities still hang over this ancient

document, giving rise to conflicting views in regard to the details, many of them highly conjectural. Fresh discoveries from time to time bring new light. Shinar has only in recent times been identified with Sumer, a part of Babylonia. Accad, unknown till still more recent times, is now become a household word as the name of a state or region. Yet as late as 1883 Schrader wrote that "as the name of a city, Accad has not hitherto been indicated in the inscriptions";[17] but in that same year Hormuzd Rassam found an inscription on a granite block, giving it as the name also of a city.[18] The statement that "the beginning" of the Babylonish kingdom was earlier than that of the Ninevitish (verses 10, 11) is now confirmed, contrary to the former supposition. It is only since the explorations of Loftus (1857) that Erech (v. 11) has been definitely identified with the ruins of Warka, on the Euphrates. The situation of the city Calah (v. 11), unknown till within a few years, is, as Schrader remarks, firmly settled by the inscriptions, being also identified with the ruins called Nimrud in the angle formed by the junction of the Tigris with the Zab; Assurnatsirpal relating that the city was rebuilt by him (883-859), but was built by Shalmaneser (about 1300 B. C.).[19] Sayce announces that in the winter of 1894 he had discovered, in a hieroglyphic geographical list recently excavated at the temple of Kom Ombo, the two Scripture names of Caphtor

---

17 Keilinschriften, p. 95.
18 Hilprecht, cited in Delitzsch, i., 324. See also Dillmann in loco.
19 Keilinschriften, p. 97.

and Calushim, in the places Kaptar and Kalushet.[20]

Of course it would be impracticable to enter here on a full statement, much less a discussion of this table of the nations, as it has been termed, which has been the subject of protracted dissertations and even of volumes, by such scholars as Bunsen, Knobel, Ebers, Schrader, Fried. Delitzsch, Dillmann, George Rawlinson, Brugsch, Sayce and others. A few hints only are admissible, and with regard to the descendants of Japheth.

Gomer is confidently (and now almost universally) identified with the Kimmerii("Cimmerians")[21] of Homer, Herodotus and Æschylus, in the obscure region north of the Black Sea, whose name was once found in the "Kimmerian Bosphorus" and remains in the "Crimea." Many writers go further and find traces of the race in the Cimbri (Kimbri)[22] and even the Kymry; while Josephus[23] would include the Galatians (Gauls?), and George Rawlinson uses arguments for finding among their descendants the Celtic race. If this last view could be maintained, it would singularly aid in explaining the great phenomenon of the migrations.[24] But though accepted by some (e. g. Ebrard), it has not been generally sustained. Yet the identification with the Kimmerii stands fast, though, as always, with

---

[20] The Higher Criticism, p. 173.

[21] The consonants of the words are the same, the sonant G being practically identical with the surd K. But scriptural and other historical indications concur. The race is also the Gimmarrai of the Assyrian inscriptions.

[22] With Diodorus Siculus, v., 32, and Strabo, vii., 2 seq.

[23] Antiquities, i., 6. His detailed statement would apply to the Galli in general.

[24] Rawlinson's Herodotus, iii., 150 seq.

some dissent.[25] The identification of Magog with the Scythians is, for historical reasons, generally accepted, as originally suggested by Josephus; of whom it is stated by Herodotus that they had early driven the Kimmerii into Asia. Their original seat after the dispersion is assigned to the tract between the Caucasus and Mesopotamia, where, in the seventh century B. C., they appear for a time to have been the dominant race. Rawlinson would find the Slavs as their descendants, but this is perhaps more than doubtful. Madai without dissent represents the Median race. Javan is equally beyond dispute the Ionian (or Hellenic) race. Meshech and Tubal are with perhaps as little hesitation recognized in the Moschi and Tibareni of Herodotus, and the Tabal and Muski of the Assyrian monuments.[26] Their location was understood to be south or southeast of the Black Sea, nations once powerful, but declining in power from 1100 B. C., and unknown in their descendants. Tiras is more questionable; regarded by Rawlinson (after Josephus, Eusebius and Jerome) as the Thracians; by Tuch, Dillmann and others as the Tyrseni or Pelasgic people, and by Delitzsch as the dwellers on the Tyras or the Dniester—all concurring, however, in assigning them a location beyond the Euxine.

A few words may be added in regard to Javan. The consonants of the Hebrew word are the same with those of the Greek "Ionians," when the proper Greek termination is dropped and the digamma re-

---
[25] Halevy, Kiepert and G. Wahl are cited as dissenting.
[26] Schrader, pp. 82, 84; and other writers.

tained. The location, both as indicated in the table itself and in the inscription of Sargon II. (727-705 B. C.), which mentions Javnai,[27] corresponds. Kalisch gives his authorities for finding their names, in the Sanscrit *Iavana* and the *Jounan* of the inscription of Rosetta;[28] and Sayce claims that the name occurs "letter for letter" in one of the Tell Amarna tablets (No. 42, Berlin), and that in the days when the monarchs of the sixth dynasty were erecting their pyramids, the Mediterranean was already known as the great circle of the "Uinivu" or Ionians.[29] At all events, the identification appears to be thoroughly settled. Of the subordinate details it is agreed that Chittim designates the Cyprians, or inhabitants of Cyprus; the island being called Chetima in the time of Josephus,[30] its capital termed Kition by the Greeks, and its king being represented by Homer as giving a suit of armor to Agamemnon.[31] Cesnola finds that (with the exception of the Argive colony of Curium) the Greek settlers chose the north and west sides of the island, and that of the west kingdoms of Cyprus only two were distinctly Phenician.

Tarshish was undoubtedly the Tartessus of the Greeks, probably at the western limit of the Mediterranean, and supposed to have been not far from Gibraltar. Elisha is by the greater weight of

---

27 Schrader, p. 81.
28 Commentary, Genesis, p. 212.
29 The Higher Criticism, p. 20.
30 Antiq., i., 6.
31 Iliad, xii., 19.

authority understood of the Æolians.[32] Dodanim of the common text has been found in the Dardanians;[33] but if it be Rodanim,[34] as in the marginal reading (with Septuagint and some other authorities), then the inhabitants of Rhodes and the islands of the Ægean.

These specimens illustrate the general and confident agreement upon the main lines of the table; and also, owing to the defectiveness of modern knowledge, the difficulty attending many of the subordinate details, where conjectures are more abundant than known facts. Very likely more light is to come.

Without entering on further details of this table, it is to be observed how in the main it explains the radiation of these several branches of the family of nations. It shows us the race of Ham located largely in Africa, but also early (as they can be traced) in Babylonia and Assyria,[35] as well as in Arabia and Canaan; the race of Shem less widely dispersed in Elam, Syria and Assyria, in which last country they subsequently encroached upon the Hamites; and the Japhethites on their way to a far more remarkable dispersion, the Medes to the southeast, the Ionians to the southwest along the Mediterranean towards Italy, and Gomer, Magog and Tiras to the west and the northwest, where they subsequently crowded one another from behind to-

---

[32] Josephus, Knobel, Rawlinson, Delitzsch, Smith's Bible Dict. But Kalisch and Sayce say Hellas, and Dillmann dissents from both.

[33] Gesenius, Knobel, Bunsen, Delitzsch.

[34] Dillmann, Rawlinson, Strack.

[35] The attempt to limit Cush to Ethiopia was abandoned many years ago.

wards the Atlantic Ocean. It is manifestly a great historic chart, obscure in subordinate points because of our present ignorance, but clear and firm in its main outlines.[36]

---

[36] See note xvi., Appendix.

CHAPTER VII

THE DELUGE

The time has gone by when any well-read man can afford to speak lightly of the Scriptural account of the Deluge. It is beyond rational dispute that such an event took place, and that this narrative is the one sober, consistent account of it. In dealing with the subject, four points deserve attention: (1) The evidence of the fact; (2) the characteristics of the narrative of it; (3) the extent of it; (4) the method. Strictly speaking, there is no necessity for an explanation of the method, if the fact is sustained. Proved facts are ultimate, whether explicable or not.

I. The fact. Nothing in regard to the early history of mankind is better sustained. The proof is found in the widespread traditions of the human race, inexplicable except as commemorating such a fact, and also corroborated by late geological evidence.

The traditions of the deluge, while not universal—as could not reasonably be expected—are yet of the widest extent, being found in various parts of both continents. Although in some instances they may have been imported, in many cases such a supposition is not only unsupported but clearly inadmissible. As Alexander von Humboldt long ago remarked, the local coloring in each, together with the extreme isolation of many of these peoples (as, for example, in the forests of Orinoco), renders it impossible to ascribe the traditions to outside influences.[1] The most succinct, and possibly discriminating statement, is that of the oriental scholar Lenormant. His opening assertion is this: "Among all the traditions which concern the history of primitive humanity, the most universal is that of the Deluge. It would be going too far to assert that this tradition is found among all nations, but it does reappear among all the great races of men, saving only in one instance—an exception which it is important to note—and that is the black race, traces of it having been vainly sought either among the African tribes or the dusky populations of Oceanica."[2] This exception, however, appears to be taken away by other testimony. For Delitzsch affirms in his New Commentary, that the legend of the flood (mingled also with traces of the revolt against heaven) was found in southwest African Damara, he having received the information personally from the missionary superintendent C. Hugo Hahn, who assured him that "it was original, for that no white man and no missionary had come in contact with that people before himself."[3] Williams and Calvert assert the existence of a similar tradition in the Fiji Islands, its details including even

---

[1] Cited in Reusch's Nature and the Bible, i., p. 405.
[2] Beginnings of History, p. 382.
[3] New Commentary, Vol. i., p. 247, Eng. trans.

the rescue of eight persons from the general destruction.[4]

In recent times no little effort has been expended in reducing the instances by endeavoring to discriminate original from alleged "imported" traditions, and real from "pseudo" ones, that is, from those regarded by the writers as referring, not to a general destruction, but to a local phenomenon. These discriminations are of course largely matters of individual opinion. But after all attempted and claimed reductions, the reminiscences branded into the life of the nations are found to be too widespread and consentient, as well as characteristic, to be set aside. Thus Raymond De Girard, who, in his three volumes devoted to this theme, has subjected the various claims to a searching and unhesitating criticism, confidently affirms that even "the minimum is such that, resting on it alone, the tradition argument holds good. The traditional consensus proves the historic reality of the Deluge."[5] The distinguished and careful Delitzsch, in his New Commentary (his last), though grown somewhat cautious, if not timid, in his advanced years, and under the pressure of bold attempts to reduce the testimony, and omitting the extensive details of his earlier editions, yet finds the "legend of the flood starting from the region of the Tigris and Euphrates, and spreading westwards over Anterior Asia and thence to Greece, and eastward to the Indians,

---

[4] Williams and Calvert's Fiji and Fijians, p. 212.
[5] De Girard, Le Deluge, i., p. 310.

after they had advanced from Hindukuh along the Indus as far as the sea, acquiring everywhere fresh national coloring and attaching itself to different localities." He admits there is no means of checking the statement of Josephus, who cited two authorities that it was found among the Phenicians; concedes that it occurs in the Bundehesh of the Persians; so, too, in the Scandinavian and German mythologies, and in the Welsh Triads. He proceeds to mention the "surprising" fact that traditions of the Flood strikingly like the ancient ones in their details are found among the Mexicans, the inhabitants of Cuba, the Peruvians, the Tamanaki, and almost all the tribes of the Upper Orinoco, the Tahitians and other islands of the Society Archipelago, and the Macusi Indians of South America.[6] He might have added, on the authority of Schoolcraft, most of the tribes of North American Indians.[7] He also cites an Egyptian tradition, given by Brugsch, of the destruction of a sin-corrupted world, not by a flood, which in Egypt would have been a blessing, but by a slaughter.[8]

One of the most recent, as well as most rigid and uncompromising investigations of this whole subject, appears to have been made by Richard Andrée, not alone in collecting the facts, but in scrutinizing their relations, whether in his view original or imported, whether actual or "pseudo"—the last dis-

---

[6] Vol. i., pp. 245-6.

[7] Schoolcraft, History and Condition of the Indian Tribes, i., p. 17. Schoolcraft gives the detailed statements.

[8] Brugsch, Steininschrift, p. 47.

tinction being better expressed as general or local. He finds the tradition in not less than eighty-seven widely scattered tribes or races; and although he endeavors to reduce them all, with the exception of three or four (the chief of which is the Chaldean), to the two classes of imported or local, the effort speaks for itself in view of the fact that forty-seven of them are found in the American continent, all the way from the Esquimaux on the north to Brazil on the south.[9] No theory of origin can hide the great fact; and that can be explained only by the reality of the event.

Very extraordinary among these accounts is the Chaldean one of Berosus, which has long been known; and even more remarkable was the discovery by George Smith in 1872 of another account contained in some tablets in the British Museum which had been exhumed from the ruins of Nineveh. The date assigned to it by Smith and by Boscawen is about 2000 B. C. There are marked resemblances and some marked differences between it and the Scripture account,—on which we need not dwell at present.

The substance of these various traditions, with more or less of expansion or of omission, is as follows: A wicked world destroyed for its wickedness; one righteous family saved in an ark or boat,

---

[9] Andree's results are tabulated by De Girard at the end of Vol. i. The absurdly haphazard and helpless way in which some writers vainly endeavor to break the force of this wide consensus is illustrated in the case of Diestel, whose results are also tabulated by Girard. He finds the tradition in seventy-seven different tribes or races, recognizes one as original and genuine, and without even taking the trouble to divide the remainder into two classes, he blurs the matter over by pronouncing *each instance* to be *either* imported or local. He cannot say which.

together with animals; the ark resting on a mountain; birds sent out to learn the condition of the earth; an altar built and sacrifices offered.[10]

The details usually have a local coloring;[11] but, as Kalisch remarks, "there is scarcely a single feature in the Biblical account which is not discovered in one or several of these traditions." It may be safely affirmed that some such deluge as is described by it is among the best sustained facts in the ancient history of mankind.

To the weight of these wide-spread and concurrent traditions, may now be added the results of recent scientific observations, as set forth by authorities like Prof. Edward Suess of Vienna, Prestwich of England and Sir Henry Howorth. But we reserve these for the present. The *local extent* of the Deluge is also deferred for later consideration.

II. The characteristics of the Scripture account of the Flood are such as of themselves to make the strongest impression of its truthfulness.

1. Its exactness of statement. There is no looseness nor vagueness; all is precise. We have the materials, the dimensions, the internal arrangement of the ark, provision for light, constant dates and intervals of time (ch. vii. 4, 6, 10, 11, 12, 13, 17, 24; viii. 4, 5, 6, 10, 12, 13, 14), the depth of water at some point (vii. 20), and the relative number of the animals (vii. 9).

2. Its sobriety and consistency: (a) a long warn-

---

[10] See note xvii., Appendix.

[11] In the tradition of Michuacan, e. g., the humming-bird takes the place of the dove, and brings a twig in its mouth.

ing and preparation (vi. 3); (b) the duration, a year and ten days—the Chaldean account allowing but seven days; (c) the gradual progress of the flood, in regard to its height, cessation, decline and complete withdrawal; (d) the agency, not merely rain, but the breaking up of the fountains of the great deep; (e) the size and structure of the ark: taking what Gen. Sir Henry James found to be the cubit of Memphis, and of the Nilometers at Cairo and Elephantine (20.7 inches),[12] the ark would have been 517 feet long, 86¼ wide, and 51¾ high, corresponding very closely in breadth and height to the famous British Great Eastern, but shorter and therefore so far more seaworthy, the dimensions of the latter being 691 by 83 by 58; whereas the Chaldean story of Berosus gives the preposterous length of five stadia and the breadth of two stadia; (f) made of gopher or pitch wood, which is abundant in the region of the Caucasus and in Armenia; (g) tightened with bitumen, which is found at various points in the vicinity of the Euphrates; (h) constructed in stories and cells, and with light; (i) the whole structure pre-supposing the skill in the use of metals already indicated in the Scripture narrative. It may be added that the "olive" of the passage is found in Armenia. The narrative has a complete inner and outer consistency. The attempt to

---

[12] Notes on the Great Pyramids of Memphis (1869), p. 10. If this were not the precise length of the cubit, the proportions would be the same, corresponding favorably to those of the vessel built by the Mistress of the Seas in 1857, then the largest ship in the world. What human being, thousands, or even hundreds of years ago, was competent to give such proportions, except as describing a fact? Supposing the figures to have passed through the hands of Moses, they would naturally be reckoned in cubits of the pyramids.

find a contradiction, as of two conflicting accounts, in the direction to take of the clean beasts by seven and of the beasts that are not clean by two, male and female (both stated in one verse, vii. 2), even though in the first and preliminary announcement only the general principle of "two of every sort" is mentioned, is transparently futile.

3. Its pure monotheism, in marked contrast to the low polytheism of the lately discovered Chaldean account, which represents the gods as fleeing in terror before the whirlwind and storm and "like dogs lying down in a heap" (and "in a *kennel*," Davis and Boscawen). Almost equally marked is the contrast between the direct simplicity of the Scripture account and the wearisome repetitions and trivial details of what is called the Chaldean Epic.

4. Its marks of personal participation, and description at first-hand. This suggestion is not new. Kurtz spoke of the narrative many years ago as bearing "all the marks of being a carefully kept diary." Tayler Lewis spoke of its being "as optically described by some one in the ark." Dr. Dawson has called it a "log." More than sixty years ago Herder, with his quick instinct, recognized it as a journal of what took place in the ark, "true and authentic." Reusch substantially accepts the suggestion. The suggestion, once made, commends itself in the strongest manner to the thoughtful student, especially of the original text, in which the optional traits are most distinctly seen.[13]

---

[13] Kurtz, History of the Old Covenant, i., p. 102. Lewis, in Lange's Genesis, p. 321. Dawson, The Meeting Place of Geology and History, p. 139. Herder's Hebrew Poetry, i., p. 253. Reusch's Nature and the Bible, i., p. 403.

The very precision of statement, already mentioned, running through the entire narrative, and that too in regard to some things (e. g. the dimensions of the ark) which no human being from that day to the present century was capable of inventing without ludicrous mistakes, and which, it might be added, even the phenomenal memory of early non-reading communities could hardly have retained for any great length of time without the aid of writing (which antedates all historic knowledge), is of itself a powerful argument in favor of the suggestion.

But in addition to this, there are expressions and slight touches of description, which in their vividness, child-like minuteness, and even exclamatory character, belong only to the scene as actually witnessed, and would have been lost in a merely far-off outline. Thus the narrator is so impressed with the startling fact of the beginning inrush of the "fountains of the great deep," and the rainfall, that he gives not only the year, the month and the day, but he adds that it was "on the same day," literally, in the Hebrew, "in the bone of that day" (chap. vi. 11). How vividly he describes the steady rising of the waters and the effect (vii. 17-20)! They "increased," "bare up the ark" till "it was lift up above the earth," and still "the waters prevailed" and "increased greatly" till "the ark went" (walked) "upon the face of the waters." So again of the failing waters (viii. 3, 5, 9, 11, 13, 14), which "returned from off the earth continually" (literally, going and returning), "decreased continually" (going and decreasing), though still lying "on the face of the whole earth," but at length known to be "abated from off the earth," then "dried" (ver. 13), but only after another month and twenty days completely "dried"—as expressed by another word (ver. 13, 14). Some of the extremely minute touches of description are such as only a witness and actor in the transaction would have recorded: Noah "opened the window" to send forth the birds, and when the dove returned, he "*put forth his hand* and took her and pulled her in unto him in the ark." There are the optical descriptions: first (ver. 19), "*all the high hills under the whole heaven* were covered," and "*the mountains* were covered;" and after the waters began to abate, "the *tops* of the mountains *were seen.*" Here too are the expressions of the pleased surprise of the eye-witness: when the dove returned the second time, "*lo*, in her mouth was an olive leaf pluckt off" (margin "fresh olive leaf"); and later, he "removed the covering of the ark and *looked*, and behold (*lo*), the face of the earth was dry." Such slight but expressive touches come naturally and only from a participant. This circumstance, as will presently appear, is not without its bearing on the interpretation of the narrative.

The recently discovered Chaldean or Babylonian account has many points of resemblance to the Biblical statement, sufficient to show that they refer to the same event. It represents the Flood to be a punishment for sin, and describes the previous announcement, the building of a huge vessel (made tight with bitumen),the conveyance of animals into it for preservation, the tremendous storm, the birds (dove, swallow and raven), the landing on a mountain, the sacrifice, and other corresponding circumstances. Its divergences also are sufficient, as has been said by Boscawen, to indicate "a separate version," and thus to serve as a historical corroboration.

The relations of the two have been repeatedly discussed; and while some have supposed them to be derived from a common source, others have been ready to make the Chaldean to be the original and the Hebrew a derived version. This last view, it would seem, can hardly be maintained: if for no other reason, because while the Hebrew account could easily have degenerated in transmission into the incongruities and impossibilities of the Babylonian, it is not readily supposable that the latter could have been rectified and elevated into the dignity and consistency of the former. Thus, the whole time assigned to the event in the Babylonian is the proposterously short time of seven days. No mention is made of any other source of the waters than the rain. The dimensions of the ship, though doubtful as to the length, are now given by Professor Davis on the authority of Haupt as 140 cubits in width and the same in height. This, reckoning the cubit at but eighteen inches, would make it not only 220 feet wide, but 220 feet high.[14] This huge affair is entrusted to the charge of a pilot or boatman. The builder and hero of the adventure, when told to build, expresses the fear that the children of the people will laugh at him; but eventually he finishes the work and takes into it, not only his manservants and maid-servants and chests or baskets of food (carried on the heads of the bearers), but his gold and silver and "wine like waters of the river." The polytheism of the story has been already mentioned

These striking differences and inferiorities, and partly impossible details, when compared with the sober and dignified statements of the Bible, would seem to show decidedly which was the genuine and true account, and which, if either, was a loose and rambling distortion of the other. It would have been not difficult for the Hebrew narrative to be thus transformed in the lapse of time, and possibly by oral transmission, but hardly could even a Moses have made the consistent Bible narrative out of such raw materials. Brought suddenly to light after being hidden away for some twenty-five hundred years, the Chaldean epic is, even more than any of the similar and allied traditions, a striking confirmation of the Biblical narrative, to which it stands in the relation of the shadow to the substance; and it is a very noteworthy fact that this one Chal-

---

[14] Geo. Smith, Chaldean Genesis, p. 280, gives 60 cubits for the width and height; but Haupt's authority is later and better. Smith gives 600 cubits for the length, which Haupt thinks probable. Boscawen omits all figures (p. 115). Haupt's figures are given by Davis, Genesis and Semitic Tradition, p. 117.

dean account contains portions of the narrative which the modern analysts have divided between two writers, the Jehovist and the Elohist.[15]

III. The extent of the Deluge. Delitzsch has expressed the view now prevalent among sober expositors when he says, "The Scripture demands the universality of the flood only for the earth as inhabited, not for the earth as such." This opinion or its equivalent was long ago expressed by Stillingfleet and Poole, and is now adopted by commentators of various evangelical communions, such as Turner, Murphy, Tayler Lewis, Lange, the Speaker's Commentary, the Handy Commentary, Strack, and others. Dillmann calls attention to the fact that such a limitation is indicated on a close examination of the narrative itself. Some of the reasons that may be given are as follows:

1. The end announced, which was the destruction of mankind. The entire submergence of the whole earth would be a superfluous process, such as even the Divine Being is not wont to perform. It would also, as will presently appear, involve an accumulation of miracles of which there not only is no intimation, but which would seem to be precluded by the explanation given in the narrative.

2. The optical nature of the description, already

---

[15] The larger part of the Biblical account is ascribed by the critics to the Elohist. But the following things are found by them only in the Jehovist: The prediction of the rain. vii. 4; the shutting into the ark, verse 16; the sending forth of the dove and its return; the sending of the raven and its non-return; the building of an altar, the offering of a sacrifice, and the smelling of a sweet savor;—although the "epic" characteristically adds, "The gods like flies over the Master the sacrifice gathered." Boscawen shows these things conveniently tabulated in his book, as they are distinctly given by Kautzsch. Thus the critics make two of what the Epic and the Bible make one.

shown, limits the phraseology. For an eye-witness to recognize and say that all the high hills and mountains under the whole heaven were covered, that is, through the whole horizon, or as far as the eye can reach, is quite different from a scientific record that all the mountains over the entire earth were covered. The point or mode of view restricts the description.

3. The narrative itself makes one great deduction from the general breadth of the phraseology when it says (vii. 22), "All that was on the dry land died."

4. The dimensions of the ark, as given, constitute a necessary limitation. The attempt was formerly made by Sir Walter Raleigh, and has since been occasionally repeated, to show that the ark could contain a pair of each living species and seven of each clean species of animals from all parts of the earth, with a year's supply of food. Raleigh reckons on the basis of a hundred distinct species only. The number of species now known renders the supposition impossible.[16]

5. A deluge, covering the entire earth and all its mountains to the depth of fifteen cubits, would involve the following superfluous and stupendous miracles, of which no intimation can be found in the narrative, some of which are precluded by the methods specified in the narrative:

---

[16] The number, as given forty years ago, was 1658 species of mammals (including 1,062 clean species), 600 species of birds, 644 of reptiles. The "Zoological Record" now gives the species of mammals as 2,500, birds 12,500, reptiles and batrachians 4,400, crustaceans 20,000—to mention no others; and the entire number of distinct species, including insects, 366,000.

(1) The creation or procurement of eight times the present amount of water on the globe, and then its destruction or removal.[16]

(2) Provision of extraordinary, if not impossible, means of transportation of the animals across intervening continents and oceans, and their return.

(3) The preservation of many species of animals, tropical and arctic and others, away from their proper habitats, climate and food.

(4) The re-creation of the large portions of sea fish (e. g. corals) and perhaps all fresh-water fish, and nearly all vegetation, which would have been destroyed by such a long-continued inundation and mingling of salt water and fresh.

Now the narrative leaves room for none of these suppositions. It expressly conflicts with some of them. Thus it attributes the phenomenon to existing causes, namely, the fountains of the great deep and the rain from the windows of heaven, and these only. These considerations would seem to control and interpret the case.

The general or universal phraseology might at first appear to stand in the way. Scripture usage, however, relieves the difficulty. For we not only have here the limitation of the optical description, and of the end in view, and other indications mentioned; but we find elsewhere equally wide phraseology similarly restricted in detail. Sometimes it is simply understood in a restricted sense as well-known popular usage; as when we read (Matt. iii.

---

[16] Edward Hitchcock's Religion and Geology, p. 128.

5, 6), that all Jerusalem, and all Judea, and all the region round about went out to John and were baptized of him—everybody went, as we now sometimes say—or (Luke ii. 1), there went out a decree from Cæsar Augustus that all the world—all the Roman world—should be taxed. These instances are understood without any explanation being given. Sometimes the broad statement is made and limited in the next breath; as when we read (Gen. xli. 54) that "the dearth was in all lands, but in the land of Egypt there was bread." Sometimes the limitation appears later; as we read (Ex. ix. 25) how the hail smote every herb of the field and broke every tree of the field, and again (x. 15) how the locusts did eat every herb of the land and all the fruit of the trees which the hail had left. As to the Flood also, the needful limitations are involved in the circumstances and implications of the narrative. The suggestion of Tayler Lewis that the scale would at once be reduced to our imagination by translating "the whole *land*" instead of the whole "earth" (which, he adds, would be "very justifiable"), is not necessary.

We may thus properly understand, as now recognized, a deluge covering the earth's surface as inhabited by or known to man, and an unknown region beyond. The area needed not to have been a very large part of the earth's whole surface. For it has been the course of history that nations scatter only under the pressure of necessity, chiefly as they have crowded upon each other. But if we accept as complete the list of ten generations, from Adam to Noah (which, however, may be doubted), with five as the ratio of increase, it would give a population of not more than five millions, which could find room in an area not larger than the British Islands, or even in Palestine—which latter country is but about 180 miles in length, and from the Jordan to the sea rarely more than 50 miles in breadth. But a circle 800 miles in diameter, having its center at Mosul, would extend but about fifty miles into the Black, Caspian and Mediterranean seas, and would accommodate a vastly larger population than we have mentioned; and if, as many suppose, the human race had been much longer upon the earth, and had become much more numerous, the area to be covered by a destructive flood would still be comparatively limited.

IV. The method of the Deluge. If the Deluge be, as has been shown, a well substantiated fact, we are by no means bound to explain the method. We are obliged to accept facts as such, constantly, without explanation. But fortunately modern researches have made it possible to suggest at least a proximate explanation. The Scripture describes it by saying that "the fountains of the great deep were broken up and the windows of heaven were opened;" and that it was terminated by a reversal of this process;[17] although in the latter case there is the additional statement of the noticeable external phenom-

---

[17] One of the representations most unworthy of a scientific man is the statement of Draper (Conflict of Science and Religion, p. 63): "Having accomplished its purpose, the water was dried up by a wind." This is given as though the whole Scripture account of the termination of the Deluge.

enon that "God made a wind to pass over the earth." While the narrative naturally mentions the most striking phenomena of the case, namely, the violent rain (or, as some very unnecessarily conjecture, water spouts), and the wind, it can hardly be doubted that the main agency was that which is first mentioned, the breaking up of the fountains of the great deep, that is, in some way the inrushing of the ocean. Rainfall, however continuous, amounts at the utmost to but a few inches in a day, and forty days' rain, however impressive to the senses, would have been the least of the causes. The deluge was due mainly to the "fountains of the great deep," the irruption of the ocean.

Such a result, it is now known, could be accomplished on a larger or a smaller scale by the subsidence and re-elevation of the earth's surface. Nothing in regard to the history of the earth is more certain than the fact of vast elevations and depressions of its surface, both protracted and sudden, some of them going on even now, but more of them in the past, at dates that can only be stated proximately, and in geological measures.

These changes of level may be described as (1) gradual and secular; such as the slow rising of nearly the whole of Norway and Sweden, where, while south of Stockholm there has been a slight depression, the whole coast north of it has risen from 100 to 600 feet;[19] the raised breaches of Chili and Patagonia for a thousand miles on the eastern

---

[19] Le Conte, Geology (1891), p. 135.

shore and 2,075 miles on the western, lifted from 100 to 1,300, and even nearly 3,000 feet;[20] the supposed subsidence of the coral region of the Pacific through an area of 6,000 miles by 1,000 or 2,000, to a depth of 3,000 and in some places 5,000 feet[21]—not to enumerate many known cases of less remarkable change. These have been slow. Greenland, for 600 miles north and south, has been sinking for four hundred years. (2) Sudden elevations or depressions in connection with earthquakes, of greater or less extent. Instances are given in the modern geological treatises, and more numerously by De Girard.[22] Geikie mentions the raising of the coast of Chili for a long distance by the terrible earthquake of 1822, and further upraising of the same coastline by subsequent earthquake shocks; and on the other hand the sudden sinking of sixty-four square miles beneath the sea by the Bengal earthquake of 1762.[23] On a larger scale, Dana and Le Conte both cite the earthquake of 1819, which shook the whole region round the mouth of the Indus, whereby a tract of land of 2,000 square miles became a salt lagoon, while another area fifty miles long and ten to sixteen miles wide was elevated ten feet.[24] The latter author, after giving

---

20 Ib., p. 134.

21 Dana, Geology (1895), p. 350; Le Conte, p. 152. Le Conte, however, mentions that some have doubted the necessity of this explanation, and Geikie, in his Geology (1893), p. 290, remarks that the phenomena of the coral reefs "*in some cases*, at least, are capable of explanation without subsidence." But Dana in 1895 retains the statement given. Geikie, however, asserts other instances of subsidence.

22 La Sismique Theorie du Deluge.

23 Geology, pp. 278, 279.

24 Le Conte, p. 112; Dana, p. 349.

several other instances, adds, "We might multiply examples, if necessary." (3) Vast geological successive changes of level, as when in the glacial epoch on the northern portion of this continent the elevation was from 2,000 to 3,000 feet above the present level, and when in the Champlain epoch the downward movement carried the depression from 500 to 1,000 feet below the same level and was followed by the upward movement of the Terrace epoch. There was a time when the region of the great lakes was one immense lake, extending its waters south over Ohio, Indiana and Illinois, and the sea was five hundred feet deep at Montreal, when the whale left his bones on the borders of Lake Champlain, and north of Lake Ontario 440 feet above the present level of the sea.[25] About the same time the land in Scotland was depressed 2,000 feet below the present level of the sea, Great Britain was an archipelago, and a great part of northern Europe was submerged.[26] (4) Rapid and extensive inundations such as have been recently affirmed by Prestwich and Sir Henry Howorth, presently to be mentioned. Whether they are to be regarded as connected with the last-mentioned class does not distinctly appear.

Facts like these go to prove such a catastrophe as the Deluge to be entirely within the range of natural phenomena, if we choose to take that view; and at all events within the use of the Power that works behind the wheels of nature.

---

25 Dana, pp. 982, 983.   26 Le Conte, p. 572.

Now many years ago Hugh Miller called attention to a remarkable state of things in the extensive region lying east and south of Mt. Ararat, and extending easterly beyond the Caspian and Aral Seas, and southward in the direction of the Persian Gulf![27] The shore line of the Caspian is eighty-three feet below the level of the Black Sea, and the steppes around it are about thirty feet below the level of the Baltic; while vast plains, white with salt and charged with sea-shells, show the Caspian to have been once far more extensive than now. While the human race was still included within the general region of its original home, suppose a depression, such as those actually on record elsewhere, to have taken place for forty days, from the Euxine Sea and Persian Gulf on the one hand and the Gulf of Finland on the other. This "breaking up of the fountains of the great deep" would slowly and surely have submerged that whole region of perhaps 2,000 miles each way, sinking it far enough at the center to cover all the hills of the district "under the whole heaven." Meanwhile, even if volcanic action did not accompany, the atmosphere might have been so filled with long and drenching rains as to have made this the most apprehensible feature of the case. Add the supposition that after a hundred and fifty days the depressed hollow began slowly to rise till it resumed its former level—and we have all the phenomena of the case.

In singular but unintentional confirmation of the

---

[27] Testimony of the Rocks, Am. Ed., p. 358 seq.

entire possibility of such a supposition, we read in Le Conte's Geology that at a time which he refers to the Champlain epoch "the northern portion of Asia and the lake region of that continent were submerged. The Caspian Sea, Lake Aral, and other lakes in that region were probably united into one great inland sea, connected either with the Black Sea, or the greatly extended Arctic Ocean, or with both."[28] Dana says the same.[29] The fact is sufficiently remarkable.

Recent researches bring us still nearer to a definite explanation and scientific substantiation of the Biblical account. Sir Henry Howorth in his learned and careful work[30] claims to have established certain great facts which may be summarily stated thus: (1) A great and general cataclysm or catastrophe at the close of the mammoth period, by which that animal and its associates were overwhelmed, over a large part of the earth's surface. (2) This involved a widespread flood of water, which not only killed the animals, but also buried them under continuous beds of loam or gravel. (3) It was accompanied by a very great and sudden change of climate in Siberia, by which the animals were frozen in their flesh under ground and have remained frozen ever since. (4) It took place when man was already occupying the earth, and constitutes the gap which exists between palæolithic and neolithic man. (5) This is in all probability the

---

28 Geology, p. 573. He cites three authorities.
29 Geology, p. 995.   30 Howorth, The Mammoth and the Flood.

same event pointed out in the traditions of so many races, as the primeval flood; and it "forms a great break in human continuity, and is the great divide when history really begins." As substantially concurring in this view—which, as will be perceived, is of wider extent than is required for the Scripture Deluge, so far at least as the occurrence of a great flood suddenly destructive of animal life—he cites several eminent names, including the Duke of Argyll. Sir J. W. Dawson appears to accept the entire view.[31]

To the same purport and with even greater definiteness was a paper of the eminent and veteran geologist, Joseph Prestwich, read before the Victoria Institute March 19, 1894.[32] After years of investigation and inquiry, extending over Great Britain and the Continent, and the coasts of the Mediterranean, and including France, Gibraltar, Sicily, Malta, Greece, Asia Minor, North Africa, Egypt, his conclusions fully coincide in the main points with those of Sir Henry Howorth, but with this significant addition, that the depression and elevation took place *in a very brief period*. "These concurrent conditions seem to me, however startling may be the conclusion, to be only explicable upon the hypothesis of a widespread though local and short submergence followed by early re-elevation; and this hypothesis will, I think, be found to satisfy

---

[31] The Meeting Place of Geology and History.

[32] Journal of the Victoria Institute, 1894, pp. 263-284. It was discussed by other geologists with some criticism and objections. But the author answered the critics and adhered to his position.

all the important conditions of the problem." He maintains that the opinion long held by him, that the close of the glacial period (which was followed by a great inundation) comes down to within about 10,000 or 12,000 years of our time,"is forced on us on archæological grounds alone." He proceeds: "We have in the widespread catastrophe involved in the foregoing hypothesis a more adequate cause for the tradition of the Flood than any local or land flood, however great it may have been; an inundation of continental dimensions and destructive to large populations of men and animals. The few who resorted to the heights and mountain summits, could alone have escaped, and from these centers peopled afresh the surrounding areas. Although our knowledge of all the phenomena is still very imperfect, it is remarkable how in all the leading points the facts agree with the tradition. The geological phenomena have also led me to suppose that the submergence was, as in the tradition, of *short duration*, and the retreat of the waters comparatively gradual, while the destruction of animal life is sufficiently shown in the numerous remains preserved in the different forms of the Rubble-drift, wherever the conditions were favorable. That man lived at the time we are speaking of is now a question not necessary to argue, since the fact of the existence of paleolithic or Quaternary man, over the whole area we have described, is at the present day a well established fact. Therefore, that man must have suffered in this great catastrophe, may be taken for granted."

Sir J. W. Dawson substantially accords with this statement of facts and the conclusion, recognizing the comparatively recent date of palæolithic man, the disappearance of a large number of animals simultaneously with him, the separation of the neolithic from the palæolithic races by a somewhat rapid physical change of the nature of a submergence, or by a series of changes locally sudden and not long continued, this being the basis of all the traditions and historic accounts of the Deluge. He regards the Biblical Deluge as the "record of a submergence of a vast region of Eur-Asia and northern Africa," and holds it "certain that the post-glacial subsidence which closed the era of palæocosmic man and his companion animals must have been one of the most transient on record. On the other hand, we need not limit the entire duration of the Noachic submergence to the single year whose record has been preserved to us. Local subsidence may have been in progress throughout the later Antediluvian age, and the experience of the narrator in Genesis may have related only to its culmination in the central district of human residence."[33]

So Dillmann, in the sixth and last edition of his commentary (1892), accepts the fact of a brief inundation of a limited area, and after the introduction of the human race. "The specifications of the text itself indicate only a partial submergence of the earth, and indeed within the memory of man, and there is no reason to doubt its possibility.

---
[33] The Meeting Place, etc., pp. 128, 12, 9148.

Many instances of seismic-cyclonic floods in lands lying near the sea have been collected by Suess from historic times. There must have been a mighty flood of this kind in high antiquity, to which reference is here made." He concludes that all indications point to east Armenia as the scene.

Dillmann's reference to Suess suggests the somewhat definite explanation reached by that writer in his treatise, "Die Sintfluth"(1883). He holds that it was a natural phenomenon beginning on the lower Euphrates, a great and terrible inundation covering the lowlands of Mesopotamia; the principal cause was a violent earthquake in the Persian Gulf or the neighboring region, preceded by other slighter shocks; and that probably during the most violent shocks a cyclone set in from the south to increase its ravages, and that under these influences the ark would be carried, as it was, northward to be stranded on the northern hills.[34] De Girard defends this theory, supporting it by additional details.[35] Delitzsch says: "The circumstances of the Deluge have as yet been better represented by no one than Edward Suess in a geological study," of which Delitzsch recapitulates the chief points.

It will be observed that while some of these writers assign a wider range than others to the phenomenon, they all agree on somewhat definite facts which would make it fully meet the requirements of the Biblical narrative. And it is no objection

---

[34] The explanation by Suess is cited from De Girard.

[35] La Theorie Sismique (1892), pp. 58 seq. Le Caractere Naturel du Deluge, p. 120.

that their discussions proceed entirely on the basis of natural phenomena, but all the more satisfactory; inasmuch as the Scripture expressly declares natural agencies to have been the means employed by God. Nor should any of their special subordinate opinions and theories cause us to overlook their united testimony to the facts.

The result of all these various facts stands fast. The Scripture narrative of the Deluge is a sober historical account of one of the greatest and most ineffaceable events in the history of the human race; true, whether explicable or not, yet entirely explicable by well known facts in the phenomena of the earth's surface. In the words of Howorth, we find "induction from paleontology and archæology compelling the same conclusion as the legendary myths and stories of the children of men. All points unmistakably, as it seems to me, to a widespread catastrophe, involving a flood on a great scale. I do not see how the historian, the archæologist, the paleontologist can avoid making this conclusion in future a prime factor in their discussions, and I venture to think that before long it will be universally accepted as unanswerable; not only as unanswerable, but as alone explaining some at least of the difficulties which crowd upon us when we study the ethnography of the human race."[36]

---

[36] The Mammoth and the Flood, p. 463.

CHAPTER VIII

ANTEDILUVIAN LIFE

THE sacred narrative prepares the way for its account of the Deluge by tracing the generations down from Adam through Seth to Noah. The genealogy, as Ryle remarks, "could hardly be simpler. Besides the names of the patriarchs we are told nothing but their ages, both at the time of their first-born and at the time of their death, and the fact that each of the patriarchs begat sons and daughters. Of the patriarch Enoch alone is any further description given."

This extreme brevity would be naturally explained by its great antiquity, itself made portable by its simplicity. The condition in which its numbers have come down would countenance the supposition. It is certainly the occasion of very great difficulties, which no skill in investigation or conjecture on the part of many ingenious men has been able to remove, or to explain even on any theory which has been generally accepted. The fundamental difficulty is the immense length of life ascribed to these men, amounting in the case of Methuselah to 969 years. Accordingly some have, with Bunsen, pronounced it "intrinsically impossible;" and Ryle contends that the unhistorical character of this genealogy should be as freely admitted as that of the legends alluded to in the authorities cited by Josephus.[1] This last summary dismissal of the whole genealogy, characteristic as it is of no little modern exposition, is as reasonable as it would be to discard the whole history of Egpyt as unfounded because Mariette Bey dates the beginning of the Anicent Empire B. C. 5004; Boeckh puts it a 5702; Brugsch, 4453; Lepsius, 3892; Bunsen, 3623; Birch, 3000, and Wilkinson, 2320. The precariousness of numbers, both in the ascertainment and the transmission, is notorious. The figures may be erroneous and the list incomplete (as many suppose it to be), and yet the genealogy historical. There lies before me a genealogical book tracing an American family down from its distant English ancestry, in which some of the figures are incorrect, and one whole American generation of the last century omitted; yet the table is historical, and the line is brought truly down to the present generation.

In regard to the ages of the antediluvians the figures have been an uncertain quantity for two thousand years or more; and we not only do not know that we are sure of them, but we know somewhat definitely that we are not. For this reason: there are three very different and divergent sets of numbers. The numbers of the Hebrew text give a total of 1656 years from Adam to the Flood; the Samaritan text, of a date not certainly settled, gives 1307, and the Septuagint, of which Genesis was

---
[1] Ryle, The Early Narratives of Genesis, p. 88.

translated some two hundred and fifty years before Christ, gives 2242, and according to another reading 2262. The fact speaks for itself; the original numbers have been in some way, and for some reason, labored with, or accidentally modified, possibly on account of their difficulty. They may have been lost and conjecturally restored. But such is the fact; we have no absolute certainty. Early in the Christian Era the numbers of the Septuagint were more commonly accepted, and they have been advocated by some in recent times. The prevailing opinion now is probably in favor of the Hebrew. But the problem is for the present incapable of certain solution. Under the circumstances, therefore, the simple and obvious method of dealing with the problem would be to dismiss it with a mere statement of the actual fact that we do not know. We are satisfied to rest the case there. But inasmuch as many may desire to know what solutions have been proposed, we will mention them.

1. Some have suggested shorter years, as short even as one month. This seems inadmissible for two reasons: first, because it would make Enos a father at about the age of $7\frac{1}{2}$ years, and Canaan at $5\frac{3}{8}$; and, secondly, because the antediluvian year is virtually determined in the next chapter, where we read of the 27th day of the month, and of the tenth month, and a comparison of the several dates indicates a year of 360 days. The supposition of a year of three months, or any less than twelve, is baseless.

2. Some, with Bunsen, have understood that the names designate, not persons, but "epochs"; sometimes explained as the ascendency of a family, as that of Seth, and so on. Or they have been called "cyclical periods." But the statement in each instance of the age at which the individual became a father, and the particular cases of Enoch, Lamech and Noah, appear incompatible with the view. Yet Delitzsch, in the last edition of his commentary, speaks of these numbers of Adam, Enos and Jared, as though "they designate epochs of antediluvian history which are named after their chief representatives, and the period of these epochs is allotted to the individual life of these chief representatives, as though it had extended over the whole period."

3. An ingenious scheme is cited by Prof. Alexander Winchell[2] as devised by Rev. T. P. Crawford. It interprets in each case the first number as giving the actual life of the individual, the second that of the continued ascendency of his family; thus Adam lived but 130 years, and appointed Seth (in the place of Abel) to be his successor, the family rule being continued 800 years more, in all 930 years, when Enos succeeded in like manner. The speculation has this much of support, that the Old Testament elsewhere invariably uses a different phraseology to designate the age of a man at any definite time, namely, not that he had "lived" so many years, but that he was "the son of" those

---

[2] Winchell's Preadamite Man, p. 449 seq.

years. It would also extend the time from Adam to Christ to 12,500 years. But it labors heavily in several points: in interpreting "begot" as *appointed* or constituted (though referring to Ps. ii. 7); in the twofold meaning ascribed to "lived"; in understanding the words "likeness" and "image" to mean character and office.

4. On the other hand, there are still writers of high character who, notwithstanding the three different editions of the numbers, adhere to the Hebrew text and its more obvious interpretation. They adduce the following considerations:

(1) The *prima facie* aspect of the several statements.

(2) The existence of widespread traditions of the greatest ancient longevity. Thus Lenormant, who regards the figures as "cyclic numbers," asserts "the belief common to all nations in an extreme longevity among the earliest ancestors of the race." He refers to the well-known statement of Josephus that Hesiod, Hecatæus, Hellanicos, Acousilaos, as well as Ephorus and Nicolas (of Damascus), every one relate that the men of antiquity lived a thousand years; the assertion of Hesiod[3] that in the silver age men remained with their mothers in the state of childhood for a hundred years; the belief of the Thynians that their ancestor lived 500 years, and of the Illyrians that their first two princes lived 600 and 800 years respectively.[4] It calls for ex-

---
3 Works and Days, 129, 130.
4 Lenormant, Beginnings of History, pp. 292, 294.

planation how these widespread notions arose, unless as a reminiscence of the actual past.

(3) The fact would explain the early great progress in the arts, which we shall have occasion to mention later. With the long contemporaneous lives skill would be accumulated and inherited. Methuselah would have been long contemporary with both Adam and Noah.

(4) It accords with the apparent reduction of the length of life according to the Scripture narrative. Three classes of long life are given, in a descending scale: of the antediluvians, ranging (except Enoch) between 777 and 969; of Noah's earlier descendants, from 230 to 600; of Abraham and his earlier descendants, less than 200 years, namely, Abraham 175, Isaac 180, Ishmael 137, Jacob 147, Joseph 110, Moses 120, while Jacob at 130 pronounced his days "few and evil" and less than those of his fathers.

(5) An admissible, or at least possible, explanation of the change, namely, the resistance to decay long offered by the body in its primitive condition, and prior to the effects of steady abuse of the human system through ages of inherited degeneration. The wonder is that men live now so long, in their luxury, vices, and intemperance of every kind. For though there are modern well authenticated instances of lives extending much beyond a century, if not nearer two centuries,[5] vast numbers through personal habits and inherited decay are worn out

---

[5] See Appendix, note xviii.

early, and whole lines of ancient aristocratic families, like those of the Duke of Northumberland and the Earl of Warwick in England, have failed of all lineal descendants. And on the other hand, better sanitary arrangements, together with better medical and surgical methods, have actually raised the average length of human life in such countries as England and the United States.

In truth, as Kurtz, Reusch, Delitzsch, Zoeckler, Strack and others have well remarked, no man is capable of saying what length of life was "possible" when the human constitution was in its primitive strength, and under very different circumstances and conditions from those which now prevail—and originally made, perhaps, to pass away, not by disease and death, but by such a transfiguration as that apparently of Enoch and Elijah. Strack makes a remark also, which may or may not have weight, that this length of life is not ascribed to all men, but only to the prominent personages of the Sethite or godly race, while the silence concerning the limits of life in the Cainite family may well be regarded as significant. He accepts the suggestion of Zoeckler that this long life of the antediluvians was "the after-glow of the glory of paradise."

The difficulty of pronouncing summarily on the possible length of life under changed conditions is well illustrated in the case of tree life, or even animal life. One who is accustomed only to trees like the poplar or the maple, decaying perhaps within less than a century, might assert very confidently that it was impossible for a tree to live two thousand years; but we have the great authority of Professor Whitney and Asa Gray that the Sequoia of California has attained more than that age,[6] while it is also to be noted that such a growth and age are to be found now *only under those conditions*, and in those very regions. The olive is a hardy fruit tree, but it will thrive only in certain parts of the Spanish peninsula; and while in France the severe winter of 1709 killed all the olive trees in that country and the adjacent parts of Italy, there is near Nice a tree thirty-eight feet in diameter, recorded as an old tree in 1516, and another at Pescio said to be 700 years old, and some at Jerusalem undoubtedly far older. Animal life is for the most part short, much of it very short. far within the lifetime of man. Yet it is Sir John Lubbock who reminds us how little we know of the age to which animals can or actually do live. He proceeds cautiously thus: "The camel is said to reach 100 years, the elephant 200, the Greenland whale 400(?). A pike is said to have been taken in Suabia in 1499 with a ring inscribed with a date and statement which would make it 267 years old. A tortoise is said to have reached 500 years."

Such facts and admonitions as these strongly suggest the necessity of caution in saying what can and what cannot be. So do the very latest discoveries in regard to the functions of light, electricity

---

[6] See an article by Asa Gray in Johnson's Cyclopædia, 2nd Edition, vol. vii., p. 133.

and sound. For any man to say what was impossible as to human life many thousand years ago, under what may, and what purports to, have been very different conditions, is not merely idle, it is presumptuous.

The conclusion to which we may come is that we are at liberty, if we choose, to hold to the figures of the Hebrew text, saying that, notwithstanding the objections, there are some important considerations in its favor; or to take the ground that the changes of the three sets of numbers and their present divergence are such as to forbid any positive decision or solution. The latter may be the wiser course.

Another matter connected with this early history calls for attention. The brief and therefore somewhat obscure account prefixed to the narrative of the Flood has been made the occasion of strange ingenuity. The marriage of the "sons of God and the daughters of men" is interpreted by a whole class of writers, who pronounce the early history of the Scriptures to be mythical, and by many others in deference to their authority, as describing a sexual union between angels and women—although most of these writers discard the supernatural. The attempt to burden the narrative with such an absurdity is needless.

A perfectly simple and consistent interpretation is the one commonly accepted by the evangelical churches. It is entirely defensible. The account joins on easily and directly to the history where it was interrupted by the insertion of the "generations" or genealogy of the sons of Adam. The last verse preceding (ch. iv. 26) had said, "Then began men to call upon the name of Jehovah"—men of the Sethite race. The passage immediately following this interruption speaks of the "sons of God," and most naturally refers to this same pious race, these worshipers of Jehovah, and it becomes a continuous account. The daughters of men, so called by contrast, are the worldly and sensual line of Cain. It was a grave error, and attended with the grave results immediately announced—the "mighty men," and the earth filled with violence. There is no special difficulty with the first phrase, "sons of God." (1) It is prepared for by the statement in iv. 26, from which it is separated only by the genealogy. (2) The equivalent idea of the divine sonship of God's chosen seed occurs in the early Scriptures (Ex. iv. 2; Deut. xiv. 1; xxxii. 5; Is. l, 2; Ps. lxxiii. 15; Hos. i. 10). It has been objected that the phrase here employed is not children of God, but of Jehovah. It hardly seems a weighty difference, and does not hold good of Deut. xxxii. 5 and Hos. i. 10. True, the term, sons of God, is in some instances applied to the angels (Job i. 6; ii. 1; Ps. xxix. 11; xxxix. 7, R. V.), and these passages have been made the basis for the singular interpretation. But it is spoken of them in their high spiritual character, not of fallen, seducing spirits as they would be on this supposition. (3) The narrative itself does not speak of illicit connections, as would be assumed in the false interpretation, but of permanent marriages—"took them wives." (4) The notion of a union between angels and women of earth is so absurd as scarcely to need the assertion of the Savior that in heaven they neither marry nor are given in marriage, *but are as the angels of God.* (5) The results predicated correspond to the natural interpretation. The combination of the long-lived and vigorous Sethites with the progressive and inventive Cainites was, as seen in the mingling of other remarkable races, a race of "mighty men, men of renown," but also of insurgent wickedness. (6) The subjects of punishment sustain the natural interpretation. God is not described as punishing angels or their offspring, but wicked and violent men.

These various considerations make the present interpretation not only clear, but well nigh unavoidable. No parade of learned names need shake confidence in it. The main objection that can be urged is founded on the antithetic phrase, "daughters of men." This has been pronounced "decisive." But it certainly is not. The antithesis is natural and obvious, between those who belong to the line of God's children, still holding a filial relation to their Maker, and those who had willfully broken the Divine relationship and become distinctively and only human. It tells the story in a word. If it be said that the addition of the word "other," so as to read "other men," would have avoided ambiguity, it is to be replied, the word is here both inadmissible and unnecessary. Inadmissible, because it had just been said that men had multiplied and daughters were born to them—to *these* men, not to other men. Unnecessary, if admissible, because such careful precision does not belong to this brief and simple style. Moreover, such omissions are not uncommon. Thus (Gen. xiv. 16) we read of "the women and the people," that is, the rest of the people; so (Jer. xxxii. 20) "in Israel and among men," that is, as the word is supplied in the rendering, other men; and (Ps. lxxxiii. 5) "they are not in trouble as men," other men, "neither are they plagued like men." Similar usages of exceptions not stated in form, because anticipated in substance, are sufficiently common in the Scriptures.

Without further discussion, we need not hesitate to say, if not, with Strack, that this is the only possible interpretation, yet that it is the only natural and admissible one. When so understood, the narrative presents no monstrous myth, but a series of events as credible and seemingly historical in their character and consequences as the invasion of England by the Danes.

CHAPTER IX

ANTEDILUVIAN OCCUPATIONS

In reviewing the glimpses given of the condition and occupations of the race in antediluvian times, we are pushing still farther back of all other history, and must judge of it by its consistency and its correspondence with such fragmentary indications as we can trace from the remotest ages. And here the narrative will stand the test.

It is very noteworthy how different is the condition of man in paradise from that of man of "the golden age." Ovid, writing in the Augustan age and at the capital of the world, described a time of absolute idleness, when the untilled soil produced its heavy crops, with the absurd addition of rivers flowing now with milk and now with nectar, and the yellow honey dripping from the green oak. The Scripture gives the first man, what man must have, something to do. But it is, as it must have been, of the simplest kind, the care of the garden. Skin clothing, also ascribed to him, is the common form of primitive dress as found in the caves at Mentone and Cromagnon, among the North American Indians, or even now among the Russian peasants in winter. The first man is represented only as having a capacity for speech, developed, however, in the most natural mode, naming the animals brought to his attention. He has strong conjugal instincts, and an experience which exposes him to temptation and fall.

The next stage of life shows progress, but limited still. One of the second generation has his small cattle only, sheep (and goats), an employment of the simplest kind. The other has begun to cultivate the soil. The offering of the sacrifices, and the use of milk from the flock, might imply the use of fire, and perhaps, but not necessarily, of pottery. As a matter of fact, although some (like Lubbock) have been inclined to doubt the possession of fire by the paleolithic man, it is now asserted on apparently abundant evidence by Winchell, Nadaillac, Joly and Quatrefages.[1] This also conforms to the classic story that Prometheus stole it from heaven. Pottery, though denied by some to paleolithic times, has certainly been found in connection with the bones of the mammoth and the cave bear.[2] How graphically true is the brief account of the most terrible fruit of the fall, the first murder: the envy, the anger, the fatal deed, the remorse, the terror, the removal, and the stronghold inspired by terror! The "city" which he built has been properly understood in the general and loose sense in which the word is used in the early narrative. Thus there were 124 cities in Judah's portion of the land of Palestine, and 119 in the rest of the territory

---
[1] Joly, Man Before Metals, p. 189. Quatrefages, The Human Species, pp. 152, 319. Nadaillac, Prehistoric Peoples, p. 101. Winchell, Preadamite Man, p. 415, expresses, however, only an opinion. Lubbock, Prehistoric Times, p. 558, speaks his doubt hesitatingly.

[2] Joly, p. 307; Nadaillac, pp. 96, 97.

west of the Jordan. In Isaiah i. 8 it designates a watch-tower. In much later days the stronghold of Troy was of small compass, as was that of Lachish, recently excavated. The enclosure of the conical hill at the Egyptian mines of Wady Maghara was but 600 by 260 feet. Gesenius and Fuerst both suggest in this narrative simply a nomad encampment, defended perhaps by a ditch or wall, as the former suggests, for protection. This "city" implies also permanency, and that facilitated the remarkable progress which is recorded as subsequently taking place in the line of Cain's descendants. For while we learn that there was one line of the early race that began to call upon the name of Jehovah, the great worldly development in the arts is recorded, as we might expect, in the line of Cain.

The consistency of the narrative also appears in the fact that the great progress did not come till after seven recorded generations from Adam. It was in the remarkable family of Lamech. Any one who should incline to doubt the possibility of such a wide and apparently rapid outburst has but to recall the history of Europe in the half century from 1450 to 1500 A. D., or the still more extraordinary physical progress of the century about to close.

First is mentioned Jabal as the head or leader of those that dwell in the tents and have cattle. The advance from the keeping of sheep and goats to that of larger cattle is a marked and consistent account of progress. The dwelling in tents naturally involves the art of spinning and weaving, as the Bedaween of the present day dwell in tents spun and woven from the hair of their domestic animals. The art of weaving antedates all historic knowledge. While we do not find evidence of it among the cave-dwellers of Europe, woven cloth appears in the Lake Dwellings. The best linen of Egypt, according to the testimony of both Wilkinson and Erman, was not inferior to our cambric, and in smoothness and softness almost comparable to our silk.[3] This is true of its quality as early as the sixth dynasty, and nothing is known of its beginning. Cotton and woolen garments were also made. Equally remote is the care of cattle. In almost every tomb of the Old Empire we meet with the herdsman and his animals, and even then there were fancy breeds.[4]

The narrator walks on equally sure ground when he assigns the harp and pipe (R. V.), or wind and stringed instruments, to the remotest antiquity. Paintings in the Egyptian tombs, both of the earlier and the later times, show a very great number of such instruments, of both kinds: single pipe, double pipe, flute, lyre, lute and harp, as well as drums, tambourines, cymbals. The stringed instruments were singularly various in shape, size and number of strings, from the light lyre of three strings to the tall harp exceeding the height of a

---

[3] Wilkinson's Ancient Egyptians, ii., p. 161. Erman's Life in Ancient Egypt, pp. 448.

[4] Wilkinson, i., p. 431 seq. Erman, p. 262 seq.

man. The paintings represent harps with four, six, seven, eight, nine, ten, eleven, twelve, fourteen, seventeen, twenty, twenty-one and twenty-two strings, although not all of the Old Empire.[5] Some of them come down from the earliest period of known history. The Assyrian sculptures, though of less ancient date, show the harp, double pipe and drum.[6]

It was a bold statement of the sacred writer to assign the forging of instruments of iron and brass, or rather copper (R. V., margin), to that early age. But in Egypt the use of copper is older than our historic knowledge. Copper mines were wrought by the Egyptians at Wady Maghara in Sinai before the building of the great pyramid, as is attested by the cartouch of king Snefru at that place, and the ore and slag found there. And even the manufacture of bronze took place under the Old Empire, and was carried to a perfection indicating long practice.[7] The Babylonians also used copper early and abundantly. Loftus found at Tell Sifr what appeared to be the stock in trade of a coppersmith, supposed by Rawlinson, from the accompanying tables, to be about 1500 B. C. The great variety of these objects, and the skill exhibited, also involved long continued use and practice: "large chaldrons, vases, small dishes, hammers, chisels, adzes and hatchets; a large assortment of knives and daggers of various sizes and shapes—all unfin-

---
[5] Wilkinson, i., pp. 435-493.
[6] Layard's Babylon and Nineveh, p. 456.
[7] Erman, pp. 460, 461.

ished; massive and small rings; a pair of prisoner's fetters; three links of a strong chain; a ring weight; several plates resembling horses' shoes, divided at the head for the insertion of a handle, and having two holes in each for the insertion of links; other plates of a different shape; an ingot of copper; and a great weight of dross from the same smelted metal."[8] And in 1888 the expedition of the University of Pennsylvania discovered in their excavations at Nuffar, among a vast number of other things, objects of bronze, which would appear from their connection to be of far older date.[9] At Hissarlik not only do copper and bronze occur in the second city, the Troy stratum, but bronze objects were found in the still older city of the first stratum.[10] The use of copper and even of bronze thus recedes to a period beyond all historic knowledge.

The statement concerning the working of iron is still bolder. For until recently it has been doubted, though now conceded, that iron was used in early Egypt. It occurs there only in small quantities. Not only were iron deposits of any considerable extent remote from Egypt, but the difficulty of smelting it was not easily overcome. And though at Wady Maghara and Surabit el Khadim there is iron in the ore and the slag, it does not appear to have been smelted when the copper was extracted.[11]

---

8 Loftus, Chaldea and Susiana, p. 269.
9 Hilprecht in Recent Research in Bible Lands, p. 62.
10 Schuchhardt's Schliemann's Excavations, pp. 63, 69, 37.
11 A piece of slag brought by the writer from Wady Maghara contained 23 per cent of iron and less than one-tenth per cent of copper. Ore from Surabit el Khadim contained 31 per cent of copper and 12 per cent of iron.

So in Greece. It was but quite recently that two lumps of iron were found in the second or Homeric city at Hissarlik; and in the graves at Mycenæ it has been found only in the form of a few finger-rings,[12] although known to Homer as used for both tools and weapons.[13] But when we reach western Asia, where the early population had its home, where the narrative had its origin, and where also the metal exists in the mountains, we find iron in the earliest times to which we can penetrate, and in comparatively free use. At Nineveh, in the northwest palace at Nimroud, the oldest of all, dating probably nearly nine hundred years before Christ, Layard found in one chamber "a large quantity of iron" and "recognized it as scales of the armor represented on the sculptures. Each scale was separate and was of iron, two or three inches in length, rounded at one end and squared at the other, with a raised or embossed line in the center." Though badly decomposed, there were several baskets full of these relics. As the earth was removed, other portions of armor were discovered, some of copper, some of iron, others of iron inlaid with copper. Several iron helmets of various shapes were found, although so rusted that they fell to pieces.[14] It is needless to say that such articles involve a long previous process of manufacture. The direct proof is not wanting. Thothmes III. of Egypt, whom Brugsch assigns to 1600 B. C., has recorded in his

---

12 Schuchhardt, pp. 332, 396.
13 Iliad, vii., 141; viii., 15; vi., 48. Od., i., 204; ix., 391, etc.
14 Nineveh and its Remains, ii., pp. 277, 278.

great inscription at Karnak the spoil brought by him from his warlike expeditions into western Asia. Among them were two suits of iron armor, and iron vessels from the king of Megiddo, an iron suit of armor decorated with gold from the kings of Ruthen, vessels of iron and bronze from Tunip, iron suits of armor and fine iron helmets from Naharain (Mesopotamia), iron from the land of Punt, and, once more, iron suits of armor and weapons from Naharain.[15] These records show an extensive use and skillful manufacture, necessarily involving a long preceding use. Thus this ancient historic record of the Scriptures points back into a still more remote past, in confirmation of the remote invention. In still further harmony with the record is the fact that not only do iron mines abound in the Tyari mountains of Armenia,[16] but iron is found in great quantities scattered on the sides of the mountains three or four days from Mosul.[17] An additional consistency in the whole narrative is seen in the fact that such a structure as the ark at a later time would require the progress in metallurgy here indicated. Certainly the one would in part explain the other. It has been shrewdly suggested, of course with much less cogency, that the homicide or murder for which Lamech expected to go unpunished, may have been one of the consequences of this forging of "every cutting instrument of copper and iron," it being mentioned in the immediate sequel.

---

15 Brugsch, History of Egypt, pp. 364, 373-385.
16 Layard's Nineveh, i., p. 190.   17 Id., ii., p. 315.

The song which Lamech addresses to his wives accords with the historic fact that the beginnings of music have been early coupled with the sister art of song. In its subject-matter it shows "a titanic arrogance" in crime founded on the impunity of the first murder, preparing the way for and necessitating, not only the subsequent destruction of the race for its great wickedness, but a reconstruction with a new legislation inflicting the death penalty for murder.

But while the worldly career and the rapid development of the arts of living and luxury are going on in the line of Cain, and that family is dismissed from the view, the promise of the Maker (presently to be discussed) begins to find its fulfillment, not only in the last words of the common mother, but in the religious revival in the line of Seth—however transient it may have been—when men began to call upon the name of Jehovah. Here, apparently, are found "the sons of God" who are spoken of in the narrative of chapter vi.

CHAPTER X

THE PRIMITIVE CONDITION

In thus tracing the Scripture narrative upwards we reach the account of the temptation and fall, which, however, cannot well be considered before an examination of their previous condition. The history of the work of creation must also be deferred, though at some disadvantage.

The account of creation in the first chapter of Genesis is followed by a brief explanatory statement concerning man, preliminary to the subsequent narrative, and alluding only to such points as bear on the writer's purpose. These points are selected, not in the order of sequence, as in the creation narrative, but by the laws of association, as connected with the destiny of man, which now becomes the theme, man himself being the center. First we are told specifically of man's twofold nature (ii. 7), formed not only of the dust of the ground but with the inbreathing of God, in contradistinction from the animal world made "out of the ground" only. This is preceded, however, by a reference to the changed condition of things from the time when there was no man because the earth was not prepared for his residence (verses 5, 6). These allusions are preparatory to the Eden narrative. The endeavor to find here a second, and especially a conflicting, narrative is unnecessary. The well-known change from the use of Elohim to Jehovah Elohim, is as well explained by saying that it purposely identifies the God of creation with the God of Israel, as by supposing a different writer; and the omission of all details not required for the object in view, and the mention of those that are given in their present relations rather than their previous sequence, is the simple, natural and wise method. The proceeding is no more peculiar than the brief retrospective notices and recapitulations with which other narrators often commence a new chapter to make a connection; as, for example, in the opening of the third and fourth chapters of Macaulay's History of England, and any number of instances. It is a narrowness of view to make so much of this very simple and common thing as has been done by some writers.

At the same time a use of older documents, adopted and thereby sanctioned by an author, no more detracts from his proper authorship, than is the similar method of Bancroft and other historians inconsistent with their historic function. As has been already intimated, there are good reasons and somewhat clear indications for the belief that such was the fact in regard to the narrative of Genesis. There is no valid reason for holding, even if Moses was the responsible author of the book, that all the facts antecedent to his time, any more than those of his own time, were miraculously revealed to him, when there are indications or probabilities of natural methods. It has never been God's way to supersede natural methods by supernatural when the former were sufficient. But the practicability of dividing up and accurately sorting out all these sources, and especially of detruding them from a high antiquity and authentic value, is a very different thing. We are at present concerned only with the truthfulness of the narrative; and so far as that is sustained, the other questions are comparatively unimportant. In the present instance it would be a matter of indifference whether here are one or two narratives, provided they are not in conflict, as under any fair treatment they are not. All the phenomena, however, may be perfectly explained on the supposition of one continuous narrative. It is idle to expect a writer to go over all the details of a narrative a second time; equally idle to require or expect him in his allusions to his former account, for a very different purpose and from an entirely different standpoint, to refer to them in the same order.

The writer alludes to facts already mentioned just so far as they concern this new portion of the history, and no farther. He refers to man's peculiar diversity from the animal world and yet his relation to them, and no more; to the plants and herbs (ii. 5) generally, saying nothing of their bearing seed or fruit; to the trees of the garden where man was to be placed, and no others; to the cattle, fowls and beasts with which the man was brought in connection, and not to the immense sea life and great monsters (i. 20, 21) with which he is not now concerned. Why any one should insist on finding a different and second narrative in this discretionary and discreet reference is not very obvious. But it is said that there is an actual conflict; that, according to verse 19 of chapter second, man was made before the animals, contrary to the previous statement. Certainly the creation of the animals is mentioned after the mention of Adam's being placed in the garden; so also is the making of the trees of the garden to grow mentioned not till after the man was placed in it. But that order of events does not follow in the one case more than in the other.

One thing perhaps calls for a little further notice. It is strenuously insisted that an actual contradiction of the order of creation is found (ii. 19) where we are told, in immediate succession, that God formed and brought the animals to the man, and therefore the writer here places the Creation of the animals after that of man, whereas in the first chapter the process was the opposite of this. What is the insuperable difficulty of recognizing here the briefest possible reference to the previous creation of these animals, with the addition that these animals are now brought by their Creator to the presence and attention of the man for the purpose immediately specified? This is the rendering made and defended by Strack (1894): "Therefore Jehovah God brought all beasts of the field and all fowls of heaven which he had formed out of the ground to the man," etc.¹

The question of the location of the first pair has its difficulties, due apparently rather to our ignorance than to any uncertainty in the original description. The writer defines it boldly, and by careful specifications of locality, boundary and, in one instance, production. It carries every appearance of an undoubted, undoubting historic statement. But in its remoteness and our historic ignorance it is partly beyond the limit of our recognition. In recent times we have gained more knowledge, and some of our difficulties have been removed. Certain negative and some positive results have been reached. An important achievement was accomplished when Friedrich Delitzsch demolished what he calls "Paradise in Utopia,"² that is, the lawless theories which freely made the most impossible combinations, as of the Nile with the Tigris and the Ganges; which, among them, proposed as many as seventeen different streams for the Pison, and thirteen for the Gihon; and which located Eden at various points from the Canary Isles to China or the Baltic Sea. A chief occasion of this confusion was the mistaken belief that the land of Cush, so

---

1 Dr. Driver summarily declares, "The rendering 'had formed' is contrary to idiom." But Delitzsch in his latest edition reverses his own former opinion, and affirms that this mode of expression is not only conformed to Hebrew style, but necessitated by the purpose and method of this narrative. He cites Hitzig (Jeremiah, p. 288, 2nd ed.) in support of such a construction. Dr. Green takes the same ground (Unity of Genesis, p. 7). Dillmann in his latest edition (1892) concedes the mode of construction to be admissible, but objects to it here on the ground that the previous statement, "I will make an helpmeet," forces us to understand also that the animals are now to be made; which does not follow. See Appendix, note xix.

2 Wo lag das Paradies (1881).

rendered properly in our Revised Version, was only the land of Ethiopia, as rendered in the English Version of James. The removal of this long-continued ignorance has brought the problem to a proximate solution, and removed the last excuse (if ever there was one) for bringing the Nile and Ethiopia into this connection. Gesenius, who had opposed the acceptance of an Asiatic Cush in the earlier part of his great work, the Thesaurus, changed his opinion before its completion and recognized a Cush in Arabia. Robinson extended the view and assigned to the Cushites the "immense region stretching from Assyria in the northeast, through eastern Arabia into Africa." Fuerst admits the same wide extent, as far as to the land east of Babylonia. Rawlinson pointed out a remarkable connection between the Cushites of Ethiopia and the early inhabitants of Babylonia. Lenormant, Maspero and Brugsch take a similar position; and in 1895 Professor Hommel sustains the decision of Glaser as "the only correct view," that in the earliest time the Kassites (as he designates them) dwelt in Elam, whence they invaded Babylonia about 1700 B. C.[3] Indeed, it is a singular phenomenon that any one should ever have attributed to a Hebrew writer or compiler at any stage of history such ignorance as to assign to the Nile, which flows from the south to the north, an origin in the vicinity of the Euphrates and Tigris.

[3] The references are to the Thesaurus in the articles on Cush and Raamah, Robinson's translations of Gesenius' Lexicon, Fuerst's Lexicon, Rawlinson's Herodotus, i., p. 353; Lenormant's Chaldean Magic, pp. 347-357; Maspero, Histoire Ancienne, p. 147; Brugsch's Steininschrift und Bibelwort, p. 58; Hommel in Recent Research, p. 154.

Notwithstanding the present difficulty of settling some of the details of the description, others of them are clear. And among the indications of the historic character of the description and its former intelligibleness are these: the general locality, "eastward," naturally from the place where the narrative took its final form; the designation of two rivers about which there is no question, the Euphrates and Tigris; the mention of the perfectly well-known one of these rivers without explanation, and of the others with descriptions; the minuteness of the description, especially in the case of the Pison, including not only the land it compassed, but the products of the land and the particular fact that its gold was "good"; the designation of a region, somewhere about the Euphrates and Tigris, a region not only generally adapted to human residence, but in conformity to the now prevalent belief that in western Asia was the cradle of the human race, as has been set forth in a previous chapter. There is thus positive reason for recognizing its historic character, and no valid reason for doubting it.

When we descend to the details, some things are certain, and some are, and possibly must remain, unsettled. There is no dissent as to the two great rivers; and it is known that one main branch of the Tigris rises within about two miles of the Euphrates.[4] The latter is 1,600 miles long, and the former about 1,146 miles before its junction with the

---

[4] Delitzsch, Genesis (New Com.), i., p. 133.

Euphrates. As to the Pison and Gihon a considerable diversity of opinions still prevails, each view being open to objections not easily overcome. Waiving, therefore, any argument for or against any one of them, we fix upon the settled facts, the two unquestioned rivers.

In conformity with this assignment of locality, divested of all doubtful details, is the fact as stated by Wright and Pinches,[5] that the more reasonable theories as to the position of paradise may be roughly divided into two classes: namely, "those which place the garden of Eden below the junction of the Tigris and the Euphrates, and seek the Pison and Gihon among the many natural or artificial tributaries of those streams; and those which locate the site in the high tablelands of Armenia, where so many noble streams have their origin." It was somewhere along the line of the Euphrates, higher or lower. Either of these regions would well satisfy the conditions. The southern portion of it is the congenial soil for the cereals, and has been the seat of population and power from the remotest antiquity. The tablelands of Armenia give rise to four noble rivers,[6] all springing from sources not far from each other, and discharging into three different seas; and the country is described by the British engineer. Colonel Chesney, as adapted to the growth of "every tree that is pleasant and good for food," interspersed with beautiful valleys

---

[5] Smith's Dictionary of the Bible, 2nd Ed., i., p. 846.

[6] Besides the Euphrates and Tigris, the Araxes, 1,000 miles long, and the Halys or Kizil Irmak, 700 miles long. See note xx. in the Appendix.

and fertile plains, and overspread with "groves, orchards, vineyards, gardens and villages."[7] In either region the fig of the sacred narrative would grow. Here, then, the account is beyond impeachment. It is perhaps not wise to lay any stress upon certain traditions—one cherished in the valleys of central Armenia that Eden extended from the pashalik of Mosul to a point near Erzeroom and from Tocat to beyond Lake Van,[8] and one in Harpoot that paradise was in the neighboring plain;[9] nor on the name "Paradise Mountain" that lingers on a lofty peak of the Caucasus above the sources of the Rion or Phasis.[10] They are not necessary. Nor is it needful to dwell on the statement of Sayce that "the land on the western bank of the Euphrates (in southern Babylonia) went under the general name of "*Edinna*," the Eden of Scripture—the sacred grove and garden in the neighborhood of Eridu, at the junction of the Tigris and Euphrates, being the garden of Genesis;"[11] or that of Friedrich Delitzsch, that the name Eden came from the Accadian "*edinu*," which, as he claims, was applied to a part of Babylonia, the word meaning "field, land, desert," and applied to this region as *the* land preeminently.[12] It is sufficient that the general and growing consensus of scholars who do not hold to the Utopian theory, locates the site of the garden

---

7 Chesney's Euphrates and Tigris, i., p. 270.
8 Chesney, i., p. 267.
9 H. N. Wheeler, Letters from Eden, pp. 15, 16.
10 Freshfield, Central Caucasus, p. 277.
11 Sayce's Ancient Empires of the East, p. 95.
12 Wo lag das Paradies, pp. 79, 80. See note xx.

somewhere along the region of the Euphrates, higher or lower; that the conditions of the region are entirely consistent with the supposition; and the various indications of the dispersion of the human race, as already mentioned, point to western Asia as their original home. All these things go to support the historical character of the narrative as a whole, whatever details are still beyond our means of investigation.

Man's primitive condition is described in a mode which bears the closest scrutiny, even in circumstances to which objections have sometimes been made. (1) He has employment; he could not be happy otherwise. (2) His employment is of the simplest kind, belonging to the most primitive state of things, to "dress the garden and to keep it." (3) He has intelligence and the capacity of speech, used first in the most natural way of recognizing and naming the animals that present themselves to his notice. (4) He is a social being, and longs for companionship. (5) He is from the first under moral relations—privilege and prohibition, each of the simplest kind: a sacramental tree, so to call it, and a test tree. (6) The test to which he was subjected was precisely conformed to his condition. Some such test was the only natural one, we may say the only practicable one. The objection sometimes raised or felt, to making obedience, or disobedience with penalty, hinge upon keeping from the fruit of a tree, singularly misapprehends the state of the case. The nature of the prohibition is the best guaranty of the truth of the narrative. It was not only in keeping with that first mode of life, but it was of almost the only kind which the situation admitted.

The great crimes of the modern statute book, such as theft, robbery, arson, adultery, and the like, were impossible; murder and violence at first inconceivable. Even if it had been the object to make the trial of him in his relations to man rather than to God, those relations were mainly still wanting. It only remained to select a test from the actual life and environment. The spirit of obedience, of obedience to his Maker, could be as well determined by the one selected as by any other. Thus, when carefully considered, the complete conformity of the narrative to the condition and surroundings of the man is the best evidence available of its fundamental truth, while the whole series of facts, even to the matter of clothing, is stated with a verisimilitude apprehensible to all mankind. Surely there is no need nor justification of finding a myth in such a naive and consistent history.

The account of woman's creation and union to the man is, of course, attended with difficulties in detail, owing to the reticence of the narrative, and the utter absence of all other sources of knowledge. It must also be borne in mind that no possible explanation of the relationship can be clear of difficulties; the tracing of origins is a plunge into mystery, after all is said. The fact of sex, not only in the human species, but throughout animated life, and its unfailing adjustment from the beginning, is a fact before which, when fairly considered, the most enthusiastic evolutionist has nothing satisfactory to offer. So infinite are the probabilities against a single individual appearing in exactly the right time and with the right constitution to be in perfect correlation to another individual for the continuation of the species, and so inconceivably infinite against this occurrence taking place through the hundreds of thousands of species and countless millions of individuals, and in such wise as to insure its never-failing continuance, that one need hardly hesitate to pronounce the statement of the direct creation of the first woman to be the most simple and the most probable explanation. Nothing certain can be alleged against it, and nothing certain, if anything probable, can be advanced instead of it.

Furthermore, the scriptural statement of the relation thus established is, as we shall presently see, absolutely faultless in its lofty ideal, above all criticism. The difficulty is in regard to the process, and consists mainly in its obscurity; obscurity in a matter which, very possibly, must in any case have remained obscure, like other ultimate facts of natural science. Whatever the exact nature of the process, the significance of it is clear, and has been clear to the whole world in all ages. We will not, therefore, minutely discuss the several theories of the process, except to say that the word translated "rib" is indeterminate. It is so translated nowhere else in the Old Testament, but in its frequent use has the generic meaning "side"—the side of various objects.[13] While some have supposed it to be actually a rib, others have conjectured some unknown part of the body, or some part made for the purpose, and even (as Maimonides and the Talmud) one half of an androgynous being. In each case, it is life from previous life, and so far reasonable.

It may be added that another view of the transaction is suggested by the narrative itself, which gives it the same significance, namely, that it was a symbolical transaction in a vision. We read that Adam was first cast into a "deep sleep"; the same word being used as concerning Abram's state when he had the vision of the smoking furnace, and the word used in Job iv. 13, where it speaks of "visions of the night when *deep sleep* falleth upon man." The account would thus seem to permit, if not distinctly to suggest, that here may be a vision in this state of deep sleep, as in the case of Abram, described as it presented itself, phenomenally, in the one case as in the other. For those who may prefer, this mode of conception is apparently admissible.

But whether this transaction was an inner or an outer vision, the meaning is the same—equally distinct, remarkable and noble, the highest possible conception of the relation of husband and wife.

---

[13] The side of a mountain, of the tabernacle, the ark, an altar, of a double door, of the heavens, a side chamber. In 1 Kings vi. 15, 16; vii. 3 it means beams or joists of a building here only approximating to the signification "rib."

Taken in connection with Adam's own exclamation, "This is bone of my bone and flesh of my flesh," here is a declaration not only of similarity, but of identity of origin, nature and interest, of sympathy and of intimacy as in no other human relation. Even the beautiful and striking description of the relation in Ephesians v. 21-31 is but its paraphrase. The narrative, then, presents an ideal of marriage not only far above the prevailing Jewish standard in Christ's time, but above the practice of their venerated ancestors, and higher than the requirements of their great law-giver. As such it speaks for itself, for the fundamental truth of the narrative, and, we may add, for its superhuman origin.

Add to this the announcement (in ii. 24) of the great and perpetual law of marriage which the Savior Himself only reaffirmed; and we behold an extraordinary phenomenon: this second chapter of the Pentateuch establishes the two great institutions which lie at the foundation of the family life and the religious life of the world, namely, the Sabbath, and marriage in its highest ideal. In the presence of these two fundamental facts there is no occasion to make apologies for this narrative, nor to talk of myths.

It should also be said that the supposition of a late origin of this account supposes two insupposable things: first, that some late Jewish writer or writers invented an early legislation which condemned the practice of their two most boasted ancestors; second, that there was some Jew in the days of comparative disorder in the eighth or ninth century B. C., or indeed in any later time before the coming of Christ, capable of rising to such a height.

CHAPTER XI

THE TEMPTATION AND FALL

This part of the early narrative confessedly presents many difficulties. They are reduced by remembering that the style is popular, and that here, as in the first chapter (presently to be considered), the description is phenomenal, representing things as they appeared, and in the language of common and oriental life.

The cardinal points of the narrative are these: An original state of innocence; a subsequent state of sin and sorrow, brought about by disobedience to the law of God.

The first of these is so far beyond the reach of all other historical records that it comes down only in the unwritten history, the tradition of the nations—the recognition of a "golden age" when the gods held converse with men, and there was neither sin nor care nor painful labor and sorrow. The proof of this tradition is abundant. The cautious Dillmann describes it as a belief spread through all antiquity, and he instances in detail the classic nations, India, Persia and Egypt, in which last country, as is well known, it took the form of a protracted reign of the gods. Zoeckler makes a more extensive enumeration, and finds the tradition (combined with other traits of the Biblical narrative) among the Chinese, Mongolians and Japanese, Karens, early inhabitants of India, ancient Eranians, Egyptians, Phenicians, Malayo-Polynesians, Babylonians, Etruscans, Germans and Greeks. He states his conclusion thus: "A golden age, followed by a gradual descent to the want and wretchedness of the present state, a Paradise sun with long waning light, is in fact a common possession of all the older peoples."[1] The reader of the classics need not be reminded of the representations found in Hesiod and Ovid. And in the trivial and, in part, foolish details of the latter author, though written in the Augustan age, he will perceive the marvelous contrast to the dignity of the Hebrew book that even then could have been found in Rome beyond the Tiber.

No fair-minded person can fail to recognize the immense weight of this consensus of antiquity, this concurrent reminiscence descending as a common heir-loom of the oldest nations of the world. It is inexplicable except as testimonies admitting no collusion. Many persons, no doubt, would be more impressed by a parallel narrative, were such a one found at Niffur, as old as the time of Sargon I., but it would not carry a tithe of the weight.

This portion of the sacred history and of general unrecorded history, of course, will naturally find denial from those who hold to the rise of the human race from a lower, indeed the lowest, order of being. Their denial will deserve a more careful con-

---

[1] Zoeckler, Urstand des Menschen, pp. 84-112.

sideration when several things shall have been proved that are now unproved; as, for example, that living substance has come from non-living substance, that sentient life has come from non-sentient, that man has actually come from any non-human being. Till then the consentient testimonies of antiquity must hold good against speculations, or the speculations must somehow find room for the testimonies.

The second point, that the human race through all recorded history has been in a state of sin and of suffering, needs no argument. But it is to be observed that not only is sin universal, but it shows itself contemporaneously with responsible action. Whatever benign influences may be combined in the environments, and whatever may be said by fanciful writers of the perfect innocence of infancy, we can look upon any child in the cradle and confidently predict that when conscious moral agency begins, it will be accompanied by wrong-doing in some form; and the prediction will never be found false. The fallen man "begat a son in his own likeness after his own image."

The third fundamental point, that the evil condition of the human race has its origin in disobedience to the law of God and of righteousness, is equally unquestionable. It is a truism that man is his own worst enemy, and his next worst enemy is his fellowman. What are all the follies, vices and crimes that destroy the welfare of the individual, the family, society, the nation and the world, but the various outbursts of disobedience to the great law of righteousness and God?

On these three fundamental matters, the record appears to be historic and irrefutable. When we come to the transition from innocence and well-being to sin and woe, the chief difficulty presents itself; but then, be it observed, not in the process described so much as in the form. As to the inner process and progress of the temptation, the record is singularly true to human experience and observation. Nothing could be better. First is suggested a sense of the hardship of the restraint and the exaggeration of the case: "Yea, hath God said, Ye shall not eat of any tree[2] of the garden?" Then, when parleying with temptation begins, next comes a lowering of motive to the danger incurred, and the danger discounted: "*lest* ye die." Then follows a disbelief of the evil consequences: "Ye shall not surely die." On the contrary, some great gain: "Your eyes shall be opened, and ye shall be as God, knowing good and evil"—where the mingling of specious truth and fatal falsehood reminds us of the echo in our great poet:

> "Juggling fiends, no more to be believed,
> That palter with us in a double sense;
> That keep the word of promise to our ear,
> And break it to our hope."

The persistent brooding over the attractiveness of the forbidden object continues—"when the woman saw that the tree was good for food, and that it was a delight to the eyes, and that the tree

---
[2] So the Revised Version, in accordance with the Hebrew usage and the best expositors.

was to be desired to make one wise"—till the end came as always after such a dallying. How true to fact! Also true in that the temptation to an innocent being comes from without, and first to the more emotional nature.

The consequences ascribed to this temptation and fall are found to be equally in harmony with fact. These cannot well be considered without a few previous words as to the method of the temptation; in which, let it be observed, is found the only difficulty and ground of questioning. If this were regarded as a parable or a figure, as some would have it, or a dramatic representation, it would still leave unimpaired the truthfulness of the facts so conveyed.[3] But it seems not necessary and apparently not admissible so to regard it.

In discussing the method, several writers (Ebrard, Dillmann, Strack) have called attention to the consistency of the narrative in referring the seduction to an outer source, since it could not well originate in an innocent being, nor then have come from other human beings. So those who hold to the absolute innocence of infancy endeavor to explain sin by "environment." Who then was the real tempter? According to the New Testament it was "that old serpent called the devil and Satan" (Rev. xii. 9; xx. 2), who, as the Savior said, "was a murderer from the beginning" and "a liar" (John viii. 44), who has "the power of death" (Heb. ii. 13), so that

---

[3] Perhaps no one has more strongly emphasized the truthfulness to nature and the essentially philosophical character of the whole narrative than Dillmann in his commentary, p. 189. Ebrard makes a similar showing; Apologetics, i., pp. 311-313.

"the Son of God was manifested that He might destroy the works of the devil" (John iii. 8), with the assurance that "the God of peace shall bruise Satan under your feet shortly" (Rev. xvi. 8). The same connection of the serpent with Satan is implied by the Savior in Luke x. 17-19, and more distinctly when He termed His wicked opponents children of the devil (John viii. 38, 44; Mark xiii. 38). The antagonism predicted in Gen. iii. 15 is broadly stated by Christ as the conflict between the kingdom of Satan and the kingdom of God (Luke xi. 17-20), and was exemplified in the temptation which Satan was permitted to offer to the Son of God, the second Adam. If we accept the authority of the New Testament, and even of Christ, it would seem that we must accept this explanation. Many in these days incline to doubt or deny the existence of such a being. But they cannot well deny that Christ distinctly taught it, not merely as an exoteric doctrine, or an unmeaning concession to a popular notion, but in his personal and private instruction to His chosen disciples.[4] And it is very noteworthy that even Mr. Huxley, in his contemptuous arraignment of what he calls the story of the Gadarene swine, is obliged to confess that he has "no *a priori* objection to offer. . . . I declare as plainly as I can, that I am unable to show cause why these transferable devils should not exist."[5] Certainly an active agency is quite as comprehensible as an

---

[4] Matt. x. 8; xvi. 19, 20; Mark ix. 28, 29; Luke ix. 1; x. 17-19. Christ distinguishes between casting out evil spirits and healing diseases, as Luke xx. 1, etc.

[5] Science and Hebrew Tradition, p. 226.

"environment," and much more to the point.

But granting, what cannot be denied, the philosophic truthfulness of the underlying lesson, we may be expected to meet the question, Was there, as the instrument, an actual serpent or form of a serpent? This appears to be involved in verses 1 and 14 of the narrative, and to be the understanding in 2 Cor. xi. 3. That the writer of the narrative knew the actual agent that was behind this appearance does not appear. Here, as elsewhere, he describes *the phenomenon;* in the words of Delitzsch, he "confines himself to the external appearance of what took place, without lifting the veil from the reality behind it."

Now, whatever difficulties may attend this portion of the narrative, it finds a remarkable confirmation in early traditions. Says Kalisch in his commentary, "Almost throughout the East the serpent was used as an emblem of the evil principle, the spirit of disobedience and contumacy. A few exceptions only can be discovered." Probably a larger margin should be allowed for exceptions; the statement is substantially correct. Sometimes the serpent was worshiped as an object of fear. Lenormant, who makes all necessary exceptions, asserts, and with illustrative instances, that "we find in all mythologies a gigantic serpent personifying the nocturnal power, the evil principle, material darkness and moral wickedness." And as the result of several pages of examples he concludes by saying that "the great serpent, among all the highly civilized peoples whose traditions we have scrutinized, is symbolical of this dark and evil power in its broadest conception."[6] Turning to one of these nations as described by another high authority: Brugsch affirms that "through the mythical traditions belonging to all periods of the Egyptian monumental world down to the Christian era, there enters like a red thread the representation of the serpent as the symbol of evil; . . . the tree of life and in its vicinity the serpent are in the old Egyptian representations inseparable from each other."[7] Lenormant follows this last line of double suggestion with several similar illustrations, one of which, previously cited by George Smith in his "Chaldean Genesis," is sufficiently striking to be described in his own words: "A man and a woman, the first wearing on his head the kind of turban peculiar to the Babylonians, seated face to face on either side of a tree with horizontal branches, from which hang two large branches of fruit, one in front of each of these personages, who are in the act of stretching out their hands to pluck them. Behind the woman a serpent uprears itself."[8] Now, notwithstanding two or three minor objections, such as that it is not certain that these two persons are man and woman rather than two men, that one is not actually handing the fruit to the other, and even the very peculiar one that the serpent "may have

---

6 Lenormant's Beginnings of History, pp. 103, 114.

7 Brugsch's Steininschrift, pp. 24, 25. See also Wilkinson's Ancient Egyptians, iii., pp. 121, 152, Birch's edition.

8 Lenormant, pp. 98, 99.

been introduced for the purpose of ornament,"[9] a writer who gathers up these objections to show that the reference to the temptation is doubtful, is constrained to concede that "the picture at once strikes the beholder as a representation of the temptation"; while such authorities as Lenormant and Friedrich Delitzsch declare it to be capable of no other explanation,[10] and W. St. Chad Boscawen also regards it as an "indication" of the story of the Fall.[11] The case is made still stronger by other pictorial representations, a very large number showing the sacred tree with various surroundings and a less number showing the serpent-cultus. George Smith gives a cut from the seal of a Syrian chief of the ninth century B. C., representing the sacred tree with attendant figures and eagle-headed men. To omit other references, Ohnefalsch-Richter, in his elaborate work,[12] devotes 196 folio pages to the discussion of the tree cultus and its connections, accompanied by scores of cuts of the tree, from the crudest and often conventional forms up to an occasional delineation of branches, leaves and fruit, and attended by a variety of figures, human, animal and imaginary, from the commonly crude drawings up to that on a Greek vase where two human figures are somewhat gracefully outlined, and the well-drawn serpent opens his mouth towards the one that holds a fruit in the hand, it may be as an offering (Plate

---

[9] Prof. J. D. Davis, Genesis and Hebrew Tradition, p. 67.
[10] Lenormant, p. 99. Fr. Delitzsch's Chaldaeische Genesis, p. 305.
[11] Boscawen, The Bible and the Monuments, p. 89.
[12] Kypros, Die Bibel und Homer, 2 vols. (1893).

cxxiii., Fig. 3). The same writer has a brief excursus[13] on the serpent cultus (and a promise of a more complete discussion hereafter), in which he refers to twenty cuts of this nature, exhibited in his tables, and derived from Egypt, Babylonia, Persia, Cyprus, Crete, and elsewhere, many of which he contends cannot have been otherwise than independent in their origin, and some of them of the greatest antiquity.

In view of these concurrent indications, it is not those who accept the view of an external transaction here recorded that are bound to show cause, but rather those who reject it. There are questions concerning some of its details which cannot be answered. But whatever our decision as to the form of the occurrence, the truthfulness of its teaching cannot be denied. Professor Ryle, who does not express clearly his belief of the personality of the spirit of evil, yet in speaking of "the story of the fall" declares that "the Paradise narrative brings a message pregnant with evangelic truth."

Equally true and remarkable is the delineation of the consequences as immediately set forth. The penalty of disobedience was announced in these terms: "In the day that thou eatest thereof thou shalt surely die." This death evidently was not primarily physical death, for that did not take place on that day nor for long years after, as the writer proceeds immediately to show. But he does describe a series of consequences constituting that

---

[13] Ib., pp. 442, 443. Note xxi.

spiritual death so abundantly indicated in the Scriptures, and well described by Augustine when he said that death of the body consists in the separation of the body from the soul, but death of the soul in the separation of the soul from God. In the very act of transgression that separation took place. Its several elements are implicitly presented in the sequel: first the sense of guilty shame, then the shrinking and endeavor to hide from God's presence, painful dependence of the woman on the husband and suffering in the parental relation, and for the man anxious and disappointing toil, all closed and crowned by a return to the dust of the earth.

How soberly and terribly true is the statement of the changes wrought by the curse of sin, whereby the labor that was to have been a pleasure becomes a burden, the woman's loving dependence so often a galling chain, and the family a scene of conjugal trouble, filial wickedness, and parental sorrow! All this, set forth not in abstract but in concrete terms, is how sadly true as the fruit of sin, alienation from God! The press of modern times teems with the proof.

A few words as to the details of the curse. They are wholly concrete and illustrative, rather than technically inclusive. The serpent's doom is readily understood when the real agent is borne in mind, according to the New Testament interpretation. It is addressed to the arch enemy, and couched in terms drawn from the form he had assumed; a serpent's form he had taken, and a serpent's fate shall be his, a groveling and dirt-eating career; enmity between his "seed," the "children of the wicked one" (Luke xiii. 38), the "offspring of vipers" (Matt. iii. 7), and the promised "seed of the woman," Christ and Christ's—the children of light and of God. And though a wound of the heel, a dangerous wound, was inflicted on the one side, a bruising of the head, a final overthrow, should fall on the other—a conflict now hopefully going on, Christ having come "that He might destroy the works of the devil." This apprehension of the curse renders it unnecessary to understand any change in the serpent form itself from an upright to a prone position, a change that would require a reconstruction of every portion of its body; but it assumes the prone position and motion as the fitting symbol of the curse. The sentences of the man and of the woman are announced, after the common mode of the Scriptures and of the Savior, by specimen. The pains of parturition are but the beginning and illustration of the sorrows that sin has brought upon the wife and mother. The contention with "thorns and thistles" is but a type and foretaste of the painful and often fruitless struggles of man's life. One is tempted to attach a more sweeping range to the utterance, "Cursed is the ground for thy sake," or on thy account, when he looks over the world and sees what vast regions, once fertile, flourishing and populous, as in the Fayoom, Babylonia, Assyria, Palestine, and other lands, have been made desolate for ages by human wickedness, and how other lands, almost all the lands of the earth, have been devastated for generations by human vice, passion and violence. The billions that a generation ago carried such destruction over the soil of the southern states of this Union, were enough, if spent in economic, literary and artistic improvements, to have converted the region into a kind of terrestrial paradise.

Thus, in all its fundamental features, this account of the temptation and fall and the consequences is eminently rational and truthful; and the only questions at issue are minor ones of mode and detail, in which also the concurrence of ancient and widespread tradition supports the more obvious interpretation of the narrative.

CHAPTER XII

THE CREATION NARRATIVE

PERHAPS no part of the Sacred Scriptures has suffered more from foes and friends than the history of creation. It has been the subject of hasty assault and hasty surrender. Some men of scientific attainments—not grasping the character and method of this simple history—have charged it with grave errors of fact; and Christian writers, overawed by this seeming authority, have timidly conceded the case, and it has become too customary to excuse the alleged "mistakes" on the ground that it was not the function of Genesis to teach science, or that the writer shared the erroneous notions of his contemporaries. Others have resorted to the view that it is legend, saga, myth, parable, or poetry. One writer has elaborately defended it as a "Psalm of Creation"—ignoring the palpable narrative nature of the statements, and the immense difference between it and such a composition as the one hundred and fourth psalm, which is an actual psalm of creation, the one so eulogized by Von Humboldt.

Now, we hold that this is neither poetry, saga nor science, but *a popular and truthful narration*, and we propose to show that when fairly treated, that is, when *interpreted by its mode of narration and standard of style*, it is sustained by the statements of the best modern scientific authorities. It is neither Huxley's "pure fiction," nor the absurd travesty of facts with which Professor Draper entertained himself.

It is quite remarkable how much is conceded to this narrative even by those critics who find difficulties and discrepancies in it. Dr. Driver terms it a dignified and sublime representation, in marked contrast to the other ancient cosmogonies. Among its declarations on which he lays great stress as of the utmost weight amid the crude and false notions then universal, are these: (1) That the world was called into existence, and brought gradually into its present state, at the will of a Spiritual Being, prior to it, independent of it, deliberately planning each stage of its development—a fact which no scientific progress can affect or disprove; (2) its object is to afford a true view in conception, if not in detail, of the origin of the earth as we know it, and not in an abstract and confused form which may soon be forgotten, but in a series of *representative pictures* which may impress themselves on the imagination, teaching, in terms which all can understand, the same truth which is the outcome of the wisest philosophy, that the world in which we live cannot be comprehended, cannot become an intelligible object of knowledge, except as dependent on a supreme Mind; (3) the distinctive pre-eminence of man as endowed with that highest of gifts, *self-conscious reason*, with all its implied intellectual faculties, with will power, with the ability to enter into relations of sympathy, affection, compassion, and love, with the capacity for character, and with the power of knowing and loving God and receiving the knowledge of God and the purposes of His grace. All this is stated in his own words, though abbreviated at great disadvantage to the impression.[1] In thus ascribing to the narrative these supreme truths, in declaring that they are in accord with the wisest philosophy, disclosed in representative pictures which all can understand and which impress themselves upon the memory; when he also adds in his detailed statement, that the narration "groups the living creatures under great subdivisions which appeal to the eye," and even in regard to the word "day" says that it is "reasonable on the whole to concede its metaphorical use here"[2] —a concession at which Mr. Huxley sneered in his lectures in New York—Dr. Driver actually announces or implies all the principles of interpretation which, as we shall presently see, remove the difficulties which he finds remaining.

Professor Ryle, who, while calling this a "matchless introduction to the whole history," indulges in similar objections to its "scientific accuracy," yet in the strongest terms eulogizes its representation of three "fundamental conceptions," namely, the physical universe, mankind, and the Godhead. The first, he says, agrees in its highest conceptions

---
[1] Driver's Sermons on the Old Testament, pp. 171 seq.
[2] See note xxii., Appendix.

with the teaching of the purest philosophy of religion; in regard to the second, every item of the description is in harmony with the highest religious conception of man revealed to us in the teaching of the incarnation; in regard to the third, even more striking does this exaltation of conception appear in the description of the Godhead. These propositions, stated in his own words, he expands in detail.[3] Professor Ladd, who gives no little attention to the "lapses and errors" in it, prefaces his discussion with the declaration that "the noble simplicity of style, the loftiness and purity in theological conception of this masterpiece, are acknowledged by all, both critics and casual readers." He proceeds to specify "the more important elements of doctrine designed to be taught," which are made more impressive by his exposition in detail, briefly stated thus: (1) That the universe is dependent for its existence and present order upon the will of God; (2) the divine qualities of power and wisdom as evinced in preparing the world of physical substances, of living creatures, and of moral subjects made in the divine image, are prominent in the thought and narrative of the author; (3) the divine qualities in their creative activity penetrate every detail of creation; (4) the divine institution of the Mosaic Sabbath; (5) man at the head of creation, and the center of creation; (6) the universe constituted by God through successive acts of creation, an orderly and progressive whole.[4] Prebendary

---

[3] Ryle's Early Narratives of Genesis, pp. 10-12.
[4] Ladd's The Doctrine of Sacred Scriptures, i., pp. 253-259.

Row goes so far as to say of the statements of the Biblical narration that "while in some minute points they are not absolutely consistent with scientific facts, yet they make a marvelously near approach to them."[5]

Thus these writers affirm the singular truthfulness of the narrative in the great fundamental points, but here they pause and turn to certain stereotyped objections or alleged minor inaccuracies. It is proposed to show that these "inaccuracies," so constantly rehearsed by rote, disappear when the narrative is fairly treated, *and its actual method fully recognized*. The mistake of its critics and the oversight of many of its defenders consist in failing to take clear notice of the method and style of narration. Dr. Driver was on the verge of discovering it and thus disposing of his own criticism, when he spoke of its being given "*in representative pictures*" for all men to understand and to remember, its description by groups under the great subdivisions which appeal to the eye, and the metaphorical use of the word "day."

It becomes necessary first of all to call attention to the method and style of the narrative, and, because of the persistent oversight, to do so somewhat in detail in order to make it clear. And let it be observed that we are not advancing theories about the narrative, but stating *the facts of the case*.

Now, every composition must be judged and interpreted from its own aim, standpoint and method,

---
[5] Row's Bampton Lectures, p. 461.

whether mathematics, science, poetry, metaphysics, history or biography; and history itself by aim, recognizable mode, and its intended readers. Dickens' Child's History of England and Hallam's Constitutional History cannot be criticised on the same specific grounds.

This narrative was written and fitted for all mankind; for all lands, ages, classes and conditions of men. Its intent was not primarily intellectual education, nor completeness of science, but moral and religious impression and the uses of piety, and particularly as introductory to the history of the Revelation of God and the Redemption of man. These two governing considerations, universality of adaptation, and subordinateness of purpose, account for and necessitate two striking traits, *facts*, in the method of the narration, which have not received the attention they require, namely, its brevity, and its purely popular quality.

First, its brevity, absolutely unparalleled; the history of many millions of years, according to the scientists, told in thirty verses; the merest outline sketch. It is like compressing the map of a continent into less than a square inch. This marvelous brevity necessitates several things of the utmost importance for fair treatment of the account, several of the most important being steadily overlooked: (1) Omission of details, exceptions, modifications, in its broad and characterizing outlines; (2) a dismissal of facts once narrated, and a continuous forward movement, the narrative marking each new stage and then passing to the next without reverting or alluding to the former—although they move on together; (3) the announcement of each new movement, law, order of things, therefore, *in its totality or completeness.* This was also the needful mode of connecting the history with the creation known to the reader. The method, as matter of fact, runs through the whole narration, as, for example, in the case of the continents, vegetation, animal life, and other things that will be mentioned in their place. It is a perfectly obvious fact, when attention is called to it, but the overlooking of it has been the chief weak spot of the attack and the defense.

The universal adaptation of the history gives rise necessarily to these traits: (1) The absence of all technical terms, not alone, because the Hebrews had none such, but because they would have been inadmissible. Hence the visible universe (τὸ πᾶν) is "the heaven and the earth"; the vegetable kingdom is "the grass, the herb yielding seed, the fruit-tree yielding fruit"; chaos is "without form and void," or emptiness and desolation; there is no chemical action, but the Spirit of God moving, or brooding; no cosmic gas or chemical elements, but the deep, the waters, and so on. (2) Popular modes of statement always; scientific statements would have been stumbling blocks down to the present time. Not even the process is described, but only the results, and that usually by visible marks of changes the most stupendous, such as the appearance of light, and "the firmament." Instead of God's volitions we read that "God said." The Creator communes with Himself, "let us"; "calls" things by names, and sees that they are "good"—all in the human, vivid and universally intelligible mode. So also in speaking of the stages of creation, instead of talking of a geological epoch or era (if the Hebrew had had any such word), or attempting to state a length of time, incomprehensible at best, it simply describes these stages after the human mode as so many days' work, that is, of God's working. (3) For the same reason the descriptions are phenomenal, of things as they appeared or would have appeared. It is not necessary, though perhaps admissible, to suppose (with Miller, Kurtz, Godet, Reusch, Row) a series of visions, or a moving diorama. But clearly the method, it is important to observe, is the popular one of describing things not as they are interiorly, but phenomenally, as they appeared. On this point the sun and moon are a test case; the one a luminary, the other a dark reflecting body, but described alike as they appeared, the one to rule the day, the other to rule the night. The same trait appears throughout; in the visible "heaven," sky or welkin, in the separation of the waters from the waters, in the *obvious* forms of vegetation, in the monsters, literally "stretched out" creatures, the fowl flying *on the face of heaven*, and everything that *creepeth* on the earth; all phenomenal and even optical descriptions.

These traits of the narrative need but to be distinctly stated to be recognized; but the failure to recognize some of them has caused the chief criticisms of the narrative. Even the use of the word "day" is not a defect, but an excellence, in a narrative written in the simplest form for all men. The criticisms have made it necessary to point out these traits very distinctly and in detail, although they are recognizable at a glance when attention is directed to the facts. To enumerate them, however rendered necessary, is like analyzing a dandelion.

Bearing in mind the unquestionable aim and character of the narrative, let us proceed to test it by the latest results attained. It is worthy of mention, meanwhile, what Professor Arnold Guyot relates of himself: "In the beginning of the winter of 1840, having just finished writing a lecture which was to be part of a course which I was then delivering at Neuchatel, Switzerland, it flashed upon my mind that the outlines I had been tracing, guided by the results of scientific inquiry then available, were precisely those of the grand history given in the first chapter of Genesis. In the same hour I explained this remarkable coincidence to the intelligent audience which it was my privilege to address."[6] Forty-three years afterwards he adhered to the same view of the complete harmony between the narrative and the results of scientific inquiry, and published it to the world.

We proceed to the narrative itself. The first verse asserts the creation by God of the visible uni-

---
6 Guyot's Creation, Preface.

verse, that is, its absolute origination. The Hebrew word, much like our word "create," though the proper word for origination, might not of itself necessarily carry that force. The full meaning of the word is favored by the fact that (in this Hebrew conjugation) it is elsewhere used only concerning God's doings, and in this chapter employed but three times (vs. 1, 21, 27), in regard to the universe as a whole, the introduction of animal life and the origin of man—matter, life, spirit—and is made decisive by the fact that all the plastic processes subsequently performed on this material, are so complete and exhaustive as to admit only origination here. Science has nothing to say against it, while some scientists both admit and insist upon it.[7] The alternative would be to hold with Plato to the eternity of matter; thus making it so far the equal of God. This brief sentence, as has been well said, cuts off Atheism, Polytheism, Pantheism, Dualism, Materialism and Fatalism.

In verse second it is important to notice that the narrative leaves the universe in general and limits itself to the earth, with an unknown interval of time between. It presents the earth in a chaotic condition, "waste and void" (R. V.); a summary and dignified statement—how different from the absurd details of Ovid! And in the added clause, "and darkness was on the face of the deep," the "deep" is obviously this same chaotic mass, and the darkness carries us to a condition prior to chemical com-

---

[7] See note xxiii., Appendix.

bination, inasmuch as chemical action, when intense, produces light and heat. When Professor Ladd objects that this is incorrect because "light by its very nature belongs to that condition of the earth mass with which the hypothesis of science begins," he forgets that though scientists may commonly go no further back than to speak of this earth mass in its incandescent state, their fundamental principles involve the recognition of elements, atoms, molecules, which by their combination and interaction produce that incandescence. And science has now gone so far in the hands of Raoul Pictet as to prove that at certain very low temperatures (from $-125°$ to $-175°$) the most powerful chemical agents (even nitric acid) are inert. An uncombined and therefore dark state is not only assumable, but proximately provable. Professor Dana virtually says this very thing when he says that the beginning of activity in matter "would show itself by a flash of light through the universe."[8] Here, then, is the fact of activity begun, contained in the announcement, "Let there be light." How simple and apprehensible this slight stroke of a phenomenal description—a result perceived—which tells the story of enormous and unimaginable combinations! Any child can apprehend the statement; no man can fully comprehend the process; and while Voltaire might be excused in his day for objecting that light could not have existed prior to the action of the sun, it was hardly excusable for a writer (C. W. Goodwin, M. A.) in

---

[8] Dana's Geology, 2nd edition, p. 766.

the noted Oxford Essays and Reviews to repeat an objection which a schoolboy could then have answered.

But this intense activity is referred to its divine cause in the preceding verse: "The Spirit of God moved," or more strictly (R. V. margin), *was brooding*, the word which (Deut. xxxii. 11) describes the action of the eagle fluttering over her young, and denotes a steady activity not necessarily limited to the beginning of the work, but perhaps applicable throughout. He moved upon "the face of the waters," the term "the deep" being now exchanged for "the waters," and this last evidently but another term for the "waste and void" condition. Language and thought could hardly furnish more vivid phraseology for the vastness of this heaving mass than "the deep" or ocean, or than "the waters" for its unstable condition. The vaporous mass is conjectured by Sir W. Dawson to have had a diameter two thousand times greater than its present one,[9] its brilliancy becoming like that of the sun. This immense change, so simply told, fills the first epoch or "day"—a word to be considered later. When God "divided the light from the darkness," He established a permanent condition or relation, very simply stated.

Next comes the "firmament," or, more properly, *expanse*, to separate the waters "under" it from those "above" it. It is to be observed that the narrative has now left the universe and limited itself

---

[9] Dawson's Story of the Earth and Man, p. 9.

to the earth; and therefore it seems inadmissible to find here the resolution of a nebula into our solar system.[10] "Firmament" is the critical word, meaning, literally, *expanse*,[11] and in verse 8 defined as "heaven," that is, the sky or welkin; and thus in the most simple and popular mode there is presented the scene of a sky with a sheet of waters below and dense water-clouds above. This one brief stroke, purely phenomenal, addressed to the eye, tells the story of other immense changes, including the cooling of the earth's surface to a crust and the reduction of its temperature till water will lie upon it; and also such a disengagement of the elements as to form an atmosphere, though laden not only with dense vapors, but with much else that has been since absorbed and combined. It would be the change produced by ages of gradual radiation, summed up in a sentence. This signal change marks the second stage or day.

Next, in verses 9-12, are contained two great events. First comes the appearance of dry land, by the formation of continents and oceans. This implies a time when the surface of the earth was covered by waters; a fact abundantly asserted by the geologists.[12] The formation of the continents, though here summarily described at the beginning of it, actually continued through the several geo-

---

10 As Guyot and Dana give it.
11 So the margin of R. V.; "expansion" in margin of A. V. The Hebrew verb from which the noun comes usually means to expand, not to make solid as the *firmamentum* of the Vulgate.
12 Dana, 4th edition, p. 44. Van Cotta, Geologie, p. 219. Guyot, Creation p. 79. Dawson, The Story of the Earth and Man, p. 12.

logical epochs, even down through the Tertiary; the original Archean land in this country lying mainly (though not solely) north of the St. Lawrence.[13] Just so the previous day's result was a protracted process, described in its completeness. This method, as will be seen, runs through the whole chapter and is to be distinctly recognized, since it furnishes a key to the next description, and answers the most specious objection that has been raised to the correctness of the account.

For on the same third day are introduced "grass, the herb yielding seed, and the fruit tree yielding fruit after his kind"; a popular description of the vegetable kingdom, as we call it, by the forms visible to the eye and known to all mankind. Here, as before and after, and in keeping with the method which we are bound to recognize as running through the whole chapter, the vegetable system is mentioned as a whole, in its completeness, not to be alluded to again. It is only by overlooking this unquestionable fact of the entire method that Mr. Huxley and Professor Ladd have charged an anachronism upon it, inasmuch as the cereals and fruit trees occur only very late in the history of the earth. With the recognition of this unquestionable method the objection vanishes.[14]

---

[13] Le Conte, Revised Edition (1891), p. 292. C. H. Hitchcock, Geology of N. H., i., p. 511. Dana, 2nd edition, p. 147; 4th ed., p. 440. These writers speak of the ocean as nearly or quite universal. Geikie, however, in his 3rd edition (1893), p. 14, doubts its absolute universality, though affirming the present surface contours to be of comparatively recent date.

[14] Guyot calls attention distinctly to this characteristic of the narrative (Creation, pp. 89, 90). Dawson overlooked it (Modern Science in Bible Lands, p. 17), to his disadvantage, as did Mr. Gladstone in his discussion with Professor Huxley.

The introduction of vegetable life, as here announced, prior to that of animal life, is well sustained. For while, from their perishable nature and the high temperature of the period of metamorphic rocks, no plants in their original form are, or could be expected to be, found in the Archean rocks, their early existence is a matter of plain and direct inference, or, as Dawson puts it, "a trite conclusion to natural science." For (1) the temperature and condition of the water and the air would admit vegetable before animal life; (2) animals require plants for food; (3) the existence of graphite,[15] anthracite, and certain iron ores in great quantities in the Archean rocks, indicates abundant early vegetable life, primarily sea-weeds.[16] A question has been raised as to the possibility of vegetation before the incoming of solar light; whereas the growth of vegetables in the dark (for the most part colorless) is a familiar fact, and Godet mentions that M. Famazin in all his experiments upon algæ never made use of any light but a gas lamp. The same writer also cites the botanist Karl Mueller, who attributes the immense change and progress of vegetation after the Carboniferous era "to the solar light."[17] Evidently the earth was not yet prepared for the higher animal life. The Archean era, dur-

---

[15] Dana (2nd edition, p. 157) says that some layers of the Archean (Laurentian) contain twenty per cent of graphite. While admitting (pp. 67-146) that graphite and bog-iron ore are results in connection with vegetation, not so exclusively as to prove it, he characterizes (p. 144) anthracite as "a most highly mineralized form of vegetation." Le Conte, Dana, Dawson and Hitchcock regard the graphite as clear evidence, and raise no doubt as to the bog-iron ore.

[16] Dana, p. 454; Le Conte, 288, 304, Revised Edition.

[17] Godet, Creation and Life, pp. 32, 33, 48.

ing which vegetable life is supposed to have been predominant, was relatively the longest in the earth's geological history; according to Le Conte, longer than all subsequent eras.

The fourth stage or day (verses 14-19) brings, as already stated, the test proof that the description is phenomenal, addressed to the eye; the sun and moon described alike, as they appear, to rule the day and the night, though their actual function is so unlike, the one being a luminary, the other an opaque reflector. Here, then, is a visible phenomenon, the appearance or disclosure of the sun and moon in their relations and functions to the earth. The special word "create" is not employed here; they had been already created as part of the heaven and earth, and now "God said, Let there be lights in the firmament." The "setting" them in the heavens is part of the same optical description; and the word "made," in the summary statement, is in the Hebrew, as in the popular English, a word of wide range, covering the meanings of appointing, constituting, establishing, as (Ex. vii. 1), "I have made thee a god to Pharaoh." When, therefore, Dr. Driver insists that this verse affirms the "formation of the heavenly bodies not merely after the creation of the earth, but after the appearance on it of vegetation," he not only disregards the clearly phenomenal nature of the representation, but puts himself in direct conflict with the first verse of the chapter, which records the creation of "the heaven" and the earth. And when in his preceding sentence he remarks, as an objection to the order in the narrative, which puts vegetation prior to animal life, that "plant life from the beginning, in its earliest and humblest forms, was accompanied by similar humble types of animal life," it would be difficult for him to prove the remark by competent authority.

But this visible token, the full disclosure of the heavenly bodies, indicates an immense progress. How was it brought about? The question is virtually answered by Le Conte,[18] when he speaks of the withdrawal of the "aqueous vapor and carbonic acid" that had been "a double blanket" to the earth, and by Dana when he says that it was "after the vapors which till then had shrouded the sphere were withdrawn."[19] The intervening resultant changes were vast, and the process long-continued, and, from the nature of it, difficult to assign to a very definite period. Dr. Dawson appears to place it after the Laurentian,[20] Hugh Miller after the Devonian, if not after the Carboniferous.[21] It is perhaps definite enough to say with Dana, "It must have preceded the animal system, since the sun is the grand source of activity throughout nature on the earth, and is essential to the existence of life except in its lowest forms,"[22] as well as for the additional reason assigned by Le Conte,[23] that "the progressive purification of the atmosphere by the withdrawal of the superabundant carbonic acid and returning the pure oxygen fitted it for the purposes of higher and

---

18 Geology, p. 382.
19 Geology, 2nd ed., p. 769.
20 Origin of the World, p. 204.
21 Testimony of the Rocks, p. 203-4, 208.
22 Geology, 2nd ed., p. 766.
23 Geology, p. 382.

higher animals." The process, though long continued, is described as usual in its completeness. The record is unassailable. And in its mention of the practical uses of these chief luminaries, as marking off the years, months, days and "seasons" of various kinds, the popular nature of the narrative is still manifest; they are the world's great chronometer.

The fifth stage or day (vs. 20-25) is characterized by animal life in three forms:[24] (1) Marine life, verse 20; (2) winged creatures (not "fowl"), verse 20; (3) monsters, verse 21, not "whales" (A. V.) nor "sea-monsters" alone (R. V.), as will presently be shown, but "stretched-out" creatures. This is a brief statement of facts as now known, and in the same general order, although that last is not to be regarded as a vital point. (1) Marine life. The primordial rocks, says Dana, have afforded evidence only of marine life.[25] As to its abundance Le Conte unconsciously echoes the very words of Genesis, which reads (R. V., margin), "Let the waters swarm with swarms of living creatures," while the geologist writes concerning the Silurian age, "These seas

---

[24] A singular objection is that of Prof. Ladd (Doctrine of Sacred Scripture, i., p. 262), that the narrative does not deal with "the impossibility of separating the lower grades of vegetable from those of animal life." This is the demand that a bold outline sketch, phenomenal in character, and for mankind at large, shall enter into certain minutiæ of a scientific character, unrecognizable by mankind at large. Dr. Asa Gray, however, to whom he refers, though speaking of the "close connection of the lower with the higher forms," does yet distinguish between the vegetable and the animal (Natural Science and Religion, pp. 32, 33). The separation is palpable enough to the average man, for whom the narrative was written. It may be that the *Eozoon Canadense* of Dawson, found in the Laurentian, is an animal, though strongly disputed (see Geikie, pp. 694, 695). If so, exceptional instances would not invalidate a characterizing description of the predominant condition, as distinguished from the equally remarkable outburst of animal life at the fifth stage.

[25] Dana, 2nd ed., p. 169; 4th ed., p. 469.

literally swarmed with living beings," mentioning over 10,000 species as having been described from the Silurian alone, and these to be regarded as a small fragment of the actual fauna of that age.[26] In the Devonian came the great outburst of fishes.

Here let it be observed that it would not mar the correctness of this general, *outline* description, if exceptional instances of marine life were found in the huge mass of earlier vegetation, or before the full shining of the sun. It is also to be observed that here too the new order is described as a whole, although every species of the earlier marine life has disappeared, to be succeeded by different species; but no further allusion is made to the fact.

(2) The "flying" creatures, not necessarily fowls, but "what flies" (Fuerst). The geological history of the world actually shows the incoming of the winged tribes after that of marine life. Without making any account of the earliest of the winged creatures, namely winged insects, which were somewhat numerous in the Devonian,[27] and in the Carboniferous attained a spread of wings of twenty-six inches,[28] we encounter in the Jurassic the peculiar feathered creature called the archæopteryx, with wings of three feet spread; and at least twenty species of true birds in the Cretaceous of New Jersey and Kansas alone.[29] But the most extraordinary phenomenon in this line appears in the bat-like or lizard-like creatures called pterosaurs, of several genera, one genus of them called pterodactyles.

---
26 Le Conte, p. 302. 28 Id., p. 398.
27 Id., p. 334. 29 Id., 488.

They begin apparently in the Jurassic, and were of many kinds, having an extent of wings ranging from two or three feet up to twenty and twenty-five. Seven species were found in the western Cretaceous, one with a spread of eighteen feet and two of twenty-five feet;[30] and ten species in Great Britain, one having a spread of twenty-five feet.[31] Whatever aspects the earth might present at this stage, nothing could be more striking than these huge winged creatures darkening the sky. They occur from the Jurassic into the Cretaceous.

(3) The third characteristic of this stage or day is what the common version renders wrongly "whales," and the Revised Version inadequately "sea-monsters," while Gesenius, more in accordance with the facts, makes it include the land serpent, dragon, monster, as the actual usage requires (Ex. vii. 9; x. 12; Deut. xxxii. 33; Ps. xci. 13; Jer. li. 34), adding that it is so called from its extension or length, being derived from a verb meaning to stretch out. Tuch, Knobel, Dillmann, Delitzsch, all give it as the "long stretched out" animals, among which Delitzsch specifies the saurian. The serpent into which the rod of Moses was changed (Ex. vii. 9), and the dragon of the other three passages above cited, are called by this name, all apparently land animals, one of them certainly a reptile.

Now there is a long period of geological history, beginning somewhat before and extending through the Mesozoic. which the geologists term the "era

---

[30] Id., pp. 442, 445, 446. [31] Geikie, p. 931.

of reptiles" from the extraordinary profusion of reptile life, as well as the immense size of its species.[32] The size of some of these species is given by Geikie as follows: Hadrosaur, 28 feet in length; ornithotarsus, 35; ceratops, 30; dinosaur, 40; cetiosaur, 50; mososaur, 75; atlantosaur, 100.[33] Le Conte gives additional statements: Ichthyosaur, 30 to 40 feet; plesiosaur, 40; megalosaur, 50; atlantosaur, 115.[34] Sir John Lubbock gives the titanosaur the length of 100 feet.[35] Some of these were sea-monsters, some land animals, and some amphibious. Not only was their size enormous, but their numbers were great. At least fifty species of mososaurs have been found in the Cretaceous of America, fifteen or twenty species of dinosaurs have been described by Professor Marsh, and there are sixteen of plesiosaurs in Great Britain alone.[36] "There are now on the whole face of the earth," writes Professor Le Conte, "only six reptiles over fifteen feet long," whereas "in the Cretaceous of the United States alone one hundred and fifty species of reptiles have been found, most of them of gigantic size"; and "the fossil fauna of any period is but a fragment of the actual fauna of that period." What fact in the earth's earlier condition could be more striking?

Looking now at these three phenomena, partly

---
[32] Lyell, Miller, Le Conte, Dana, Agassiz, Geikie.
[33] Geikie, pp. 892, 933.
[34] Le Conte, 1st ed. In the 2nd edition the length of the atlantosaur is not given.
[35] Lubbock, Address before the British Association of Science.
[36] Le Conte, pp. 439, 487, 460.

successive and partly contemporaneous, what three bold strokes could so well describe that state of things as these three: the waters swarming with marine life, the face of the heavens darkened by such flying creatures, and the stretched out monsters under whose ponderous forms the earth groaned?[37]

The sixth day's work (verses 24-31), like the third, is twofold. In the first section are "cattle, beast of the earth, and creeping thing." It is a purely popular description, universally intelligible, and very well explained by Guyot: "In the Tertiary the herbivorous animals, domesticated by man, are named cattle, while the others, including the carnivorous, are called the beasts of the earth or wild beasts, and the smaller ones the creeping things."[38] These evidently include the greater and smaller mammals, as we now call them. The geologists have designated the Tertiary as the "age of mammals"; but the narrative no more uses that term than in the previous period the word reptiles or amphibians. The larger animals are mentioned in the two most obvious divisions, and the smaller are characterized as they would appear to the eye, "creeping upon the earth." Dr. Driver has well said of this narrative: "It groups the living creatures under the great subdivisions which appeal to the eye." The geologists in their designation of this period are in accord with Genesis, in the *general* characterization, and as such it would not be

---

[37] Geikie (p. 892) gives the estimated weight of the brontosaur, though but 50 feet in length, at twenty tons.
[38] Guyot, Creation, p. 119.

impaired by any previous limited introduction of semi-oviparous animals, or even oviparous (if such were discovered). As an outline sketch for its purpose, and for the world, the case could not be better stated. Mr. Huxley, however, in order to force a misrepresentation upon the writer, insists on pressing upon the term "creeping thing" a technical meaning which would designate a lizard or reptile.[39] But (1) the reptile species have already been dismissed; (2) the Hebrew word is elsewhere applied to the motion of all land animals whatever (Gen. vii. 2; ix. 3; Ps. civ. 20); (3) the interpretation here given perfectly accords with the writer's method throughout, describing by the most obvious marks—the larger animals in two marked groups, and the smaller in another group as they appear on the landscape creeping upon the earth. Homer, with the same picturesqueness, speaks of "all things that breathe and *creep upon the earth.*"[40]

While this first half of the sixth stage actually describes the introduction and predominance of what we call mammal life, it is to be observed that the writer does not commit himself to any such definition nor limitation. But the stage described is all the more remarkable in two respects: (1) It was preceded by the extinction of the huge reptilian fauna of the Mesozoic, a "destruction great, worldwide, and one of the most marvelous events in the geological history";[41] (2) the incoming of the new

---
[39] Huxley, Science and Hebrew Tradition, pp. 170 seq. He refers to Lev. x. 29, where, however, a different word is used.
[40] Iliad, xvii., 446. [41] Dana, p. 877.

order of life in the Tertiary was a great and somewhat sudden outburst, "a rapid and most extraordinary change in the life system,"[42] at once distinguished both by the number of species ("all the main divisions") and the size of some of them.[43] In the Miocene of the Siwalik Hills, India, are found remains of eighty-four species of mammals, including three species of mastodons, seven of elephants, five of rhinoceros, from four to seven of hippopotamus, and three of the horse family.[44] In India was also the dinotherium, as large in proportion to our elephant as an elephant to an ox;[45] so that while the fauna of India is one of the noblest in the world, "it is paltry in comparison with that of the much more limited Miocene, India." In recognizing this amazing and sudden change, the narrative is surely impregnable.

The second half of this day or stage is marked by the introduction of man, the crowning work, and pre-eminently characteristic. The order accords with what is known. It would not detract from the weight of the outline sketch in recording this one great event were it found that other genera continued to be introduced after the incoming of the human race. But apparently it is not so. For while it is said that some thirty species of birds and animals have become extinct within historic times,[46]

---

[42] Le Conte, p. 501.
[43] There were what are called anticipations of mammal life in the Juvassic and Cretaceous; but probably all oviparous or semi-oviparous (Dana, p. 852), and "like mice and rats in size" (Ib., p. 768).
[44] Le Conte, p. 525, 526.
[45] Dawson, The Earth and Man, p. 251.
[46] Winchell, Preadamite Man, p. 434.

there appear on the other hand only variations of species. Man belongs to the latest life. This fact is all that is necessary for the present discussion. It is needless to specify at what precise geological epoch he appeared, or how many years ago; although it may be remarked in passing how in recent times assertions as to the early origin of the human race have been steadily growing more moderate,[47] and the demands for hundreds of thousands of years are becoming obsolete. A very significant indication is to be seen in the two editions of Le Conte's excellent Geology. The first edition (1879) said that "man's time on the earth may be 100,000 years, or it may be only 10,000, but more probably the former than the latter."[48] The revised edition (1891) repeats the numbers, but omits the opinion in favor of the larger one.

But the account of man goes much further. It not only presents him at the close of the series, but at the head of it, as man, with simple relations indeed, but in his clear and entire humanity. So all antiquarian research. While the cave men, in their remote locations, are not necessarily to be regarded as proper specimens of primitive man, they yet reveal all the qualities of true humanity, with weapons, implements, ornaments, and apparently burials and fires.

Further yet, the account assigns to man "dominion" over the whole animal world (verses 26, 27). He has always exercised it. Even the cave men

---
47 See note xxiv., Appendix.
48 Le Conte, p. 570, 1st edition; p. 619, 2nd edition.

somehow mastered the largest and fiercest wild animals, and they sketched the cave-bear on a pebble, and the mastodon on his own ivory; and they used a variety of animals for food.

The narrative rises to its highest point when it declares man to be made in the image of God: primarily in his moral nature—reason and free will; and secondarily, and partly in consequence thereof, in his intellectual nature. This is an indisputable fact, thus unfolded by Dana in the last year of his life: "There is in man therefore a spiritual element in which the brute has no share. His power of indefinite progress, his thoughts and desires that look onward even beyond time, his recognition of spiritual existence and of a Divinity above all, evince a nature that partakes of the infinite and divine."[49]

And now a few more words on the "day." It has been made a chief ground of assault. But when viewed in connection with the purpose and method of the narrative, it is of the easiest explanation and vindication. The explanation, too, is not the result of a modern sientific dilemma. Augustine in the fourth century said that it was impossible to comprehend what was God's day;[50] and the venerable Bede in the eighth century suggested that this includes "omnia volumina saeculorum."[51] The narrative itself gives warning in the use of the word before there was or could be a solar day, and by the analogy of God's day of rest, which has lasted

---
[49] Dana, p. 1018, last edition.
[50] Civitate Dei, xii., 6.
[51] Com. in Pent., ii., p. 1940. He speaks differently in the Hexaemeron.

some thousands of years. "Days of God are intended," says Delitzsh.

This leads to the simplest explanation of the use of this term, namely, it is but a part of the (so-called) anthropomorphic representation that runs throughout the narrative. Everything is described not only in the language of common life, but by human processes—"God said," "God saw," and the like; and so the series of stages in the work is described under the easy figure of human days' labor, naturally connected with the first alternation of darkness and light. So Bunsen: "The six sections of this work are conceived under the image of the earthly day as six stages of progress in light formation. Thus the earthly day is the most fitting picture, the most adequate framing. . . . . . Rightly taken, the text needs no violent interpretation; the slightly veiled view underlying it makes itself clear."[52] To the same effect Delitzsch says, "The account represents the work of God according to the image of human days. . . . It lies, however, in the nature of a copy that it should correspond only on a very reduced scale with the incommensurable greatness of the original." Dr. Driver's admission has been already cited.

The method was as wise as it was natural and simple. The lapse of time remains still unknown, and if it were known it would still be incomprehensible. Why should the human race have been perplexed with an irrelevant issue, and with statements

---
[52] Bibel Werk, i. I., p. 6.

which would for thousands of years have been a stumbling block, statements which would have been of no account for the purpose of the narrative? The thing which has been attacked as a blemish is clearly an excellence.

Guyot, Dana and Dawson have adopted a different mode of answering the objection. They point to the flexible use of the word in the narrative itself, in five different ways: first, the "day" before the function of the sun (vs. 5, 8, 13); second, the light portion of that day (v. 5); third, the solar day (v. 19); fourth, the light portion of that day (vs. 16, 18); fifth, the entire time of the creative work (ii. 4). They also refer to the popular use of the word in both the Scriptures and in common life; day of visitation, of salvation, of prosperity or of adversity, "in my day," etc. While this mode of defense is tenable, it is perhaps simpler and quite as satisfactory to rest on the other mode.

It has also been objected that the fourth commandment, requiring the observance of the seventh day in imitation of God's day of rest, limits the "day" of the narrative to the solar day. But it is an obvious and sufficient reply that the ratio or analogy remains undisturbed, and thus the example holds good; as God rested, ceased from creating, on His seventh day, so He requires man to rest on *his* seventh day. It is "a copy on a reduced scale."

It has also been asserted that the form of statement, "there was evening and there was morning, one day," requires us to understand the solar day.

But this alternation of light and darkness which suggests and underlies the mode of conception, is equally consistent with the longer as the shorter period. It but carries on the figure, denoting the beginning and the ending, and together the total of one stage, phase, or chapter of the creation.

Thus when the narrative is fairly treated, that is, interpreted *according to its own proved method*, we find not only the five or six main points of unquestionable truth which its critics have admitted, but their objections invalidated, and the following series of remarkable coincidences with the latest knowledge in the case:

1. All the present adjustments and forces of nature had a beginning. Science now traces them all back to their successive origin. The origination of matter it cannot disprove, while some eminent scientists maintain it.

2. All nature is one coherent system; a truth more and more fully confirmed.

3. There was once a condition of the globe when no life existed or could exist; fully admitted on all hands.

4. The fitting up of the globe was a progressive work. Evident.

5. Light was antecedent to and independent of the sun's performing its function for the earth. Indisputable.

6. The earth was once mainly covered with waters, and the heavens with dense vapors. Well sustained.

7. There came subsequently an emergence of the continents from the oceans. Unquestionable.

8. An early succeeding order of progress was the incoming of vegetation, as a characteristic event. Apparently well established.

9. The heavenly bodies performed their special function for the earth only at an advanced stage of its history. Unquestionable.

10. An early outburst of animal life was an immense sea life. Clearly admitted.

11. Winged creatures followed or accompanied, as a conspicuous feature. Undeniable.

12. There was then also a predominance of huge monsters. Established.

13. Later came the chief movement now called mammalian. Universally admitted.

14. The series was completed by the advent of man. Fully sustained.

15. Man made his appearance in possession of his distinctive human faculties, and as lord of the animal world. A settled fact.

Such are the statements here made, when the writer is permitted to tell his story in his own simple and *natural* way; a grand outline of the earth's story, sustained throughout by the latest knowledge of facts. A most extraordinary record it is; the more so because only within the century past could its truthfulness be authenticated. But now it stands forth, in the words of Professor Dana, "both true and divine."

If it be said, as it has been, that the ordinary

reader would not apprehend all that is covered by these statements, as, for example, the lapse of time included in the day, the reply is that the details which awaited the late discoveries of science did not hinder the apprehension and impression of the great truths taught by the narrative. Some of the facts now proved baffle the imagination of even the scientist to apprehend, and the early revelation of them would have been not only useless, but a stumbling block for several thousand years. In truth, there is no agreement now. The history is given in the most abbreviated form—"on a reduced scale."

After showing the remarkable harmony of this terse narrative with the results of modern investigation, there is no special occasion to compare it with other so-called cosmogonies. Ovid's description of creation was written while in all probability the Old Testament Scriptures may have been in Rome, and resembles the first chapter of Genesis enough to be almost a travesty, absurd in some of its details. Since the discovery of what are called the creation tablets in 1874 by George Smith, it has been somewhat customary to view them as coming from a common source with the Hebrew account, and sometimes to suggest that the latter have come from the former. The tablets found by Smith were from Nineveh and were supposed to date from about 650 B. C. Duplicates and additional fragments, since found at Borsippa and Sippara, have led some Assyrian scholars to refer them to a much earlier date, Boscawen as early as B. C. 2200-2500,[53] and Jensen

---
[53] Boscawen, p. 72.

supposing an origin of the story itself as early as 3000 B. C. Sayce, on the other hand, has expressed the opinion that they are "of late date."[54] Another Chaldean account has long been known, handed down by Berosus of the time of Alexander the Great. Space does not admit, nor does our purpose require here a full discussion of these cosmogonies. Those who most strongly advocate a connection with the Hebrew narrative find it necessary to admit very radical differences. Indeed Boscawen says that "in the curious Babylonian cosmogony preserved by Berosus is found so little resemblance to the Hebrew that it hardly enters into the field of comparison."[55]

But the Assyrian and the Babylonian tablets contain, together with fundamental differences, more resemblances in some of the details. The chief points of resemblance suggested in this tablet cosmogony are the following: (1) A primitive chaos of waters, which, however, is the origin of all else, in which occurs the Tiamat or Tiavat, which, it is conjectured, corresponds to the Hebrew Tehom, "the deep"; (2) the making of the heavenly bodies, the god Anu making an abode for the gods Ea and Bel, with great gates and side bolts and a staircase; (3) the creation of the cattle of the field, the wild beasts of the field and the creeping things of the field. It is also supposed that there must have been seven tablets corresponding to the seven days of creation, although the supposed sixth

---

[54] Records of the Past, New Series, i., p. 122.
[55] Boscawen, p. 42.

is wholly wanting at present, and only fragments of the second, third and seventh are found, while the fourth covers four printed pages with the conflict between Bel and Tiamat, in which Sayce would find the conflict between darkness and light. The great and fundamental differences are such as these: (1) The thoroughly polytheistic character of the tablet account, there even being a time when the gods did not exist, and when an early pair of gods was produced, and other gods descended from them by successive generations; (2) its materialism, the first pair of gods having been produced from the primeval waters; (3) the impossibility of grouping the tablets in parallel correspondence to the Hebrew days of creation, while no six stages of creation can be found in them except conjecturally; (4) the vagueness and diffuseness of most of the statements, in singular contrast to the terse distinctness of the Hebrew narrative. The best showing of the difference is the printing of the two side by side.

But whatever resemblance may be found between the two must not divert attention from the clear, proved truthfulness and dignity of the one and the grave errors and childishness of the other. And while the question of priority is not important when the one is found to be true and the other untrue in its very basis, yet if there is any relation to be recognized, we may ask, which is the more probable supposition, and conformed to all experience—that the simple and majestic narrative of Genesis grew out of this materialistic, polytheistic account, or that the latter was a corruption and far-off echo of the truthful story?

The tablet cosmogony, however, serves two important ends: (1) If the early date claimed for it is correct, it shows that another, the Hebrew, cosmogony may easily and naturally be as old as the time of the Exodus and far older; (2) inasmuch as it contains certain statements corresponding in some measure to those of both the so-called Elohistic and Jehovistic documents, it is so far forth an indication of the coequal antiquity of the whole of that Hebrew narrative, and a kind of voucher for it. And yet, as we have seen, the narrative needs no such voucher.

CHAPTER XIII

THE SABBATH

THE extreme antiquity of the Sabbath coincides with the Scripture account of its early and divine origin. The modern critical analysis assigns this portion of the narrative to the late Priest Code, so called. Long before this analysis some writers (e. g. Paley) held this portion of it to be an anticipatory statement of what actually took place first in connection with the fall of the manna in the wilderness. Without attempting peremptorily to decide this last question, it may be said that this interpretation supposes an unrecognizable break in a narrative otherwise continuous; and also that the recognition of the Sabbath in the wilderness (Ex. xvi. 22, seq.) favors rather the view that it was the revival of an established, though perhaps neglected, institution, than the introduction of a new one. Moreover the indications of the institution are not confined to the so-called Priest Code, but occur in the Jehovist section as well, and rest on outside support.

While, therefore, we necessarily lack the means of proving from outside sources that the Sabbath was instituted with the introduction of man—and while the most important point is that it is a Divine institution—we have strong evidence that it was of great antiquity, pointing even to its being as old as the human race, certainly beyond the range of history.

1. Early scriptural indications of the peculiarity and special prominence of the number seven, and septenary divisions. Cain was to be avenged sevenfold (Gen. iv. 15), and Lamech seventy and sevenfold (iv. 24). Noah took clean beasts by sevens (vii. 3); Abraham set apart seven ewe-lambs as witness of the covenant (xxi. 28-31); Balaam twice prepares seven altars, and offers seven oxen and seven rams (Num. xxiii., 1, 2, 29, 30). Some of these passages are assigned even by modern criticism to dates as early as 750 and 800 B. C.; and the last mentioned is concerning a non-Israelite transaction. It is not without plausibility, not to say probability, that Wayland and others have understood "the end of days" (Gen. iv. 3, Hebrew), when Cain and Abel brought their offerings apparently at the same time, to be the end of *seven* days. The interval of seven days occurs three times in the account of the deluge, in what late critics assign to the Jehovist, or oldest portion of the Pentateuch. Circumcision was to be on the eighth day, that is, after seven days (Gen. xvii. 11, 12). The Egyptian mourning for Jacob was seventy (7×10) days, and Joseph's morning at Atad seven days (l. 3, 10), showing that such was the custom with Israel in the early days in Egypt. At the Passover no leaven was to be used for seven days.

2. The embodiment of seven as a sacred number

in the structure of the Hebrew language. The word used from Genesis onward for taking a solemn oath was to "seven oneself," to use the sacred number. This carries us back apparently to the incipient stage of the language.

3. The early diffusion of the same sanctity of the number seven in the region of Babylonia. Schrader informs us that the Babylonish literature and especially the hymns, both in the original Sumirio-Accadian forms and in the Assyrio-Semitic translations, show "how deeply rooted already was the sacredness of the number seven in the being of the non-Semitic and pre-Semitic Babylonism";[1] and he cites instance upon instance. Professor Davis cites instances proving that "a seven-day period was a measure of time in vogue among the Semites in remote ages."[2] Lenormant says that the sacred character of the number seven, whence proceeds the division of the week, dates to the remotest antiquity among the Chaldæo-Babylonians.[3]

Schrader and other Assyriologists[4] go further and find the name "shabbatu" applied to the seventh, fourteenth, nineteenth, twenty-first and twenty-eighth days, accompanied with several special prohibitions; with the additional statement that the word is explained as "the day of the rest of the heart."[5] As these particular points have been questioned, and as some unsolved difficulties attend them, it is not nec-

---

[1] Schrader, p. 21.
[2] Davis, p. 31.
[3] Lenormant, p. 249.
[4] Sayce, Lenormant, Boscawen.
[5] See note xxvi., Appendix.

essary to insist upon them. The main fact of the peculiarity and sacredness of the number seven, and that of the seven-day measure of time as "an old Babylonish institution," as Schrader puts it, is well established. The fact appears in the Chaldean story of the flood: on the seventh day the storm and the flood ceased; on the next seventh day the dove was sent out; and on the altar were placed jars by sevens.

4. The wide diffusion of the week division and the prominence of the number seven should not pass unmentioned, as pointing to a common and therefore remote origin. Here, however, there is a difficulty in getting trustworthy statements. Some citations that were formerly made, as from Hesiod and Homer, must be abandoned. One of the latest and most elaborate investigations is that of Louis Thomas. He finds evidence of such a division of the week not only among the early Chaldeans, but among the Arabs before Mohammed, the ancient Peruvians, the negroes of West Africa, and perhaps the Chinese. In ancient Egypt he finds a religious respect for the "septenaire" before the institution of the decade, and as a popular and sacerdotal division of the week; among the Persians a double week, exact or approximate, related to the six creation acts; and among the early Greeks the great importance of the "septenaire." He also traces less definite (and of more uncertain date) indications of the week division, or of the peculiar value of the number seven, still more widely dif-

fused.⁶ These things join their force with the others in pointing to a very ancient origin of the seven-day division, and also to a special importance attached to seven. It may also be fairly said that the appointment would far more easily account for the institution than the common explanation that it arises from observing the changing of the moon, or from the process of naming days after five selected planets together with the sun and moon. This last mentioned grouping is so arbitrary that it must have come from some other necessity or motive behind it; while not only do the changes of the moon not mark any distinct divisions, unless it be the new moon, half moon and full moon (three in all), but the complete lunation, that is, the period during which the moon returns to the same place relative to the beholder, does not divide into four equal parts, but much more nearly into three divisions of ten days or six of five days each, as the late Richard A. Proctor has truly remarked.⁷ And Lenormant has not hesitated to say that not only does the week date from the remotest antiquity, but "it is greatly anterior to the application of the hebdomadal conception to the group of five planets with the addition of the sun and moon."⁸ As to the great antiquity of the week, and the peculiar prominence of the number seven, there can be no question.

Such are some of the ascertainable facts scattered

---
6 Le Jour du Seigneur, Paris, 1892. See note xxxi. Appendix.
7 Mr. Proctor, after arguing, in the usual mode, for the derivation of the week from the moon's motions, adds in a note, "More careful study of the moon's motions suggests six periods of five days rather than four of seven." It requires no "careful study," being an obvious fact. A complete lunation is 29 days, 12 hours, 44 minutes and 2 seconds, very nearly thirty days.
8 Lenormant, p. 249.

through the pre-historic past—all which the nature of the case admits—which go to confirm the statement that the seventh day arrangement belongs to the earliest history of the race. Nor is it irrelevant to point to the now well known fact that obviously "the Sabbath was made for man," ministering so unquestionably to the highest human welfare that it was fully worthy to have come by special appointment of his Maker. For it is well established that the proper observance of one day in seven as a day of rest, and sacred rest, is conducive to human well-being in all these respects: (1) Physically and intellectually; men can in the long run do more of both these kinds of work, and do it better, in six days than in seven; (2) socially and politically, according to the testimony of many of the ablest men that the world has seen, men of all kinds of pursuits, and of the most diverse views in other respects; (3) morally and spiritually, by the experience and testimony of the great company of the best men; and (4) philanthropically, by its indisputable relation to the origin and maintenance of the world-wide charities.

Now, as matter of historical fact, this benign institution was established before practical experience had given the knowledge of its benign influence; for it has proved itself only by long usage, and many of its influences have been clearly discerned only in quite recent times. And while these benefits do not directly prove its divine appointment, they prove its pre-eminent *fitness* to have proceeded directly from God; and they leave no other equally plausible mode of accounting for its origin. For the supposition that such ages of semi-barbarism as the school of Kuenen and Wellhausen ascribe to the early history of Israel, aided even by the later Jewish scribes as we know of them, devised an institution for mankind beyond the conception of Confucius or Gautama, or Socrates, Plato or Aristotle, is too incredible to be urged. This aspect of the case adds to the cumulative force of the other considerations to make it probable, if not provable, that the institution *came from God* in early times. And the narrative that presents such an institution to the world as coming from the God who made the world, needs no apology.

CHAPTER XIV

THE HISTORIC BASIS

We have thus far dealt only with the corroborative or collateral indications of the authenticity of the Hexateuch. We turn now to the more direct evidence. On account of its special nature it is difficult to present this in its full force, or as Dr. Henry Hayman terms it, "the enormous strength of the case." The attention is diverted by minor questions from the fundamental considerations. The real issue, however, is apprehensible by all clear-headed men. The critics have been obliged to confess in many ways that it is out of the question to determine the date by matters of style or phraseology. The latest appeal, it has been well said, is to considerations open to all intelligent men; critics speak of repetitions, contradictions, supposed late historic allusions or implications, the alleged earlier non-existence of certain institutions or observances, the presence of modes of thought which they affirm must be late. These are all matters to be weighed, not by profound erudition, but by clear, unperverted judgment. They are to be settled, not by the testimony of experts, but by the candor of the Christian jury. While Hebrew scholarship is to be held in the highest esteem in its place, the questions raised and the arguments employed of late rise far beyond its range; and the community are not to be persuaded into the notion that here lies the strength of the case.

The nature of the basis on which ancient writings rest needs to be distinctly understood. We cannot summon a living witness to testify concerning facts or writings dating three thousand years ago. Nor would a written claim of authorship attached to a document necessarily be decisive. It could be denied as easily as are a long series of statements contained in the Hexateuch. A string of successive vouchers extending down to the exile or the Christian era could readily be dismissed, in the words of Wellhausen, as a "pious make-up." It is easy enough to deny authorship. The noted Father Hardouin, who died in 1729, maintained that the plays of Terence, Virgil's Æneid, the Odes of Horace, and the histories of Livy and Tacitus were forgeries of the monks of the thirteenth century. Yet though he was a man of vast learning, and it could be truly said that we have (with slight exceptions) only medieval copies of these classics, also that they come to us through the monasteries, and that the monks had plenty of leisure time to write them, he found no following. Difficult as it would be to formulate a case in court for them, and slender as is the evidence in comparison with that of our sacred books, they are frankly accepted on the basis of the descending traditions, in the absence of conflicting claims or indications, together with the conviction that the monks were incapable of the composition—although this last point could not be proved. But when we turn our attention to what are called the "Five Books of Moses," it may be fairly said that we find all the evidence of their substantially contemporaneous origin and their authenticity which the nature of the case admits.

1. Undivided traditional testimony refers the substance of these books to the time of Moses. No one man has lived, but *a nation* has lived an unparalleled and unmixed life to bring down the testimony. And down to the Christian Era they lived in the land to which Moses led them, and in which his companions made their home. And not only there, but wherever they were dispersed, they inherited and retained the tradition of the Mosaic authorship of their institutions and their law, and of the record as an authentic narrative of the facts. It was never questioned.[1]

2. The admitted agency of Moses carries with it the fundamental facts of the narrative, and the overwhelming probability of substantially contemporaneous documents. Wellhausen, a champion critic, says that "from the historic tradition it is certain that Moses was the founder of the Torah," although he adds, "The legislative tradition cannot tell what were the contents of *his* torah."[2] Dr. Driver more generously admits that "it cannot be doubted that Moses was the ultimate founder of both the national and religious life of Israel, and that he provided his people not only with at least the nucleus of a sys-

---
[1] See note xxvii.
[2] History of Israel, p. 438.

tem of civil ordinances, but also with some system of ceremonial observances," and "it is reasonable to suppose that the teaching of Moses is preserved in its least modified form in Ex. xx.–xxxiii;" and he even supposes it not improbable that some form of priesthood would be established by Moses, would become hereditary, and would inherit from their founder some traditionary lore in matters of ceremonial observance.[3] This is well so far. But it must go farther. Moses was not only an ultimate founder, but he was a great founder. No man has ever set so deep and permanent a stamp on a people as Moses did. He was the last man to leave things at the loose ends which Wellhausen intimates, or even in the crude form which Driver suggests. The stamp he made proves that he was not. Trained in Egypt, the habit of writing was ingrained into him. He had the time of forty years to consider and write. He was founding and forming a lasting nation, with lasting institutions. For forty years he had found that nation as fickle and ungovernable as the wind. The supposition that such a man, under such circumstances, with urgent motives and aims, left his labor of forty years to be blown to the winds without written records and documents, is so improbable as to be incredible.

3. These books come to us as authentic documents through the proper channel. They come in the custody of the nation whose destiny has been bound up with them. "The rule of the municipal

---
[3] Introduction, pp. 144, 145.

law on this subject," says Professor Greenleaf of the Cambridge Law School, "is familiar, and applies with equal force to ancient writings whether documentary or otherwise. The first inquiry when an ancient document is offered in court is whether it comes from the proper depository; that is, whether it is found in the place where, and under the care of the persons with whom, such writings might naturally and reasonably be expected to be found; for it is this custody which gives authenticity to documents found within it."[4] Coming thus, and bearing no evident marks of forgery, they are admitted in evidence and regarded as genuine. They stand good unless the objector is able successfully to impeach them. He proceeds—and though having in mind directly the New Testament Scriptures, his words apply equally well to the Pentateuch—"This is precisely the case with the Sacred Writings. . . . They come to us and challenge our reception of them as genuine writings, precisely as Domesday Book, the Ancient Statutes of Wales, or any of the ancient documents which have been recently published under the British Record Commission, are received." So have the documents of the Pentateuch (or copies of them) come down to us, not gathered from some heap of waste manuscripts, nor from a palimpsest, nor from a sarcophagus, nor from some long buried and forgotten eastern ruin, but handed down through successive generations of living men, so reverentially

---

[4] Greenleaf's Testimony of the Evangelists, pp. 26, 27.

and universally that the apostle James could say to the assembled council of apostles and elders at Jerusalem, "Moses of old time hath in every city them that preach him, being read in the synagogue every sabbath day." Not only so, but the hated and hostile Samaritans had also their copies of the Pentateuch, of undetermined antiquity, but written in characters that antedate the exile, and still preserved in the same ancient Hebrew or Phenician characters in the Samaritan synagogue at Nablous. What more could be asked in the matter of custody? And what is there in the history of ancient literature that matches it?

4. A series of references and citations running through the remaining books of the Old Testament confirm the statements and show the priority and antiquity of the Pentateuch. These references include the principal facts, the teachings, sentiments and phraseology of all the five, and in the instances in which origin is indicated, refer it to "Moses." These references are admirably exhibited by Professor Stanley Leathes in his treatise on "The Law in the Prophets" (1891). They occupy (with some few comments) a hundred and eighty-seven pages, and cannot be even epitomized here. Suffice it to say that he quotes from seventeen prophetical books, and finds not far from 240 such allusions or distinct implications in Isaiah, more than 200 in Jeremiah, eighteen in Lamentations, more than eighty in Hosea, more than one hundred and eighty in Ezekiel, sixteen in Daniel, nearly thirty in Joel,

more than fifty in Amos, four in Obadiah, eight in Jonah, some forty-two in Micah, ten or more in Nahum, fourteen or more in Habakkuk, more than twenty in Zephaniah, seven in Haggai, over thirty in Zechariah, fifteen in Malachi. Should some of these references be questioned, a very large part of them are unquestionable, many of them being exact reproductions, and, in some instances, of *words* found only in the Pentateuch. They are from all the five books and from all the supposed writers of the critics, apparently including P. And as in the book of Joshua (not cited by Leathes) reference is made to "the book of the law" and "the commandment and the law which Moses the servant of the Lord charged you," so in Malachi, the last of the prophets, we read, "Remember ye the law of Moses my servant, which I commanded unto him in Horeb for all Israel, even statutes and judgments" (R. V.) Such was the continued endorsement by the later writers of the Old Testament. Inasmuch as modern criticism has disparaged the value of many of these writers on account of their alleged lateness, and taken their stand upon the two prophets Amos and Hosea, Professor Robertson has accepted their challenge, and shown at large not only that these reiterate all the main facts of the Pentateuch, but that they imply the existence of the institutions of the Pentateuch, of "statutes" and a "law" prohibiting offenses specified in that code, and the fact or the possibility of its being written copiously at the Divine command, "ten thousand precepts."[5] These two prophets belonged, the one to the southern kingdom, and the other to the northern, as early as the middle of the eighth century B. C.

The extent to which the early history is assumed in the later historical books, and the institutions and law of Israel referred to the great legislator, and the mode in which these allusions and statements are disposed of by objectors, are deferred for the present. But it may be well here to indicate the fullness of allusion in these early and unquestioned prophets, Amos and Hosea, to the matters presented in detail in the Pentateuch. We have not only references to the deliverance from Egypt, the forty years in the wilderness, and the overthrow of the Amorites (Amos ii. 9, 10), but the statement that the bringing up of Israel from Egypt was the selection of the children of Israel from all the families of the earth (iii. 2), was the adoption of Israel as a child (Hos. xi. 11), and the manifestation of Jehovah as his God, who thus established a claim to an undivided loyalty (xii. 9, xiii. 4). God had raised up of their sons as Nazarites (Am. ii. 11), had brought Israel up out of Egypt by a prophet and preserved him by a prophet (Hos. xii. 13), had made him then "dwell in tents as in the days of the solemn feasts" (xii. 10). Both prophets assert the existence of "a covenant," "a law of Jehovah," his "statutes," the "law of God" which Israel had "rejected, forgotten, transgressed" (Amos. ii. 4,

---

[5] Robertson's The Early Religion of Israel, p. 109, seq.

Hos. iv. 6, vii. 7, viii. 1, 12). These transgressions date as far back as the sin at Baal Peor (Hos. ix. 10, xi. 2), the days of Gibeah (x. 9), and continued through the times of the prophets (x. 9). The people had abandoned Jehovah for idols (iv. 17, viii. 4, xiii. 2), and for criminal lusts (iv. 14). Hosea speaks of the feast days, new moons, sabbaths and solemn feasts as institutions which God would in anger take away (ii. 11); and refers (v. 10) to the law of Deuteronomy (xix. 14, xxix. 17) in regard to the removal of the landmark; and again (iv. 10), to them "that strive with the priest" (Deut. xvii. 12). In denouncing the sins of his contemporaries, Amos apparently makes allusion, in ii. 7, to what is found in Leviticus xvi. 15, and in ii. 8 to Ex. xxii. 25, and in ii. 11, 12 to Num. vi. 2 and onward. He recognizes (iv. 4, 5) the custom of sacrifices, tithes and thank-offerings, although rebuking the ways of the worshipers, and he connects Jehovah's authoritative utterances with Jerusalem and Zion (i. 2).

Thus these oldest of the writing prophets, instead of showing ignorance of the ancient law, become witnesses to it as then binding, though perverted, as having come down from the past, as part of a religious polity which began with the deliverance from Egypt, but had its roots in the still older revelation to the patriarchs. Hosea recurs to events related in Genesis: the destruction of Admah and Zeboim (xi. 8), the birth of Jacob and his prevailing with God (xii. 3, 4), the interview at Bethel

(xii. 4), his departure to Syria, and his serving for a wife in the keeping of sheep (xii. 12), and the prophecy that Israel should be as the sand of the sea (i. 10). Amos "knows" (in Kuenen's words) of the overthrow of Sodom and Gomorrah (iv. 11), the high places of Isaac (vii. 9), and how "Edom did pursue his brother" (i. 11). They not only show their own knowledge of that early history and legislation, but make their appeal to a similar knowledge on the part of the people whom they addressed. Noticeably enough, also, their references and allusions are made indiscriminately to the several portions of the Pentateuch which modern critics designate by the letters P D J E.

5. The structure, implications and allusions of the legislative portions of the Pentateuch indicate its contemporaneousness with Moses, its recorded author. In its structure it is a mingling of permanent and transient statutes—for the wilderness, and for Palestine. While it mainly provides for the permanent national and religious life of Israel, it contains also many special enactments that could apply only to life in the wilderness and on the journey. Among these last are the abundant and minute directions concerning the camp, the march, the structure and conveyance of the tabernacle, and the location of the tribes. The directions concerning the tabernacle, for example, as plans and specifications for an actual structure are complete and precise; but as the useless fabrication of five hundred or a thousand years later they would be too

intolerably tedious even for a Pharisee or a Rabbin. Delitzsch well said, "We hold it as absolutely inconceivable that the Elohistic portions concerning the tabernacle and its furniture should be a historic fiction of the post-exilic age."[6]

The intermittent and often fragmentary character of the legislation in many parts of it, sometimes alleged to show the hand of a compiler, accords much more naturally with the circumstances of a legislator like Moses, burdened with cares and legislating as circumstances suggest and as occasional leisure is gained. It is natural as legislation, but would be poor as leisurely compilation. Even in Leviticus the instructions for the priesthood and the sacrifices are arrested from chapter xvii. to chapter xxi. by a collection of miscellaneous enactments. Among others a striking case of interruption occurs in the tenth chapter, to relate the sin of Nadab and Abihu, and interpose a law against the use of strong drink during the service of the tabernacle. Dr. Hayman has called attention to this method, or rather want of rigid method, somewhat in detail, and he proceeds thus: "How then can we account for such a tangled mass shot through in every direction with new departures? Let the sacred books tell their solemn tale in their own simple way, and the whole becomes perfectly easy and intelligible. Legislation was either called out by the occasion, or was interrupted by it, and its current diverted. Take the facts in Leviticus viii. as they are set

---

6 In his Preface to Curtiss' Levitical Priests, p. xv.

down. There was the actual consecration of Aaron and his sons to their offices, and out springs the stream of legislation *ad hoc*. An ancient and credible tradition connects the sin of Nadab and Abihu, among those sons, with over-indulgence in wine, and thus chapter tenth contains at once an injunction forbidding wine to priestly ministrants. Again the survivors, staggered by the blow of awful bereavement, omit certain of their newly enjoined details of duty. Observe how naturally Aaron pleads their recent calamity as an excuse (x. 16-20), and the emphatic prominence which through such a setting of facts these details acquire. So in xxiv. 10 we find the case of the blasphemer calling forth the edict against blasphemy; and just so in Num. xv. 32 the Sabbath-breaker's case draws out a general edict of capital punishment. Thus legislation grew with the wild growth of nature with the incidents of daily life.

"Or take such an incidental allusion as Ex. xxii. 21, xxiii. 9, where the injunction not to oppress the stranger is reinforced by the motive, 'for ye were strangers in Egypt.' Can we believe that we have here a writer or legislator of the third century B. C., suggesting as the motive of an important law which was opposed to the customs of his people, a transaction of a thousand years ago, instead of resting this law on the events of the captivity, which still burned in the memories and hearts of the people?"[7]

---

[7] Dr. Hayman, N. Y. Independent, Aug. 18, 1892.

6. The history of the Hexateuch was to a considerable extent interlocked with the later history of Israel by more or less of monumental observances, and memorial facts and localities. The burial place of Abraham has been invested with immemorial tradition, as well as credibility of circumstances. The Bethel of Jacob survives in the Beitin of the native. Rachel's tomb was a landmark in the time of Samuel and Saul (1 Sam. x. 2), and of Jeremiah (Jer. xxxi. 15-17), and has never been questioned to the present day. The passover perpetually commemorated the last night in Egypt (Ex. xiii. 9). The bones of Joseph accompanied the journey from Egypt to Palestine (Gen. l. 25) and found their memorial resting place in the parcel of ground (Josh. xxiv. 32), which the scholar still accepts, hard by the well which tradition in Christ's time still ascribed to Jacob. From the neighboring Ebal and Gerizim the modern traveler and his companion can hear each other recite the commandments antiphonally,[8] as the tribes once pronounced there the blessings and the curses. The ark of the covenant, constructed on the journey, retained its sanctity and gained even a superstitious regard, till it was brought to Jerusalem and deposited in the temple of Solomon. The brazen serpent which Moses had made in the wilderness remained till Hezekiah broke it in pieces because in those degenerate days it had become the object of idolatrous offerings (2 Sam. xviii. 4). And though, more than half a century later,

---

[8] Tristram's The Land of Israel, p. 152.

after the gross apostasy of two idolatrous reigns, corruption had gone so far that "the book of the law" and of "the covenant" had to be re-discovered by the high priest (2 Kings xxii.), the continuity with the past was not so dissolved but that the ancient worship was resumed with a remarkable celebration of the very feast appointed in Egypt (2 Kings xxiii. 21); and through all the misfortunes of the captivity, and the vicissitudes and desolations of protracted wars and oppressions, their institutions survived and maintained their coherence till the final overthrow and dispersion of the nation, according to the prophecy.

In view of all these several indications, we may well ask what more or better evidence could be furnished of the historic quality of the record, and therefore of its substantial contemporaneousness with the time of Moses.

7. The substantial contemporaneousness of the records with the events recorded in the last five books of the Hexateuch is attested directly by the books themselves. Of Joshua we read that he wrote certain "words in the book of the law of God" (Josh. xxiv. 26). In the Pentateuch we read again and again of the act of writing, as in Deut. vi. 9, xi. 20, xxiv. 1, xxvii. 3, xxxi. 19. The workmen who made the garments of the priest Aaron, adorned with a plate of gold, "wrote upon it a writing" (Ex. xxxix. 30). Moses is three times directed to write (Ex. xxxiv. 27; Num. xvii. 2, 3; Ex. xvii. 14). In the last instance it was to write

an account "for a memorial in a book." Three times it is definitely stated that he did write (Ex. xxiv. 4, Num. xxxiii. 2, Deut. xxxi. 9-22). "He made," says Professor Leathes, "special provision for the preservation and protection of those records in which he was himself concerned, Deut. xxxi. 9; and I do not know on what principle of sound criticism we are to set aside the statement that he did so."

We do not maintain, as has been already said, that Moses in person did all the writing of the Pentateuch, nor that the writings have not undergone revision more or less, on which something will be said later. We are also aware of the methods by which the testimony of the narrative is disparaged. But the narrative itself presents the following results: (1) Moses is declared to have been a writer of some things contained in the books; (2) no other writer is named or hinted at in connection with the subject matter; (3) the supposed writers J E D P and others are fictitious, wholly unknown personages, X, Y, Z, etc., if we may not call them straw men; (4) there is no knowledge or hint of any such writers; (5) there is no plausible identification of them with any known actual personage; (6) there is no showing of any person or persons, at the times supposed, capable of the work; (7) and there seems to be no limit to their production, from the eight of the "polychrome edition" of Genesis up to the seventeen or more makers of the Pentateuch required by Cornill.[6]

---
6 See note xxix.

CHAPTER XV

THE LITERARY PROBLEM

The Pentateuch presents certain literary phenomena that have caused a vast amount of acute discussion. The difficulty of the problem arises from our ignorance of the history of the Hebrew language. There are no standards with which to compare it, or by which to test it. The Moabite inscription is too limited in its extent and its theme for the purpose of comparison; but it shows that about the year 900 B. C. there was spoken in Moab a tongue, which, with some grammatical and linguistic peculiarities, was substantially identical with the Hebrew. An occasional Hebrew word incorporated into the Tell Amarna letters also lends support to the common opinion that Hebrew was the vernacular of Palestine before the conquest.

It is to be clearly understood that the date, relative or absolute, of no part of the Pentateuch can be determined by the language and style. The proof of this fact is (besides various somewhat direct admissions) twofold: First, as well stated by Professor Robertson, "what used to be regarded as the earliest of the large components of the Pentateuch, is now, by the prevailing school, made the latest, and the linguistic features have not been considered a bar to either view"; and second, the fact that the main, if not exclusive, arguments, of the modern critics turn on what they term, somewhat loosely, historical considerations, or marks of development in the institutions and modes of thought. The diverse and changing views concerning the age of several portions of the Pentateuch have tended probably to too great an undervaluing of the difference between the earlier and the later Hebrew, and too great disinclination to recognize archaisms.

It should also be understood that literary phenomena, more or less perplexing, are what might reasonably be expected in a book having the history ascribed to it by the long established view—phenomena most naturally explained by that view, as we have presented it. From the exodus to the Christian era, as now more commonly reckoned, it was thirteen hundred (1314) years; more than eight hundred to the time of "Ezra the scribe," "the ready scribe in the law of Moses which the Lord God of Israel had given." But there is reason to recognize the existence of yet other and older accounts incorporated in these books. In Numbers xxi. 14 mention is made of the "book of the wars of the Lord," and in Joshua x. 13 of "the book of Jashar" (or The Upright). We have also seen marked indications that such narratives as the fourteenth chapter of Genesis, the account of the flood, and the minute statements of the times of Joseph have come down from those very times. So we may reasonably suppose in regard to the genealogies; and the phrase, "these are the generations," occurring ten times, seems (as suggested by Lord Arthur Hervey) to mark "the existence of separate histories from which the book of Genesis was compiled."[1]

From this point of view the literary phenomena of the Pentateuch are, both in their variety and in the perplexity they cause, such as might be expected, and less rather than greater in amount. Look at the history of the English Bible. The Anglo-Saxon version of the gospels, dating about the year 995, is to the modern English reader an absolutely sealed book; he cannot read a word of it, unless it be "and," nor always even that. Wycliffe's version, completed five hundred years ago (1384), can be partly followed by an intelligent reader, but is often unintelligible without the aid of a later text. Tyndale's translation (of 1526) presents peculiarities of words and idioms, not very great, but the spelling is so diverse from the present mode that very many of the words would not be recognized except from their connection; in some verses more than half the words have an obsolete orthography. In less than a century King James's version followed, with many changes; and now in our own day comes the Revised Version, which, many say, ought also to be revised.

Such are the facts that confront us in regard to the English Bible. Is it not inevitable that similar

---
[1] So, substantially, Ellicott, Leathes, Delitzsch, and in part Dr. Green (The Unity of Genesis, p. 124). Delitzsch is cited by Prof. Bissell (Genesis in Colors, p. viii., note).

changes, more or less, should have been made in the form of the ancient Hebrew Bible, to make it intelligible to the Jew of Ezra's time? Naturally they might not have been so great—unless in case of the most ancient accounts in Genesis, which very probably may have been in a language as different from the late Hebrew as the Anglo-Saxon from the modern English. The changes from the time of Moses to that of Ezra would naturally have been comparatively less than in our own history, because the people were, and were kept, so homogeneous and comparatively secluded from foreign contact, because they occupied so limited an area, and because they were brought and held in so close contact with each other by their institutions and festivals. But in the lapse of ages, and in the natural course of things, some revision would be inevitable. And we have evidence of some such process. Such are the direct explanations in the text, giving modern names for obsolete ones, as in the fourteenth of Genesis, of Bela, En-mishpat, the vale of Siddim, and elsewhere of other places, as Hebron. Various explanatory notes, such as that in Ex. xvi. 36, showing the size of the homer, and that in Deut. i. 2, giving the distance from Horeb to Kadesh-barnea, and others, have long been recognized as the work of a later hand. So, of course, the account of the death of Moses. There are also the marginal notes suggesting corrections of the text, attributed in a general way to the Massoretes—of which the ultimate origin is not known. If they date no further back than that body of men, placed as they are in the margin without a change of text, these suggestions, taken in connection with the counting of the words in the several books, show the reverence with which these books were regarded in their day, a reverence so great that no unauthorized person, however learned, was permitted to deal directly with the text. The variations of the Septuagint and of the Samaritan from the Hebrew as we have it, are in conformity with the suggestion of a revision.

Some process of revision or modernizing of the Pentateuch may be safely assumed as indisputable. When or by whom, we have neither the certain knowledge nor the obligation to say. But it was clearly before the day of the Massoretes or of those whom they represented; and by men who had an authority which the Massoretes did not claim. Strong indications, however, point to the time and agency of Ezra, the famous scribe and priest. According to the account of him in the Scriptures, he was a learned and pious man, clothed with official and priestly authority, and a man of zeal and activity. He is represented as publicly reading and, in connection with his companions, interpreting the law to the people. Here then was an epoch, an emergency, and a man for the emergency. Later Jewish tradition, as found in the Talmud, ascribes to him some such agency, making him a second Moses. Notwithstanding the fabulous accretions which the tradition throws around Ezra and the

Great Synagogue, Ewald "cannot imagine that it is all a pure invention,"[2] and Westcott maintains that the tradition which points to Ezra and the Great Assembly as "having revised and closed the collection of sacred books is supported by strong internal probability."[3] Lord Arthur Hervey holds that the statements of the sacred narrative "give the utmost probability to the account which attributes to him a corrected edition of the Scriptures, and the circulation of such copies."[4] Even Dr. Driver recognizes that "Ezra was in some way noted for his services in connection with the law," and that "it would not be inconsistent with the terms in which he is spoken of in the Old Testament to suppose that the final redaction and completion of the Priest's Code, or even of the Pentateuch generally, was his work."[5] Thus, although in the obscurity of the past we are not bound to suggest a time or an agent for the revision which must in the ordinary course of events have taken place, we are able to point with much probability to both the time and the man. For the preparation of the older narratives of Genesis, even of such as may have come down through the line of Abraham in Babylonia, we find an adequate agency in the great man who was "learned in all the wisdom of the Egyptians," and who was born in Egypt, probably not less than half a century after so many letters from all parts of

---

[2] History of Israel, v., p. 169.
[3] The Bible in the Church, Appendix A.
[4] Smith's Dict. of the Bible, 2nd ed., ii., p. 1042.
[5] Introduction, p. xxviii.

Palestine were written to Amenophis, king of Egypt, all in the Babylonian language and text.

This historic experience of the Pentateuch is admirably illustrated on a smaller scale and within a vastly shorter limit of time, in the case of so modern a work as Bradford's History of Plymouth Colony, only two and a half centuries old. It offers very many of the same phenomena. The author's manuscript was terminated in 1646. It was known and quoted till 1767, after which it disappeared. The last definite knowledge of the manuscript itself was the fact that in 1658 it was deposited in the tower of the Old South Church in Boston, Mass. After nearly two centuries (in 1855) it was found in the Fulham Library, near London, England, and was fully identified by various indications, including the known handwriting of Bradford. It was published complete in 1856, edited by Charles Deane, Esq., of Boston. This edition presents many of the precise phenomena of revision found in our Pentateuch. Among the minor textual changes reminding us of the Massoretes, are such as these: An abandonment of the old interchange (in the manuscript) of "u" for "v"; a retention of the antiquated spelling, except where corrected in the original, e. g., "shuch," in which word the pen had been drawn through the second letter; a conformity of punctuation and capitals to modern usage; an omission of italics in many (not all) underscored passages; the incorporation into the direct text of five or six considerable paragraphs not so placed by Bradford, but written on the opposite or reverse pages. Of these slighter changes no notice is given in detail, although the Massoretes were careful to put their verbal corrections in the margin. But more significant and even more akin to the case in question are the following features of the book as we now have it:

1. Important subsequent modifications by the author himself, in his own handwriting; omissions of the text supplied on the blank or reverse pages; a few afterthoughts introduced into the text by a caret; occasional notes in the margin, and one very noteworthy, written (and dated) by him about *forty years after* the passage to which it is appended, as "a late observation"; and at the end of the manuscript a full list of the families that came in the Mayflower, together with a brief account of their families or "genealogies," brought down to the year 1650, four years beyond the History of Plymouth.

2. Editorial corrections of the language of the manuscript text. Thus, for the unintelligible "yothers" we have ye others; for "adventures," adventurers, twice; for "governor," government; for "things," thing; for "ye," he; for "with," what; for "on," one; for "contend," content; for "receiving," obtaining; for "be," by; for "they," the; for "sundry," sudden; and others like them, in three instances on other manuscript authority, in some instances from the obvious necessity of "harmonizing," so often derided of late. In some instances the note corrects the statement of the text.

In a few instances a note calls attention to the correction, in accordance with the modern custom.

3. Appended notes in addition to those of the author, explanatory or expansive. These are (1) by Prince the historian, (2) by the editor, (a) on the text, (b) on the notes of Prince. Among other noteworthy phenomena of this kind, just as the last verses of Deuteronomy record the death of Moses, so a note of Prince on Bradford's account of the families *records the death of Bradford*, and a note by the editor corrects the date assigned by Prince. It may be added that at the end of Bradford's list of the families, closing with a statement of the members still living in 1650, a later and heavier hand has continued the information to the years 1679, 1690 and 1698, or more than forty years after Bradford's death—as may be seen in the London facsimile edition of 1896.

Now here we have in circumstances that we can prove, on a larger or smaller scale, all the phenomena encountered in the Pentateuch, but with this difference between ancient and modern times, that the "glosses," as they would now be called, are many of them kept in the margin, or mentioned in the notes when introduced into the text (though not always), and that the accretions about the original text made by the author himself and his two successive revisers can usually be identified by evidence, whereas in the other case the certain knowledge is lost in the lapse of ages. It may be added that in Bradford's work there is a very perceptible diversity of style and phraseology and also of orthography; such as leters and letters; vitails, victialls and victualls; viage and vioage; and in one paragraph (p. 441) the three forms captine, captien and captaine. Add to this that whereas most of his many Scripture quotations are from the Geneva version, yet towards the close of his narrative he quotes in some instances from King James's version. All these various facts show how easy it would be, but for positive evidence to the contrary, for a generation of acute German scholarship to transform Bradford into several writers, and how uncertain is an analysis made on the basis of mere internal characteristics, no matter how numerous may be its advocates. No intelligent man need hesitate in questioning its validity. So acute and cautious, as well as liberal, a scholar as Professor Sanday, has not hesitated recently to say, "It remains to be seen how much of the current theories will be endorsed twenty years hence. Some of them, I feel sure, will have been pronounced impossible."[6] And whatever may be the final conclusion as to the composition, the question of date is entirely distinct and independent, and must be settled on evidence essentially historic and not speculative or theoretical. It can never be determined on the popular and baseless assumption as to what men were capable of at a certain time, or the assumption that all enlightenment must have been but an evolution from the forces inherent in a nation

---

[6] Sanday's Inspiration, p. 119 (1893).

itself. Such postulates, common though they have become, violate the first principles of sound thought and reasoning.

It thus appears, both from the well-known law of literary modification made necessary by the lapse of centuries, and from the actual phenomena of a parallel case, that the literary peculiarities of the Pentateuch are explicable as simply an editorial revision of very ancient documents belonging to the age of Joshua and Moses. But whatever decision may be reached in the attempt at analysis, let it be borne in mind that *the abundant proofs already given of the historic truthfulness of the narrative stand fast.*

A simple explanation founded upon and accordant with known facts precludes the necessity of refuting a highly complicated one, resting on speculation. A detailed examination of all the intricacies of the modern critical analysis would be far beyond the compass of this volume and would require a volume by itself. Dr. W. H. Green has devoted to the refutation of the dissection of Genesis alone, a work of nearly six hundred pages,[7] besides a more general discussion of the criticism of Pentateuch.[8] The reader who has the desire and the patience to follow through an elaborate and learned sifting of the whole process, is referred to those able works. Those writers who somewhat pretentiously claim the best modern scholarship for the modern analysis have thus far for the most part found it convenient to leave these and his previous discussions (in

---
7 The Unity of the Book of Genesis (1895).
8 The Higher Criticism of the Pentateuch (1895).

the Hebraica) unnoticed. The question has been asked, with some significance, how many of those who are so alert to accept the modern views and decry the older, have ever gone carefully through an investigation of the arguments, and especially their basis. While, however, it is impracticable, as well as unnecessary in the present treatise to duplicate a process so well performed in the works above mentioned, it may not be amiss to state briefly some of the grave difficulties under which the modern analysis labors.

CHAPTER XVI

THE ANALYSIS

The modern critical analysis rejects the long received view of the Pentateuch as being substantially one narrative subjected to the revisions made necessary by its great antiquity, and substitutes the theory of a series of writers extending through many hundred years, and compiled by various other writers who in the combination made such changes as they thought best in order to fit them together. It attempts to assign to these several supposed writers their separate portions of the work. The positive objections to this analysis are strong.

1. It is superfluous. All the phenomena can be accounted for on the older view of a continuous narrative more or less revised to meet the necessities created by the lapse of time. To reject a simple and natural explanation, accordant with all available evidence, for a complicated and needless one, is unphilosophical.

2. Its procedures are forced, arbitrary and inconsistent. The original basis of the division was the two names Jehovah and Elohim. But it was soon found necessary to reinforce this division by alleged corresponding differences of phraseology, and by some other things, presently to be mentioned. But though a vast amount of successive labor by the

acutest German scholars has been expended in harmonizing these two tests, they cannot be made to tally without violent measures. Elohim will occur in Jehovistic passages, and Jehovah in Elohistic. We will give but specimens. The methods of evading the difficulty are various; the redactor (R) is a very convenient resort. The last alleged principal workman (P) is found highly useful. Sometimes the case is quietly covered by ascribing a passage to J E conjointly; sometimes by a rapid see-saw process between the two. Sometimes it requires three or four of these cabalistic letters to disentangle twice as many successive verses. Occasionally a name is forcibly supplanted without a shadow of a reason except the emergency, as, in Gen. xxxi. 50, the Elohim compels Kautzsch at once to summon E to the rescue of J, while Dillmann and Kautzsch and Socin assign the one word to R, the latter authority coolly remarking that it is "the only possibility of disentangling the text." In like manner Kautzsch and Socin cut out the one word Elohim from a Jehovistic connection in vii. 9, and Kautzsch does not notice it. In verse 16 of the same chapter the interrupting phrase, "Jehovah shut him in," is transferred by both to the Jehovist. In chapter xvii. Jehovah occurs in the first verse of the continuous narrative, and Elohim nine times through the rest of the chapter; and Kautzsch and Socin give this one word and its verb to the redactor, while Kautzsch relieves the case by turning the whole passage before and after over to P. In chapter xxviii. 19-29 Kautzsch gives eight alternate changes from E to J, back and forth. In the successive ten verses from xx. 18 to xxi. 7 Kautzsch requires the united forces of E, R JP, P, EJ, J, E, in succession to adjust the difficulty. In chapter xxvii. from a continuous Elohistic passage of forty verses, verse 33 is singled out to be ascribed to J. And while in many parts of the Pentateuch the continuity and homogeneousness of the theme are such as to create no difficulty, in numerous other parts the disintegrations necessary to save the theory are very extraordinary. Besides numerous severances of single verses such as have been mentioned, sometimes into two or even three parts, there are abundant instances of dislocations on a larger scale. Thus chapter xxxvii. of Genesis is severed by Kautzsch into twenty-two fragments, by Kautzsch and Socin into thirty-two—there being but thirty-six verses in all. Chapter xvi. of Exodus is divided into fifteen fragments, chapter xiv. into thirteen.

It would be as tedious as it is impracticable to follow this process of vivisection through all its course in the several books of the Pentateuch and Joshua. We had marked numerous specimens, but even they would fail of making an adequate exhibition.[1]

So grave are the embarrassments in this attempt that the great leader, Kuenen, finds it needful to "utter a warning that far too much weight has often been laid on agreement in the use of the Divine

---

[1] Note xxvii., Appendix.

names," and to lay down this dogmatic utterance, "that in the few passages of their (Elohistic) narratives where Yahwe (Jehovah) now stands we need not hesitate to ascribe it to the later manipulation or corruption of the text." A confession if not a surrender.

For a thorough criticism of the attempts to divide up the Hexateuch by phraseology and style, the reader must be referred to the exhaustive discussion by Dr. Green, already mentioned. His examination of Genesis alone occupies several hundred pages, much of it devoted to this question. The facts already adduced in regard to the Divine names show that after the ablest scholars of Germany have spent years in culling out the text, with the most arbitrary excisions and dismemberments, they have failed to bring their divisions into harmony with their theory of the Divine names. They have used the largest liberty in sorting out their materials; assigning to some one writer words that occur but two or three times in all, also words that were necessarily restricted to the theme in hand, not seldom words not peculiar to the given writer. They have endeavored to confine the writer to certain stereotyped modes of expression, not allowing him the use of diverse expressions nearly but not necessarily quite synonymous. The graphic description of the steady rising of the waters of the flood in two successive verses (Gen. vii. 17, 18) is parted to aid in making two narratives. Over the first seven verses of Genesis xxi. Gramberg, Knobel, Hupfeld, Noeldeke, Dillmann, Budde, Ilgen, Kautzsch and Socin, Kautzsch, and Strack have expended their ingenuity, and among other results the theory constrains the majority to divide the first verse between two writers; although it requires but an ordinary intelligence to see that the two divided clauses simply state the conjoined fact that Jehovah visited Sarah, and in fulfillment of a previous promise.

The modern analysis further endeavors to strengthen itself by finding a continuity in the alleged documents. That this is a failure appears abundantly from two circumstances: First, the numerous, not to say constant references, of one supposed writer to things found only in the other; and second, the somewhat constant resort of the analysts to the supposed omissions of the redactor, with the remark that the writer in hand probably had stated, sometimes that he "must" have stated, the wanting facts.

One more resort is the allegation of parallel accounts, sometimes pronounced to be idle repetitions, sometimes discrepancies. Here the method is twofold: One is to identify distinct accounts, thus finding both repetitions and contradictions. An instance in point is that of the two concealments by Abraham of the relation between him and his wife, made perfectly distinct in Genesis, but confounded by the critics. Or, on the other hand, both contradictions and repetitions may be created by dividing one account into two. Thus in the flood narrative, as already mentioned, the rising of the waters is divided so as to make a repetition and a diversity of style; or a partition of the whole account may be made to assign a year and ten days as the duration of the flood, or but one hundred and ten days. Different phases of the same transaction, different speeches by or to the same person, different deportment on separate occasions, a combination of motives severed from each other, are all urged in support of a division of documents. But for a refutation of these devices in detail, the reader must be referred to the works already mentioned.

Severance of authorship on the ground of phraseology is one of the most precarious of proceedings. Professor Stanley Leathes compared Milton's three short poems, L'Allegro, Il Penseroso and Lycidas. The first of them contains about 450 different words, the second 578, the third 725; but there are only about 61 common to the three. He found in Tennyson's Lotos Eaters about 590 words, in his Œnone 720, but only about 230 in common.[2] Almost equally unsafe the somewhat broader test of style. Almost any trained writer who has been at work at intervals for forty years on different topics and occasions, and in different states of mind, will find that he has produced writings so diverse in style and method that neither his friends nor even himself would recognize all of them for his composition except for positive evidence. Who could recognize the author of the Ode on Immortality in the poem of Peter Bell, or the author of Webster's Plymouth and

---

[2] Cited in Edersheim's Prophecy and History (pp. 283, 284), from Professor Leathes.

Bunker Hill Orations in his letters to John Taylor? Similar diversities could be enumerated to any extent. It would not be a very difficult feat, with the help of a competent "redactor," as will presently be shown, to sort out the language of many a narrative or treatise into two or perhaps more. Thus Dr. Green shows the parables of the Good Samaritan and the Prodigal Son each divided in two; and Professor Mead the Epistle to the Romans in a fourfold division. About the same time the present writer had amused himself with a similar analysis of the well authenticated epistle to the Galatians, together with an apparatus of notes and references, to show that while largely the work of Paul, it also showed marks of Luke's hand, touches by John, indications of the author of Hebrews, and of a final redactor—all in readiness to be printed, if need be, in five colors; when he learned that a skillful German had just done a similar thing for the epistle in good earnest and had published to the world his profound lucubrations.

3. The claims of the analysts are unwarranted and inadmissible. The experience of literary men and the history of literature are here in open conflict with the pretensions of the critics. None of these scholars now claims to discover in the Pentateuch less than four main writers and a "redactor," while most of them require many more. This skill, too, is asserted in investigating a foreign and dead tongue, with no outside documents for comparison, and no knowledge of the alleged writers. Well-

known *facts* go to show that, in its least pretentious form, its claim cannot be maintained. The celebrated case of the letters of Junius is emphatically in point. For several years their author was pouring forth his invectives, right and left. The whole machinery of the government and all possible conjectures and efforts of exasperated enemies were directed to the discovery of the writer. The pursuit had these advantages, that the letters were in the vernacular of all Englishmen, that the characteristics of all supposable writers were definitely known, and that the earnest attention of all the acutest minds of Great Britain was directed to the discovery. More than a hundred volumes and pamphlets and a vast number of essays in periodicals were published on the question. The result was a scattering of opinion upon not less than forty-two different persons, and a failure for more than forty years to agree with some unanimity upon Sir Philip Francis, and then by reason of certain *external* evidence, which, though but slight, outweighed the chief *objection of the style*, which was considered to be above his ability.

We may take modern instances. Sir Walter Besant completed a novel left unfinished by a friend, and has publicly stated that no one has correctly recognized the respective portions of the work— although it was a decision, not between imaginary characters, but actual and known writers. The same thing is true of other collaborated works that might be enumerated. For example: In 1872 six

American writers, two of them so well known as Mrs. Stowe and Rev. Edward Everett Hale, published a joint production entitled "Six of One by Half a Dozen of the Other." Yet, notwithstanding the limited range for conjecture and the known qualities of several of the writers, "the guesses of the press were quite as often wrong as right," one distinguished literary journal declaring that in certain chapters written by Mr. Frederick B. Perkins the hand of Mrs. Stowe was evident from the beginning and it was impossible for her to veil it.[3] So, too, it never could have been known or conjectured that the passage enunciating the celebrated "Monroe Doctrine," in the message of President James Monroe, was taken from the instructions given by his Secretary of State, John Quincy Adams, to the Minister at the British Court. External evidence alone settles it.

Mr. W. E. H. Lecky, who, as the author of three prominent histories, should be familiar with the subject of documents, and who has no predilection in favor of the Scriptures, wrote an article in the Forum on the question how far it is possible by merely internal evidence to decompose an ancient document, resolving it into its separate elements, distinguishing its different dates and its different degrees of credibility, and he expresses himself thus on the present question:

"The reader is no doubt aware with what a rare skill this method of inquiry has been pursued in the

---

[3] The statement is made on the authority of Rev. E. E. Hale.

present century, chiefly by great German and Dutch scholars, in dealing with the early Jewish writings. At the same time, without disputing the value of their work or the importance of many of the results at which they have arrived, I may be pardoned for expressing my belief that this kind of investigation is often pursued with an exaggerated confidence. Plausible conjecture is too frequently mistaken for positive proof. Undue significance is attached to what may be mere casual coincidences, and a minuteness of accuracy is professed in discriminating between the different elements in a narrative which cannot be attained by mere internal evidence. In all writings, but especially in an age when criticism was unknown, there will be repetitions, contradictions, inconsistencies and diversities of style which do not necessarily indicate different authorship or dates."

Well-known facts justify the statement that these pretensions at the lowest point are invalid, and at their highest point they may safely be called preposterous. Nothing short of omniscience can discern and sort out eighteen or twenty different writers in one continuous narrative.

4. The actual outcome from the principles and methods of the modern analysis discredits the system. The constantly increasing extravagance of the results attained shows how vague and capricious are its principles, and acts as a *reductio ad absurdum*. It thus proves itself to be a scheme and not a system—a scheme in which there is an agree-

ment on the end to be accomplished and on the starting point, but the process is largely the application of individual and subjective notions. The whole sacred volume breaks up or breaks down into comminuted fragments. Not to speak of the New Testament, the analysis is no longer content with even two Isaiahs; but under the dissecting knife of Professor Cheyne the first Isaiah becomes reduced to a small nucleus, enveloped in three accretions, each of them composite. The second Isaiah, who is not Isaiah, has five chapters allowed him, and the remaining twenty chapters consist of some ten compositions. Happy the nation which could produce such a number of eloquent men and afford to forget all their names. The German Boehme has distributed the little book of Jonah to a Jahvist, an Elohist, a Redactor, and a Supplementer, besides minor insertions and glosses in every chapter. If this is not the "lowest deep," what is there "lower still"?

But turning our attention to the Pentateuch alone, we find a similar haste into fathomless depths. While Wellhausen, in the romance which he terms the History of Israel, rides serenely over every inconvenient statement of the Scriptures that lies in his way as "unhistorical" (if deemed worthy of notice), and Kuenen in his Hexateuch wrangles with the text or its statements or its connection or authorship, not less than a hundred and seventy times,[4] the actual and increasing dismemberment

---

[4] The author cited the pages in his manuscript, but omits them here.

of the Pentateuch proceeds on the same method and beyond the bounds of reason. Dillmann, the ablest and soberest scholar among the analysts (whose conclusions differ in important respects from those of the extremists), recognizes the fewest divisions, saying, "I can do nothing with Q^1 Q^2 Q^3 E^1 E^2 E^3 J^1 J^2 J^3, and I can see therein nothing but hypotheses of embarrassment."[5] But Dillmann's caution could not stay the movement. Kuenen adds to his J E P D R also P^1 P^2, etc., D^1 D^2, etc., "D and his followers," and "a scribe, including a whole series of his more or less independent followers," whom he numbers as high as R^5. Dr. Driver adopts D^2, would accept P^2 and P^3 but for the difficulty of defending them, recognizes H, and requires at least two compilers. Dr. B. W. Bacon in 1892 gave the "prevailing theory" in this formula: $\frac{J+E+D+(P^1+P^2+P^3)}{Rje\ Rd\ R}$. But Cornill in his Einleitung (1891) had already far outstripped this rather incomplete statement of the case, and presented the following constituents of the Hexateuch: J^1 J^2 J^3 E^1 E^2 D Dh Dp P^1 P^2 P^4 (a substitute for P^3 P^4 P^5, etc.) Rj Rd Rd Rp, and some fragments not included in them.

Now it may be safely said that the verdict of the best judge of literary questions would pronounce such discernment as this impossible, and the claim preposterous. But a scheme which renders such a procedure and such results legitimate, may itself be safely pronounced illegitimate.

---

[5] Dillmann, Exodus and Leviticus, p. vii. Most readers will know the meaning of these letters: J, Jehovist; E, Elohist; D, Deuteronomist; R, Redactor; P, Priest Code (Wellhausen's, Q).

5. The definite analysis has been virtually surrendered by some of its leading advocates. It would be in point here to instance the low estimate which some of the leaders place on one another's opinions, when different from their own. Kuenen, for example, who has not much to say to conservative interpreters, freely and intensely condemns the opposing opinions of those who are more or less kindred spirits: Riehm, Noeldeke, Colenso, Kayser, Juelicher, Hollenberg, Knobel, Schrader, Diestel, Bredenkamp, Maybaum. Among the terms which he applies to their views at times are such as these: Weak, unsatisfactory, grossly improbable, inadmissible, anything but conclusive, have no weight, intrinsically improbable and destitute of proof, harmonizing shifts, without foundation, arbitrary analysis, manufacture of a law to meet the demand, nothing short of absurd, the sorriest shifts. Occasionally he sweeps away three of them at one stroke of his pen, as Bredenkamp, Delitzsch and Curtiss (p. 294), Dillmann, Knobel and Juelicher (p. 152), Wellhausen, Julicher and Dillmann (p. 157), Knobel, Schrader and Colenso (p. 163). Even Wellhausen's reasoning is sometimes "doubtful" (p. 84), and he can make "a weak argument."

Coming directly to the analysis itself, we find a part of its process repudiated by Dillmann when he refuses to have anything to do with the subdivision of P E and J respectively into minor fragments, and declares it to be introducing hypotheses of embarrassment. In regard to the two most important documents of all, namely E and J, we have an extensive surrender by Kautzsch when he assigns long passages and whole pages to the two conjointly because they cannot be distinguished. Dr. Driver comments on the division of the two as presented by Kautzsch and Socin, that though "great pains and care have been bestowed upon the preparation of this work, the details as far as the line of demarcation between J and E, and the parts assigned to the redactor are concerned, can seldom claim more than a *relative* probability." He also criticises Dillmann for the minuteness with which he attempts to separate J and E: "It is often questionable if the phraseological criteria upon which he mainly relies warrant the conclusions which he draws from them." He repeatedly speaks of the "difficulty of disengaging the two sources," and admits that "in the details of the analysis of J E there is sometimes uncertainty, owing to the *criteria being indecisive*, and capable consequently of divergent interpretation," and because of the probability that "two writers would make use of the same expressions, such as might be used by any writer of the best historiographal style."[6]

The extinction of the individual writers becomes still more complete, and at the hands of leading representatives of the critical school. Wellhausen in his section on J E, commenting on the patriarchal history as there presented, makes this sweeping statement (which we italicize): "For the most part

---

6 Driver's Introduction, pp. 14, 18, 17, 12.

we have *the product of a countless number of narrators*, unconsciously modifying each other's work."[7] What has now become of J and E? Kuenen, in addition to numerous remarks upon the many changes which the Hexateuch has undergone, not traceable now, such as that even P "after its composition underwent a rather complicated literary process of which we know nothing with certainty except the final outcome which lies before us in the present Hexateuch,"[8] reaches the following notable result: "The true conclusion is rather that the text of the Hexateuch, not only here and there but *throughout* [our italics], was handled with a certain freedom in the third century, and yet more so previously, being still subject to what its guardians considered amendments. Now this is perfectly natural if, but only if, we think of the redaction of the Hexateuch not as an affair that was accomplished once for all, but as a labor that was only provisionally closed at first, and was *long subsequently continued* and *rounded off.* . . . The redaction of the Hexateuch, then, assumes the form of a continuous diaskeue or diorthosis, and the redactor becomes a *collective body* [his italics], headed by the scribe who united the two works above spoken of into a single whole, but also including *the whole series of his more or less independent followers.*"[9] What now has become of the individual writers? The failure and the surrender of the analysis is even more succinctly admitted in

---
7 Wellhausen's History, I, p. 327.
8 Kuenen's Hexateuch, p. 303.
9 Ib., p. 315.

one of the latest commentaries on Judges, thus: "J, E, JE, D, R, etc., represent not individual authors whose share in the work can be exactly assigned, the analysis, but *stages of the process*, in which more than one—perhaps *many*—successive hands participated, every transcription being to some extent a recension."[10] Here we reach the vanishing point of J E JE D R, "etc."[11]

After all that has been said, done and claimed by the "higher critics," this one thing remains true: Of the *actual literary history* of the Hexateuch, they are in the same condition of profound ignorance as is the rest of the world.

---

10 Moore's Judges, p. xxxiii., note.
11 Notes xxviii. and xxxii.

CHAPTER XVII

UNFOUNDED ASSUMPTIONS

SOME notice, however brief, may be expected of the considerations which are chiefly urged against the long established view of the Hexateuch. They have been drawn out in great detail by those who urge them; a detail rendered necessary by the circuitousness of the argument, and serving the threefold purpose of making an impression of extent and weight, of withdrawing scrutiny from the quality of its multitudinous references, and also of diverting attention from the invalidity of its fundamental positions. They may be followed through all these minutiæ and opposed at every stage. But space would fail, and the reader's patience too. Those who have the resolution for the process are referred to such works as those already mentioned, and several of the essays in the "Lex Mosaica." For the present purpose it is not necessary. Their value can be estimated by an exhibition of their principles and method, and specimens of their process. Meantime certain general facts regarding them should be borne in mind.

First, the analysis of the Hexateuch into separate portions does not determine the date of any portion. Nor does the style or phraseology, except in the most general way. Both these points are now generally admitted. The analysis is considered, however, as preparing the way to the question of the dates.

Again, diversity of dates would not directly affect the truth of the Hexateuch. But if the alleged documents could be proved to have originated many hundred years after the events, they would lose their weight as history, unless it could be shown that they rested on other narratives or documents coeval, or nearly so, with the events.

Once more, the fundamental question at issue at present is not whether there are minor inaccuracies in the Hexateuch as we now have it, but is it fundamentally true? Here the issue is in our time squarely joined. With different degrees of frankness, critics who assign the Levitical code and its setting to the time of the exile and to the priests, and Deuteronomy and its "code" to the time of Manasseh or Josiah, place themselves in direct conflict with the statements of the Hexateuch itself; for they affirm that God did not say and Moses and Aaron did not do a multitude of things which the Hexateuch affirms they did say and do. Whether in the bold and constant denials of Wellhausen and Kuenen, or in the equivalent declarations of Mr. W. E. Addis of Oxford, that "each (witness) in his order displays an increasing taste for the marvelous, and wanders further from the fact," giving a "history of religious ideas," but "not a history of Abraham and Jacob, and of Moses and Joshua," or in the more cautious words of Dr. Driver, that "we have before us traditions modified and colored by the associations of the age in which the author lived," and "placing speeches in the mouths of historical characters," such as he thought "consonant,"—in either form the conflict is open and undeniable.

At the foundation of the main opposition to the long established view lie three false assumptions, distinctly expressed by the leaders of the opposition, and necessarily accepted by their followers, even when not so distinctly announced.

1. It is assumed by them that the religious history of Israel must have been simply a natural and gradual evolution from the lower (or the lowest) to the higher, and that the supernatural, including revelation, is to be rejected. Dr. Bacon correctly states the position when he says, "If the judgment of historical critics is worth anything, the religious standpoint of JE is such as *cannot possibly be supposed* to antedate the great religious revival of Elijah." The assumption of extremists is that Israel started with idolatry like that of the nations around them, and worked their way upward. In a late commentary on the book of Judges we read that "Chemosh is the god of Moab, just as Yahweh is the god of Israel," and "the reality and power of the national god of Moab were no more doubted by the old Israelites than those of Yahweh himself." The same writer also says, "That Yahweh's anger as well as his favor is moral, was first distinctly taught in the eighth century." When confronted with abundant instances in the narrative to the con-

trary, such as when Jehovah passed by before Moses (Ex. xxiv. 6, 7), and proclaimed His wonderful divine character, the resort is to a denial of the date. In this particular instance, where the utterance stands between Jehovistic passages on both sides, we have in Kautzsch the exegetical legerdemain of singling out these two verses and assigning them to the redactor, R. What cannot be accomplished by such devices?

Yet on mere human grounds this principle that such and such views and practices cannot enter but by a long-continued development—for practices are also covered by the theory—cannot stand before facts. There have arisen at times originators who have changed the course and tendencies of human life and relationships. Read but the historian Green's account of what King Alfred did for England; how he "created a fleet," "began the conception of a national law," and "created English literature"—a combination of influences vastly more impressive when read in their particulars than stated in outline. Or turn to the extraordinary work of Charlemagne, giving to the German race its first political organization, carrying law and order into every province of his empire, calling teachers of music from Rome, gathering round him poets, historians and copyists, collecting the ancient songs of the minstrels, requiring sermons to be in the vernacular while he encouraged and pursued the study of the Latin and the Greek, personally watching over the interests and doings of the church and the clergy, regulating the currency, and fostering trade, industry, architecture and engineering, and founding schools that are said to have been the germs of universities. Such historic facts show the untenableness of the theory when viewed from its human standpoint, and sweep away cavils against the career and work of Moses.

But by what right do men attempt to rule out the supernatural element? They must ignore the person and work of Jesus Christ, the marvel and miracle of the ages, who so abruptly changed the whole drift of thought for the world. They equally ignore the fact that no other person in all history has made, by all admission, so deep and lasting an impression on any people as Moses made on the Jews. They may also be asked in particular about that decalogue, the antiquity of which in its shorter form is undisputed: Whence came that code which embodies in one brief summary what the combined wisdom of the world had not "evolved" even in fragments? The underlying assumption of a necessarily slow evolution is baseless.

2. Their assumption that non-mention or "silence" is equivalent to denial, is groundless. Abundantly as "the argument from silence" is employed, no assumption is more thoroughly disproved by human experience. It forms an essential part of the denial of the Hexateuch narrative. Wellhausen and Kuenen never weary of saying that such a writer "knows nothing" of some matter. A rapid but not exhaustive glance over the pages of Kue-

nen's Hexateuch detects the phrase or its equivalent occurring thirty-four times. Occasionally it is added that there is silence where mention might be expected. But who knows what might be expected of any writer? Silence often occurs in connection with the best known facts; and abundant cases in point are furnished by those who have given it any attention. Professor Robertson mentions that the contemporary monastic annals make no mention of the battle of Poitiers, though it effectually checked the spread of Mohammedanism across Europe; and the Koran makes no allusion to circumcision, which is held by the Mohammedans to be an ancient Divine institution, older than Mohammed. So Leathes points out that circumcision among the Jews is never mentioned in the minor prophets, the Psalms, Kings, Chronicles, or the post-captivity writings. The silence of participants in the battle of Bunker Hill leaves us in doubt who, if any one, exercised the chief command on that occasion. In Bradford's History of Plymouth, Morton's Memorial, Elliot's History of New England and Ellis's Puritan Age of Massachusetts, there is no allusion (unless we have overlooked it) to the universal Puritan custom of family prayers and grace at table. In Felt's Ecclesiastical History of New England, in two octavo volumes, where we might reasonably look for some allusion, perhaps, we find no reference to the latter practice, and to the former only one in a letter from England concerning servants. Such facts could be cited indefinitely. There is no more precarious assumption for an argument.

3. Another assumption on which great reliance is placed is that habitual violation or non-observance of a supposed law proves its non-existence. The weakness of this postulate is even more apparent. Its disproof is found in every age and every land. It is not alone individual violation of law, but frequently the indifference of whole communities. The statutes for the suppression of intemperance in some of the New England States are thus made ineffectual. In the straitened times caused by the American Revolution the School Laws both of New Hampshire and Massachusetts were deliberately disregarded by many whole townships, and the violation by officials sanctioned by the town vote at the annual meeting. Bishop Blomfield inquires, "Were not the second and fourth commandments, to say nothing of the sixth and seventh, habitually violated by the Israelites? It has never been supposed that medieval Popes and Cardinals 'knew nothing' of any condemnation of simony and nepotism; or that the court of Charles II. and Louis XIV. knew nothing of laws human or divine against fornication and adultery. There are parts of our own literature, as the comedies at the time of the Restoration, from which, if the assumption were not corrected by other contemporary literature, we might infer that at certain periods there were in this country no law, no church, no Bible, no God."

To bring a still closer parallel to any suspended observance of the Levitical law, he proceeds to say that "the Prayer Book of the Church of England, without taking into account the Canons annexed to it, contains a large number of regulations which have never been regularly observed, and some of which have been almost universally neglected"; of which he gives striking instances, including one in which "the practice was so obsolete that even its meaning had been forgotten, and it has consequently received the most various and contradictory interpretations. Generation after generation has gone by, and millions of copies of the Prayer Book have been printed, without a hint that all its regulations, down to the minutest, were not still *in viridi observantia*, or that any of them required note or comment."[1]

The assumption carries little weight at its best, even when non-observance can be fairly shown. But its "specific levity" in application is made more remarkable by two auxiliary devices: (1) By an elaborate sorting of texts so as to bring all allusions to the practice into what are claimed to be late writings. One writer remarked that "it is startling to find that the Priestly Code of Genesis contains no allusion to sacrifice or altar"; to which Bishop Blomfield replies: "The startling nature of this discovery is not very apparent when you remember that you have begun by removing from the Priestly Code every passage which contains such an allusion, on the very ground (among others) that it does contain it. It is startling to find a pack of cards which contains no aces; but the wonder

---

[1] Blomfield, The Old Testament, pp. 176-179.

ceases when you find that all the aces have been previously and purposely removed."² (2) Failing in this process, recourse is had to a challenge of the text as "corrupt," "a gloss," "an interpolation," "a later alteration." For example: Whereas the tabernacle of the congregation (or tent of meeting), provided for and described in Exodus xxv., is twice affirmed in Joshua (xviii. 1; xix. 51) to have been set up at Shiloh, Kuenen rules out all later allusions by pronouncing the declaration of 1 Samuel ii. 22 to be "an interpolation,"³ that 1 Kings viii. 4 "does not belong to the original account of the building of the temple," and that "the *repeated declaration* of the Chronicler [our italics] that the tabernacle of the congregation was pitched at Gibeon in David's time is never confirmed by the books of Samuel, and is contradicted by 1 Kings iii. 4,"— which last statement the investigating reader will find to be as unsustained as the last but one is "unhistorical." Again, in regard to the priestly functions, on a single page Kuenen assumes that 1 Sam. vi. 16a "is a gloss," that the Chronicler "altered the text" (of Sam. viii. 18, apparently), that 1 Kings iv. 2 is "probably a gloss."⁴ On another page he charges the Chronicler with an unfounded statement, finds a gloss again in 1 Sam. vi. 15, affirms that 2 Sam. xv. 24 is "corrupt" and "purposely altered," and 2 Sam. xv. 27 "only a post-

---

2 Blomfield, pp. 172, 179.
3 Hexateuch, p. 199.
4 Ib., p. 204.

exilian gloss."[5] Three pages later the reference to the Sabbath in Jer. xvi. 19-27 is intimated to be "an interpolation dating from after the captivity." In these modes "silence" is easily created.

In connection with unfounded assumptions we might very properly include many of what are adduced as contradictions in the various parts of the narrative, inasmuch as they are largely founded on certain assumptions, such as of the identity of different transactions, or the impossibility of concurrent actions with diversity of motives, of added reasons or communications being thereby conflicting—together with the assumed right to disintegrate or dislocate the text at pleasure. These methods are acutely exposed by Dr. Blomfield. He examines several of Dr. Driver's alleged instances of contradiction, namely, the account of the spies (Num. xiii., xiv.), the crafty procedure of the Gibeonites (Josh. ix.), the rebellion of Korah, Dathan and Abiram and of the Levites (Num. xvi.), and the oppressions of Solomon (1 Kings v., ix., xi.). In regard to the first he shows that the allegation of contradiction is untenable except on three untenable assumptions: (1) that a writer can never repeat himself; (2) that Caleb and Joshua must have said exactly the same thing when talking to the people and to Moses; (3) that when Caleb only is mentioned without mentioning Joshua, or vice versa, such mention of the one excludes the other. He also assumes that a direc-

---

[5] Ib., p. 205. Kuenen attempts to justify his treatment of 1 Sam. vi. 15 as a gloss because of its omission in the Septuagint (a slender foundation as against the Hebrew reinforced by the Vulgate), but in regard to 2 Sam. xv. 27 he has not even that defense.

tion from God to Moses to send spies precludes the desire of the people that such a course be taken. The second contradiction is made by taking the accounts of two different facts to be two accounts of the same fact. The third case fails unless it is out of the question that three parties should join in a common rebellion with as many different motives— a combination that is often illustrated. The fourth case rests on the supposition that to be a slave and to be subject to forced labor are the same thing; the latter condition being illustrated by conscription, convict labor or the Egyptian corvée of the present day.

Sometimes the difficulty is created by the transparent method of detaching a verse from its place. Thus in Ex. xii. 1-29 Dr. Driver assigns verses 1-20 to P, verses 21-27 and 29 to J and E, but the intermediate verse 28 back to P, drawing a dividing line beneath it and above its neighbors; but, as Dr. Blomfield remarks, the whole difficulty disappears if we transfer verse 28 below the line, where it has a right to be, and in the connection in which it was found. Dr. Green also has called attention to the frequency with which difficulties are fastened upon the text, though created by the analysis itself.

CHAPTER XVIII

UNSUSTAINED DENIALS

The previous examination of some unfounded assumptions in the modern criticism makes it practicable to speak the more briefly of certain facts in the history of the Jewish institutions, alleged to be in conflict with the narrative of the Hexateuch. While the leaders of the school appear to rely mainly upon the assumption that certain things could not have taken place at the time to which they are ascribed, or, in the words of Dr. Bacon, "cannot possibly be supposed to antedate" certain times and conditions, an attempt is also made to show that certain observances required by the Mosaic law and the narrative did not actually exist till long afterward. Before considering these denials it may be mentioned that two points, formerly more or less prominent, are now withdrawn from the discussion.

It is conceded by the critics, as already mentioned, that the language and style do not determine the date of the Hexateuch or of its parts. This admission became inevitable when, within about a quarter of a century, by a sudden reversal the so-called P was transformed from the oldest into the youngest of four main constituents, a descent of many hundred years. There has been a great shrinkage in the list of archaisms, and Aramaisms have been called in question,[1] there being no means of determining the history of the Hebrew language.

The allegation of anachronisms, that is, of allusions to things of later date than that of the narrative, is mostly withdrawn. The critics shall state the case. Dr. Bacon makes this remarkable statement concerning P: "No anachronism is traceable in the document, for the writer never permits himself for one moment to anticipate the course of revelation as he has mapped it out." We shall have occasion to refer to this admission later. In regard to J and E Kuenen says: "Reference to historical facts, such as might give a clue to the dates of composition, are extremely rare in the prophetic elements (J and E) of the Hexateuch." He endeavors, however, to present seven instances, the point of which is twofold: the implication that there can be not only no prophecy but no reasonable foresight or expectation; and furthermore, an insistence on finding in the passages things which are not there. To show the style of argument, though at the risk of a little wearisomeness, we cite them all. "The author of Gen. xxvii. 29-39 seq. is not only familiar with David's victories over the Edomites, but also with the rebellion of the latter under Solomon and their revolt against Jehoram ben Jehoshaphat." The reader is invited to look into these verses of Jacob's blessing and see for himself whether they speak of David, the Edomites, Solomon, Jehoram, rebellion,

---

[1] See Driver's Deuteronomy, pp. lxxxviii.-xc., where he even denies that נער as a feminine is archaic, though Delitzsch (i., p. 43) pronounces it "a veritable archaism." Driver ventures to suggest but two Aramaisms in Deuteronomy.

revolt and victories. Again: "The writer of Gen. xxi. 44 seq. in all probability had in view the wars of the Arameans and Israelites for the possession of the Transjordanic district." The reader will please see for himself what mention is made in these verses of wars, the Arameans, Israelites, or the Transjordanic district. Again: "Ex. xv. 17b was written some considerable time after the building of Solomon's temple; Num. xxiv. 7 after the institution of the monarchy; v. 17 after David's successful wars against Israel's neighbors; vs. 22-24 in the Assyrian period, presumably not earlier than the seventh century B. C. Finally, Josh. vii. 26 cannot have been written till the rebuilding of the walls of Jericho in Ahab's reign had long been a thing of the past." The first of these assertions shall be answered by Dillmann (sustained by other cited authorities), who says that the mountain of inheritance, referred to, is "not Zion, but the mountain-land of Canaan," and the "sanctuary" was not the tent set up by David on Zion, nor Solomon's temple, but "the declaration was fully accomplished after that a common sanctuary had been established at Shiloh." The objection founded on the second passage would interdict Balaam from even anticipating from the successes of the past the future exaltation of the kingdom of Israel, and from choosing his own mode of expressing it. The assertion founded on the third passage would incapacitate Balaam from alluding to the then impending conflict with Moab, which constituted his present errand, as well as to the manifest certainty of Israel's victory, and make him forget his immediate business for a meditation on events several hundred years later. The last two have weight only on condition that there is no prophetic foresight, the former of them being indeed not unnaturally suggested to an observer by the history of Assyrian invasions, the existing prevalence of Babylonian culture in Palestine, and the growing weakness of the Egyptian power in that country. These instances form his case; although he also alludes to three poetic passages as giving pretty clear indications, the value of which he admits "is impaired by our uncertainty as to the history of the incorporation of them into the Pentateuch."[2]

Some alleged geographical anachronisms presented to English readers by Dr. Samuel Davidson in his Introduction a generation ago, are indeed revived by Dr. B. W. Bacon in his Genesis of Genesis; but they are of so little account, and so little reliance is placed upon them, that we dismiss them to a note in the Appendix.[3] The main stress of the objection to the Hexateuch narrative, as has been said, rests on the position that certain observances and usages therein described and prescribed were actually of late origin.

The chief contention against the truth of the record is in regard to the central sanctuary. In Exodus xxv. and the following chapters is narrated in detail the structure of the tabernacle, and in xxxiii.

---
[2] The Hexateuch, pp. 237, 238.   [3] Note xxxi.

7 we read that Moses named it the tabernacle of the congregation, or the tent of meeting (R. V.). When finished it received the ark of the covenant, was filled with the glory of the Lord, was placed in the center of the camp, became the central object on the march and afterwards, was located at Shiloh and other places subsequently; and after its wanderings and the loss of the ark, it was finally carried to the temple, which thenceforward became the central seat of worship. But Wellhausen opens his History with the assertion that before the building of the temple "not a trace can be found of any sanctuary of exclusive legitimacy"; and Kuenen begins his gravest contention with the statement that "there is not a trace of the tabernacle in Judges-Kings," and "the restriction of worship was never so much as thought of before Hezekiah."

We must leave Wellhausen to the thorough refutaiton given him by Dr. W. L. Baxter, who, in several articles in the Thinker, has followed him at every point and shown his contention to be a singular combination of bold assertions, bold denials, unwarranted inferences, evasions of some plain Scripture declarations and arbitrary exclusion of others, together with a surprising amount of inconsistencies of his own, often amounting to contradictions. It is to be lamented that so few readers see and carefully read a refutation so elaborate and complete.

We can but briefly notice Kuenen's positions, which are substantially the same as Wellhausen's, somewhat more definitely formulated. And we will first show directly whether or not there is any trace of the tabernacle before Hezekiah. In Joshua (xviii. 1) we read that the children of Israel assembled at Shiloh and set up the tabernacle of the congregation there; and in chapter xix. 51 we also read that it was there. In Judges xviii. 31 and 1 Sam. i. 24 we read again of "the house of God in Shiloh," which 1 Sam. ii. 14, 22 identifies with the tabernacle. In 2 Sam. vii. 6 God's words through Nathan are that "since the day that I brought up the children of Israel out of Egypt, I have walked in a tent and a tabernacle." In 1 Kings viii. 4, "They brought up the ark of the Lord and the tabernacle of the congregation" to the temple; and in i. 39 mention is made of the "tent," "the tent of the Lord." The tabernacle of the Lord is also mentioned in those same words in 1 Chron. xvi. 39, xxi. 29, xxiii. 26; 2 Chron. i. 3, 5, 6, 13. In Jer. vii. 12-14 God speaks of "Shiloh where I caused my name to dwell at first."

Here are traces enough; too many to be disposed of by the argument from silence. Therefore Kuenen pronounces 1 Sam. ii. 22b "an interpolation," says that 1 Kings viii. 4 "does not belong to the original account," and that "the repeated declaration of the Chronicler is never confirmed by the books of Samuel and is contradicted by 1 Kings iii. 4." Now the assertion of the interpolation has no stronger foundation than its omission from the Septuagint, though found in all Hebrew copies and recognized without a question by the English and American revisers. The second statement, that the passage "does not belong," is his arbitrary assertion. The "*repeated*" declaration of the Chronicler *is* confirmed by both Samuel and 1 Kings, as the reader will see by the references we have given, and is *not* contradicted but confirmed by 1 Kings iii. 4.[4] The passage reads thus: "'The king went to Gibeon to sacrifice there; for that was the great high place; a thousand burnt offerings did Solomon offer on that altar." Gibeon was the great high place, of the altar, the sacrifice, and (1 Chron. xvi. 39, 40, xxi. 29; 2 Chron. i. 3-5) of the tabernacle—which last fact made it the *great* high place. It was here that God appeared to Solomon in a dream by night.

As if to remedy this failure, Kuenen turns to cite instances of sacrifices offered elsewhere than at the central sanctuary. It is a singular list. He first refers to four sacrifices offered at "the temple of the Lord at Shiloh," which was itself then the central sanctuary, as will be presently shown. He closes the list with the three instances of David's sacrificing "wherever the ark halts" on its way to Zion, which again was entirely regular, inasmuch as the ark of the covenant was the specially sacred content of the tabernacle, but had been separated from it by the capture at Aphek. Between these cases he introduces the sanctuary in Mount Ephraim

---

[4] The Chronicler finds no favor with Wellhausen and Kuenen, being constantly decried when in conflict with their assertions. But on all other occasions they make free use of him. Thus Kuenen cites him on pages 195, 196, 202, 206, 208, twice on page 206, thirteen times on page 196, and with more than twenty references on page 195.

established by Micah, who had stolen his mother's money, and established "a house of gods" with teraphim, a graven image and a molten image; that of the Danites, who carried off Micah's gods and "set up a graven image"; and the sacrifice of Saul, for which he was so sternly rebuked and condemned by Samuel. He also refers to the sacrifice at Bochim, which for aught we know may have been in close proximity to the tabernacle which was then at Shechem (Josh. xxiv. 25, 26), and at all events immediately followed the warning of "the angel of the Lord" there present; also the offerings at Mizpah, where we read that "the house of God" and "the ark" then were; Gideon's offering at Ophrah, and Manoah's at Zorah, in both which instances the angel of the Lord had first appeared and directed the offerings; and Samuel's sacrifice at Bethlehem, which the narrative says was by God's direct command. These three instances, occurring at times and places of God's special manifestation, were in accord with the original appointment, as will presently appear. Should Kuenen deny the supernatural manifestation, as very likely he would, he simply impeaches the witness on whom he relies for his facts. Samuel's building an altar at Ramah is also cited; but as it is unknown where the ark and tabernacle were at this time, we cannot tell whether this was a regular procedure, or a special one growing out of the anomalous state of things. None of the cases cited proves unrestricted freedom as to the place of sacrifice, and some of them are absurdly irrelevant.

Still more remarkable is the method of showing that "the same freedom still prevailed for centuries after the erection of the temple." One is hardly prepared to find Kuenen's sole evidence to be that Asa, Jehoshaphat, Amariah, Uzziah, Jotham, Joash and Ahaz "maintained the bamoth" or idolatrous high places. But (1) the Scripture statement is not that they maintained, but that they did not take away these high places; (2) in Kuenen's own words, "the writer of Kings registers this as a transgression"; and (3) of Joash it is also recorded that he took all the hallowed things and all the gold that was found in the treasury of the Lord and with them bought off Hazael king of Assyria, as Asa had previously done to Ben-hadad; and of Ahaz that he "made his son to pass through the fire, according to the abominations of the heathen whom the Lord had cast out before the children of Israel." Though similar things are not recorded of the others, they are all censured for the thing for which Kuenen cites their example. It is also recorded as a special merit of the good Hezekiah that he actually took away the idolatrous high places and destroyed the objects of idolatrous worship, and of Josiah that he thoroughly completed this and other religious reformations.

Kuenen might also have referred to Ahab, who reared an altar to Baal in Samaria; to Jeroboam the son of Nebat, who set up the golden calves at Bethel and Dan, and offered sacrifices to them; and to Jehu, who, though he destroyed the prophets of Baal, "departed not from the sins of Jeroboam, to wit, the golden calves at Bethel and Dan." But he forbears.

The alleged conflict as to the place of sacrifice, between Exodus on the one hand and Leviticus and Deuteronomy on the other hand, is a forced interpretation. The case is simple. In Exodus (xx. 24) God directs sacrifices "in all places where I record my name," or (R. V.) "in every place where I cause my name to be remembered," or (Kautzsch) "designate that I will be honored," or (De Wette, Robinson, Fuerst) "praised." In Deuteronomy (xii. 5), when, nearly forty years later, the Israelites were about to enter the land of promise, God indicates that there is to be "the place which the Lord your God shall choose out of all your tribes to put his name there," namely, a particular and permanent place to which they should come with their offerings and seek him. But during the journey from Sinai the one place designated by God was the tabernacle, where the cloud and the fire manifested His special presence, moving successively from place to place with the changes of encampment (Num. ix. 15-22). In Palestine the place of sacrifice continued with the tabernacle, first at Shiloh, afterwards at Shechem, Gibeon, Nob, and perhaps other places, and it accompanied the resting places of the ark when David conveyed it to Zion, till it found a permanent location when Solomon brought ark and tabernacle to the temple (1 Kings viii. 4). The separation of the ark from the tabernacle may have caused embarrassment and irregularities, especially in lawless times, but the instances of Manoah, Gideon and Samuel need not be considered irregularities, inasmuch as God saw fit to manifest Himself by the "angel of the Lord" in the first two instances and by express command in the third, directing the sacrifice.

A simple and obvious interpretation thus removes all appearance of conflict between Exodus and Deuteronomy in regard to the central sanctuary, and the contention that the difference supposes the lapse of centuries between. A similar argument in reference to certain required observances and usages equally breaks down.

For it is argued that certain feasts and sacred actions enjoined in the Priest Code do not appear to have been observed, and therefore its late origin is thus proved. The answer is that they are mentioned to as great an extent as could be expected, even as shown by the admissions of Kuenen, and by the allusions of prophets whose antiquity he is obliged to recognize. He admits that the feast of the tabernacles is frequently mentioned, and that Hosea and Amos, whose antiquity he does not dispute, speak of feasts in the plural; also that the feast of the new moon was observed from the earliest times, as proved by Amos, Hosea, Kings, Samuel and Isaiah; that the Sabbath is a very ancient institution; and that the year of release is mentioned once by Ezekiel; also that the trespass offering is not unknown, as well as the Nazarite's vow; and that circumcision appears to have been regularly practiced.[5] This is a surrender of all that is needed to invalidate the general statement, since we could not expect these writers to go into a historical inventory of things completely specified elsewhere in the proper place. He objects to some of these that they did not spring from the Tora (or law),—which is merely his assertion. He affirms that the year of jubilee is never mentioned, even in Jer. xxxiv. 9-20, although the fact that the prophet in verse 17 uses the very term employed in Lev. xxv. 10, used of the jubilee, "proclaim liberty," has led many so to understand it. He also affirms that the first celebration of the passover of which we have historical assurance, is Josiah's passover, 2 Kings xxiii. 21-23. The narrative distinctly implies the contrary; for it records that there had not been "*such* a passover from the days of the judges, nor in all the days of the kings of Israel nor of the kings of Judah,"—an unmeaning comparison except as the passover had been observed in some way during those times and in both kingdoms. Besides some minor omissions requiring no special attention, he says truly that the great Day of Atonement is never mentioned. But far more significant than direct mention is the fact that in Solomon's temple a separate and *permanent* provision was made of the most holy place (1 Kings viii. 5-11), precisely as in the tabernacle, where the ark was placed under the cherubim, this part of the tabernacle being re-

---

[5] Hexateuch, pp. 207-210.

served for *use only on the annual Day of Atonement*, and entered then by the high priest alone. This conclusively shows that it was and was to be a settled arrangement; and its very notoriety was a natural reason why it was not particularly mentioned. In what history of the United States or of New England can there be found any formal notice of the Fourth of July? Another important fact in connection with the Day of Atonement is that not only is there no mention of it in the Old Testament history, but nowhere else do we find any allusion to it till about two and perhaps three centuries after the return from the exile,[6] the time when, according to the critical theory, the Levitical code had been introduced and the observance must have been *long practiced*. Non-mention does not imply non-existence.

Thus it clearly appears that both the historical and prophetical books confirm the knowledge of the main points of the Mosaic law throughout the history of Israel, notwithstanding the disorders of many centuries, and although, as Wellhausen truly remarks, "for reasons easily explained, it is seldom that an occasion arises to describe the ritual." The denials are unsustained.

But the objectors appeal in a certain way to the earliest of the writing prophets, chiefly to Amos and Hosea, the former assigned to the northern kingdom, the latter to the southern as early as the middle of the eighth century B. C. The genuine-

---

[6] According as in Ecclesiasticus l. 50, mention is made of Simon I. or Simon II.

ness of the writings is undisputed by them, except as some extremists have ruled out certain passages in Amos that conflict with their theories. Isaiah also is cited to some extent. We have seen in a previous chapter how these prophets refer to the chief events recorded in the Hexateuch. Their brief allusions to the institutions are equally confirmatory. And Amos in speaking of the past history and of the prophets and Nazarites appeals directly to the knowledge of the people: "Is it not even so, O ye children of Israel?"[7] Both prophets speak of a covenant, a law of Jehovah, His statutes, the law of God, which Israel had forgotten, rejected, transgressed.[8] They had abandoned Jehovah for idols and for criminal lusts.[9] Hosea speaks of the feast days, new moons, sabbaths and solemn feasts as established institutions, which God in anger would take away;[10] and Amos of the custom of sacrifice, tithes and thank offerings, although rebuking the worshipers for their transgressions.[11] Hosea speaks of the sin of removing the ancient landmark, and of striving with the priest,[12] together with allusions less clear and certain. The recognition of these Mosaic regulations is so unmistakable that Wellhausen and Kuenen have resorted to the device of asserting God's rebuke of the *abuse* of the institutions to be a warfare against their use, a "polemic against the praxis." While intelligent readers will continue to see, as they always have

---

7 Amos ii. 11.
8 Am. ii. 4. Hos. iv. 6; vii. 7; viii. 1, 12.
9 Hosea iv. 12-14.
10 Ib. ii. 11.
11 Amos iv. 4, 5.
12 Hos. v. 10; iv. 4.

seen, that the rebukes are directed against, not the observance, but the hypocritical observance, the absurdity of Wellhausen's contention becomes too plain for argument when applied to one of the most striking instances, cited by him with special emphasis, namely, Isaiah l. 11-17, where God spurns, not all oblations, but "vain oblations," and their other ceremonial observances, when they are but the superficial mask of inner unrighteousness and corruption. If the closing strenuous demand for purity, repentance, justice, mercy and compassion are not sufficient, take one decisive test: when God says, "When ye make many prayers, I will not hear," does God condemn prayer, or prayer offered in such a spirit? There can be but one answer, and that answer settles the whole interpretation of Wellhausen to be absurd.

Thus far then the objections to the early existence of the Levitical code appear to have no substantial foundation. There remains one other point in that code which requires attention, which will be considered in the next chapter.

CHAPTER XIX

UNSUSTAINED DENIALS: THE PRIESTHOOD

In patriarchal times there was no special priesthood, but sacrifices apparently were offered by the head of the family, and, as some suppose, the priestly function descended to the first born. Some have recognized the family priesthood in Exodus xix. 22-24 and xxiv. 5. After the exodus, according to the narrative, the family of Aaron was set apart for a hereditary priesthood, and later the whole tribe of Levi was separated for the service of the tabernacle.

Kuenen (and others) asserts that no such exclusive qualification of the tribe of Levi existed in early times, and that the distinction between priests and Levites in general appears in the whole exilian and pre-exilian literature but once, and that in a passage which he does not accept. Thus again he endeavors to show the late origin of the Levitical code which so minutely establishes the system.

If the Biblical account be true and all the details were adjusted as prescribed, there was no reason why the later records should give any recapitulation of these details. The most that could be expected would be incidental references and, as usual, some of them so incomplete as to require for their explanation a knowledge of the original arrangement.

As matter of fact, evidence of the separation of the Levites to the service of the sanctuary is found in all stages of the history of the nation. At the entrance into Palestine, some forty years after the system is recorded to have been made, we find it in full operation. Both at the crossing of the Jordan and in the march around Jericho the priests are in sole charge of the ark of the covenant, and, as if to anticipate this very cavil, they are termed (iii. 3) "the priests the Levites." Were we to accept the critics' date of these passages (J E), they were written eight hundred years B. C. At Shechem, where Joshua built an altar and "wrote upon the stones a copy of the law of Moses," it is "the priests the Levites which bare the ark of the covenant" (viii. 33). This passage is assigned by Kautzsch to Dt of nondescript date. Twice we read in Joshua of Aaron the priest, three times of Eleazar the priest (Aaron's son), and once of "Phinehas the priest," twice called "Phinehas the son of Eleazar the priest"; and chapter xxi. is given up to the assignment of the cities of the Levites, which are summed up as "all the cities of the children of Aaron the priests." This passage is ascribed by Kautzsch to P, the latest main portion, so that the record by his showing covers many hundred years —from JE to P. Again, the congregation are told (xviii. 7), "The Levites have no part among you, for the priesthood of the Lord is their inheritance"; and the same statement is made in chapter xiii., verses 14 and 33, with the addition in both cases, "as he said unto them," obviously referring to the previous announcement in Deut. xviii. 1, 2, and that apparently to Num. xviii. 8-32. Thus these writings concur. It is not surprising that Professor Robertson Smith, in his critical argument, should say, "I exclude the book of Joshua, because it in all its parts hangs closely together with the Pentateuch." Even from the disorderly times of the judges there comes a statement to the effect (Judg. vii. 13), where Micah says, "Now know I that the Lord will do me good, since I have a Levite to be my priest." In the days of Samuel, Eli the high priest was a descendant of Aaron, and the statement meets us once more (1 Sam. ii. 27, 28) that his father's house had been chosen out of all the tribes of Israel "to be my priest, to go upon mine altar, to burn incense, to wear an ephod before me,"—priest's duties all; and his reprobate sons, Hophni and Phinehas, were in the priest's office (i. 3; ii. 27, 28) and attended on the ark of the covenant (iv. 4). The Lord's priest at Shiloh in Saul's time was Ahiah, grandson of Eli (xi. 3); and Abiathar, whom Solomon thrust out from being priest, was a descendant of Eli (1 Kings ii. 27). Zadok, his successor, was of the line of Eleazar (1 Chron. vi. 8). In Kings and Chronicles we read repeatedly of the Levites as being in charge of the ark and collecting and holding the money for the repairs of the house of the Lord. It is recorded as one of the grave wrong-doings of Jeroboam that he made priests of "those who were not of the sons of Levi."

Thus at all these various points of the history we have evidence that the sacerdotal functions, including the care of the tabernacle and the ark of the covenant, were allied to the tribe of Levi. When the progress of the ark to the city of David was for a time arrested by the punishment of Uzzah for his presumption, on the renewal of the effort David took precautions that only Levites should be its bearers; for he said, "None ought to carry the ark of God but the Levites, for them hath God chosen to carry the ark of God and to minister unto Him forever."

Kuenen endeavors to break the force of this accumulated evidence by adducing instances of the priestly function of sacrifice exercised by others than Levites. We give his complete list: Gideon, Manoah, Micah, the citizens of Beth-shemesh, Samuel, Saul and Jeroboam; and he adds, "According to Ezekiel xliv. 6-9 even foreigners were admitted to the service of the sanctuary before the captivity." The list shows both the straits to which an acute writer can be reduced, and his confidence that his readers will not scrutinize his references. The passage in Ezekiel is a denunciation of "the rebellious house of Israel" for their "abominations" in doing this very thing. Of Jeroboam's example it is hardly necessary to say that he is the notorious character steadily described as "Jeroboam the son of Nebat, which did cause Israel to sin." Micah was first a thief and then an open idolater. Saul was sternly rebuked for his presumption and disobedience, and threatened on the spot with the loss of the kingdom. Samuel, though not a descendant of Aaron, was a Levite, had a special consecration as a Nazarite before his birth, early became the assistant of Eli the high priest, wearing the ephod and sleeping in connection with the sanctuary, had a personal call and repeated communications from God to be a reformer and a prophet, and certainly in one instance a definite direction to offer sacrifice. Manoah and Gideon also at the time of their offerings were under the direction of the angel of the Lord. It does not appear that the citizens of Beth-shemesh offered their sacrifices otherwise than in the regular way, by the hands of the priests; for the record says that the Levites were there and "took down the ark of the Lord and the coffer that was in it and put them on the great stone" (1 Sam. vi. 14). If the sacrifice was made by these men personally, and not through the Levites, it would have been an extraordinary and irregular expression of their joy—for "they rejoiced"—in irregular circumstances, the ark being brought to their village by a yoke of unguided kine. Possibly this was the case, for we read that the Lord smote the men of Beth-shemesh because they had looked into the ark of the Lord. As to the remaining instances of David and Solomon, the brief statement that they offered sacrifices no more involves their direct action than when "Solomon built him an house." In the first instance cited by Kuenen in regard to David (2 Sam. 17, 18) the very next verse relates that David "dealt among all the people, among the whole multitude of Israel, as well to the women as men, to every man a cake of bread and a good piece of flesh." Did he distribute to all this multitude with his own hands? The next verse preceding also says that the ark was set in the midst of "the tabernacle which David had pitched for it," and, four verses previous, that "David brought up the ark of God." Did he carry the ark and pitch the tent with his own hands? Kuenen's first quotation in regard to Solomon's sacrifice shows the absurdity of the claim (1 Kings iii. 4): "A thousand burnt offerings did Solomon offer on that altar." If Solomon offered these thousand victims with his own hands, he was a much stronger man than Samson; "he was the very strong man Kwasind, he was the strongest of all mortals." This exhausts Kuenen's catalogue wherewith to break down the uniform testimony of the record. Further comment is needless.[1]

But it is further affirmed in objection that the distinction so emphasized in Leviticus and Deuteronomy between the priests and Levites in general does not appear previous to the exile, and that this proves "P" to be as late as the exile. The strength of the objection lies in disregarding the standing distinction between the exactness of technical or legal statements and the inexactness of popular and current phraseology. In Leviticus and Numbers we have the careful legislation. Again in 1 Chron.

---
[1] For specimens of Kuenen's style of references see Note xxx.

xxiii. 24-32 there is a re-statement of the case in entire accordance with Leviticus, as a statutory re-enactment or at least defining statement by David, in which it is said of the Levites, "Their office was to wait on the sons of Aaron for the service of the house of the Lord," accompanied with an enumeration of details. Kuenen, if he took notice of the passage, would doubtless deny its validity; but it states David's method as known to the Chronicler. That the distinction was well known even in the disorderly times of the judges appears from the fact that after Micah's bargain with the Levite, the record reads further (Judg. xvii. 12), "Micah consecrated the Levite, and the young man became his priest"; he was not already a priest by being a Levite. In 1 Kings viii. 4 the distinction is made, "the priests and the Levites." But Kuenen declares in italics that "the writer of Kings cannot have written" so, "first because he mentions the priests alone in verses 3, 6, 10, 11," which proves nothing; and "in the next place he regards all the priests as qualified for the priesthood" (1 Kings xii. 31); which passage the reader will find to be the information that *Jeroboam* "made priests of the lowest of the people, which were not of the sons of Levi." The Chronicler speaks also of "the priests and the Levites" in the reign of Jehoiada, of Joash, and of Hezekiah, where (2 Chron. xxix. 34) the distinction of functions is alluded to, and in xxxi. 9, where Azariah, the chief priest, is mentioned as "of the house of Zadok," a descendant of Aaron.

Denial of their truth does not remove the testimonies. The Chronicler (as Kuenen recognizes) always assigns to the Levites the task of bearing the ark.[2] So also does 2 Sam. xv. 24, which Kuenen dismisses as "corrupt."

The chief reliance in the denial of the distinction thus clearly specified at various stages of the history, is an appeal to a frequent usage in Deuteronomy and elsewhere, namely, "the priests the Levites," which, it is argued, makes the terms coextensive. If the order were reversed, namely, the Levites the priests, the appeal would have weight. But it is always the other order, merely adding to the word priest the tribal designation. It would show at least that the custom had sprung up of adding to the mention of this prominent class their distinctive and distinguished tribal name, superfluously but popularly. There is a similar superfluous addition in mentioning "the children of Aaron the priest, which were of the Levites" (Josh. xxi. 4), and (Ex. iv. 14) even "Aaron the Levite." It is difficult if not impracticable to classify these varying usages on any particular principle. But that the addition of the word Levite does not make all Levites priests appears, among other indications, from the fact that from the language of Malachi (ii. 1, 4, 8; iii. 3) it might just as well be argued that all Levites were priests, whereas the distinction is admitted on all hands to have been established at that time. Again, in Deuteronomy, where the

---

[2] 1 Chron. xv. 2,13, 15; 2 Chron. v. 4; xxxv. 3.

double phrase repeatedly occurs, we find the actual arrangement announced (xxvii. 9, 12, 14) for the tribe of Levi to *stand with the other tribes* at Mount Gerizim, and for the "Levites," who are called in verse 9 "the priests the Levites," to speak to those tribes with a loud voice—thus showing the distinction and separation.

It is as sound a literary as it is a legal maxim, that all brief and current references are to be interpreted by the full and definite statements, and not contrariwise. With this principle in mind we may dispense with a wearisome investigation of details, beyond the scope of this discussion, and refer to an excellent illustration given by Bishop Blomfield, and lying directly within the ecclesiastical domain. Now in Leviticus we have the high priest, the priests, and the Levites; while in much of the narrative we have summarily "the priests" or "the priests the Levites." Dr. Blomfield's illustration is this: "The ordained ministers of the Church of England are distinguished in the Prayer Book as bishops, priests and deacons; in deeds and other legal documents they are described as clerks in holy orders; in ordinary literature and in modern acts of Parliament they are denominated clergy or clergymen; in colloquial 'slang' they are spoken of as parsons. The first-named description alone recognizes their distinctive status and position; yet the third (clergy) is habitually used by those who are well aware of that distinctive character, without any confusion, and without any suspicion that the writers are ignorant of it. When it is remembered that Deuteronomy is 'the people's book,' it can cause no surprise that the more general and comprehensive term, corresponding to clergy, should be the term habitually used."

On the principles of sound reasoning, the denials, both of the separation of the Levites to the work of the sanctuary, and of the separation of the Aaronitic priesthood from the rest of the Levites, are not sustained.

CHAPTER XX

THE CODES

IT is now an established custom to speak of the Mosaic legislation as consisting of three codes, named the Covenant Code (Ex. xx.–xxiii., xxxiv.), the Deuteronomic Code and the Priest Code, extending from Ex. xxiv., with minor exceptions, through Numbers. This grouping is rather convenient and popular than precise and scientific. Not only does the narrative show the legislation to be a protracted process, but the analysts admit the codes to be more or less interrupted and fragmentary. Kuenen, while maintaining the general unity of each code, says of the first that the succession is not always natural and regular, but that some of the ordinances break the context; of the second, that the order of succession is not always what we might have expected, and cannot (with few exceptions) be explained by later insertions—his standing resort; and of the third, that they "do not form a closed and ordered whole; their arrangement leaves very much to be desired; some of the ordinances or groups might be removed without any perceptible void; some of them have the appearance *of novellæ;* and in some cases they contradict each other."[1] Dr. Driver makes the important admission in regard to P that "even of the incidents in

---
[1] The Hexateuch, pp. 49, 50.

the wilderness many appear to be introduced chiefly on account of some law or important consequence arising out of them," of which he gives a dozen instances,[2] showing that the legislation was somewhat continuous, or rather continued, but with frequent interruptions. Dr. Hayman has called attention still more strongly to the fragmentary character of the Priest Code: "It is not a code, but in many parts a set of disconnected injunctions easily accounted for as successive legislations made as occasion suggested them during the wandering, in regard to which we can in some instances discern the occasion, and anything but a systematic statute book framed by a set of otherwise unoccupied priests." After giving striking illustrations, too extensive to be quoted here, he proceeds: "To call it the Priest's Code was hardly a happy thought of the critics, codification being precisely the element which it does not present. This condition of things naturally and perfectly accords with its historic origin, and as completely conflicts with the theory of its deliberate composition by a body of priests at their leisure drawing up a code of laws for the people returning from captivity. It also shows even more strongly the devout reverence with which the code of Moses was regarded, that the priests did not venture to change this comparatively heterogeneous mass of precepts into an orderly system."

Clearly the legislation, while more or less con-

---
[2] Introduction, p. 119.

tinuous and successive, was interrupted and related to circumstances and occasions. It began at the exodus with the law of the passover, founded on the events then occurring, and the law of the first-born for a similar contemporaneous reason. Next, in connection with the manna, came the re-enactment of the Sabbath law. In the third month there was found the convenient halting place and the leisure for promulgating the fundamental principles of the law in its broader and deeper relations to God and man; beginning with the decalogue as the basis of all, immediately followed by certain moral precepts, including the treatment of servants, against violence, manslaughter and murder, in regard to accidental injury, kidnapping, theft, trespass, borrowing and lending, personal purity, treatment of the stranger, the widow, the fatherless, concerning bribery, oppression of the poor, conduct towards one's enemy, together with the duty of observing the great religious festivals, and offering the first fruits of everything to God. These primal duties are all stated, but disconnectedly, as though many of them were evoked and recorded on the occasions. The section closes (xxiii. 20-23) appropriately with an earnest exhortation, warning, and assurance of the Divine blessing on obedience.

This group, called the Covenant Code, naturally prepares the way by its closing declarations for what is called the Priest Code. It had enjoined the worship of God and the observance of the religious festivals, the latter in anticipation of the expected entrance into the promised land, which was not yet deferred by the rebellion.[3] Thus naturally followed the summons of Moses, Aaron, Nadab and Abihu, and the seventy elders, to a solemn act of worship, involving the building of an altar, the offering of sacrifices, the consecration of the people, and the covenant. The appointment of the great festivals and of sacrifices leads naturally to the regular provision for their observance as established institutions, the modes of observance, the duties of priests, the structure and arrangement of the tabernacle; in short, the ritual of the future, the so-called Priest Code. For this the nine months at Sinai were sufficient, elaborate as it is. The vast and complicated Code Napoleon of 2,281 articles was completed and promulgated between March 5, 1803, and March 30, 1804. Kuenen is constrained to admit that "in itself it is not surprising that these regulations in Leviticus i.–vi. (in regard to priests and sacrifices) should precede the first performance in the tabernacle (Lev. ix.), and even the consecration of the priests, which itself involved certain sacrifices (Lev. viii.)." Of course not; it was the proper method.

Inasmuch as the Mosaic code was promulgated in different portions, and sometimes on occasion of definite occurrences, such as the death of Nadab and Abihu, the strife and the blasphemy, it was entirely natural that among or between the portions of ceremonial legislation there should intervene

---
[3] Kautzsch would destroy this connection by breaking in on four solid pages of E and JE with the assignment of six verses (Ex. xxiii. 14-19) to K.

many moral ordinances, as in Leviticus xviii.–xx., and exhortations, threats and promises, as in Leviticus xxvi. It was equally natural, if not inevitable, that laws of permanent force should be mingled with directions limited to desert life. It was equally natural also, and for this very reason, that at the close of the wandering and after the changes of forty years, there should be modifications introduced, especially on the eve of entering the new and permanent home.

Similar and far greater modifications following changes of circumstances could be cited. An illustration falling under the immediate observation of the present writer offers itself in the school laws of New Hampshire, growing out of the movement of population *within its borders.* For a long course of years, during the sparse occupation of the townships, there was what was called the town-school system. Then, as the population spread through the townships, came the district-school system; and within a few years past, in consequence of the depopulation of the outlying territories of the townships, has come a return to the township method, and with it a system in many respects simpler than the one which it displaced.

As the Priest Code, so called, sprung up naturally with the full establishment of the worship, as narrated, so the Deuteronomic Code is the natural offspring of the circumstances stated in the narrative, and its character is thoroughly explained by those circumstances. It contains the last solemn reminders, tender words and monitory injunctions of the great lawgiver in view of his death. Its loftiness and eloquence have always been recognized. But it is important to observe that the occasion and purpose control the character of what is loosely termed the code. Dr. Driver shall state for us its purpose and spirit: "In so far as it is a law-book, Deuteronomy may be described as a manual which, without entering into technical details (almost the only exception is xiv. 3-20, which explains itself), would instruct the Israelite in the ordinary duties of life. It gives general directions as to the way in which the annual feasts are to be kept and the offerings paid. It lays down a few fundamental rules concerning sacrifice; for a case in which technical skill would be required it refers to the priests (xxiv. 8). It prescribes the general principles by which the family and domestic life is to be regulated, specifying a number of cases likely to occur. Justice is to be equally and impartially administered. It prescribes a due position in the community to the prophet, and shows how even a monarchy may be so established as not to contravene the fundamental principles of the theocracy (xvii. 14 seq.). Deuteronomy is, however, *more than a mere code of laws;* it is the expression of a profound ethical and religious spirit, which determines its character in every part. The principles of human action cannot be more profoundly stated than is here done. Nowhere else in the Old Testament do we breathe such an atmosphere of generous devotion to God, and of large-heartedness towards man; nowhere else is it shown with the same fullness of detail how these principles may be made to permeate the entire life of the community." More is said to the same effect.

We could ask no better vindication of the view in regard to Deuteronomy which Dr. Driver assails, its time, place, and authorship. It is worthy of the devout and mighty legislator about to die. It is— or rather contains—but a general rehearsal of the duties of the Israelite, specifying some "cases likely to occur," and referring to the priests for matters of "technical skill," implying the established priesthood and its well-known functions. The inculcation of the great and "true principles of human action" does not weaken its profound impression by a preponderance of details. Hence the book and the "code" as they are; and its freedom from the specializations of the Levitical law not only does not imply its earlier origin, but naturally presupposes those details to supplement its broader and simpler injunctions.

Hence also, as the closing utterance of forty years, the reply to the chief difficulties alleged, namely, "variations" from other portions of the Mosaic legislation. In the words of Driver, "old enactments are repeated, and fresh enactments to meet special cases are added." But while even repeals of previous ordinances are entirely supposable, the cases actually cited as "conflicts" hardly sustain the assertion. Some of them are general references, some are supplementary. Take the first case cited by Dr. Driver, with his own italics: "In Deuteronomy language is used implying that *fundamental institutions of P are unknown to the author.* Thus, while Lev. xxv. 39-43 enjoins the release of the Hebrew slave in the year of Jubilee, in Deut. xv. 12-18 the legislator, *without bringing his new code into relation* with the different one of Leviticus, prescribes the release of the Hebrew slave in the seventh year of his service." Here is no conflict. Both laws stand. The slave is still to be released at the Jubilee; now it is added that he shall be released at the end of his seven years' service, whether the Jubilee year has arrived or not. There is no occasion to "bring it into relation," although modern legislators go through the form of "an act supplementary to an act." The case of the priests and Levites has been already discussed.

Thus the legislation, from the first, follows a natural order entirely consistent with the history that is given of it: A beginning made on the way to Sinai; at Sinai, during the long halt, a code of fundamental principles and precepts; then in connection with the religious cultus there was organized a complete system of ecclesiastical officers and ritual observances, all the legislation containing double traces of the transient and the future home; after forty years a final series of exhortations and warnings, together with such briefer and more general references to the earlier legislation as would give point to the warnings, and some modifications after the lapse and trial of forty years, and in immediate prospect of the new home.

Perhaps a few words should be said as to the impracticability or impossibility of such an imposition as would be the introduction of the Priest's Code in Moses' name at or after the exile. No one has more keenly ridiculed the theory in its very foundation conception than Klostermann. At a time, he says in substance, when for centuries the Israelites had been visited by prophets of Jehovah who gained obedience to their preaching as the word of God, and when famous prophets had reminded the people of their disobedience to what was known to them as the law of Moses, why should this prophetic man draw off the sure garb of the prophet and put on the paper coat of Moses? especially when Moses had promised prophets like unto himself? In the same act this man expresses the confidence that the name of Moses can give authority to his claims, and the disbelief that the same name can give authority to him as the successor of Moses. And inasmuch as Moses was the acknowledged founder of the whole religious polity from antiquity, what hope could this revolutionist have of securing acceptance for his widely divergent polity by attaching to it the old label? And why would not his claims be resisted by those whose office and interest conflicted with them, and either the fraud exposed, or counter claims set up? "He had no patent whereby he alone could falsify." And why should not some true prophet strip off the mask? The greater the number in the enterprise, the greater the danger of exposure. "In short," says Klostermann, "as is the result, so is the man, incomprehensible."

These and other insuperable difficulties may be pressed with unhesitating emphasis. How was it possible for any clique or combination to impose undisputed on the whole Jewish people a burdensome code of laws and regulations, newly invented, as having come steadily down from the remotest past? The nation which Moses and the prophets had always found a "stiff-necked" people must have suddenly become a whole flock of lambs. And the exile had not obliterated all knowledge of the previous conditions and customs. Nor could a small body of priests have absorbed all the intelligence of the Hebrew race. Even if there had been no intelligent questioner or objector left among all the returning exiles, it has been well asked, why did not Sanballat and Tobiah and their company, enemies and assailants of these leaders, instead of fruitlessly fighting them, simply expose them? The world's history does not present the parallel of such a stupendous imposition. It is very easy for ingenious and recluse scholars to devise such a chimera; but not all the scholarship and all the statesmanship of Germany could convert it into a reality.

Equally marvelous would have been the skill of the imaginary composition. These priests were far greater romancers than Sir Walter Scott; for, with all his native knowledge and antiquarian lore, he was guilty of occasional lapses in regard to times not more remote than the age of Elizabeth, while, as we are told, "no anachronism is traceable in the document" P.

Furthermore, what a magnanimous company of impostors it was, to introduce a scheme that left them of all the tribes without any landed possessions beyond the suburbs of the villages in which they were to reside; and what a submissive tribe were the Levites as a body, to yield without a murmur to the dictation of one family cutting them off from their lawful share of the land! Still further, when this body of priests, by the power of combination, had wrought this great revolution, what a singular fatuity in them thenceforth to deprive themselves of the power of further combination by dispersing themselves through forty-eight villages of Palestine! Surely our critics, who begin with the elimination of the supernatural, end with its accumulation and culmination.

Four things may be said in conclusion:

1. No book in the world's annals was ever so embedded in the literature, institutions, history, character and life of a nation as the Hexateuch.

2. The assaults upon its truthfulness contain a vast amount of arbitrary assumptions and denials, capricious dislocations, reconstructions and alterations of its text, scholastic criticisms of popular

speech, and closet speculations ignoring the course of human life and action.

3. Its literary peculiarities are no more, its obscurities and difficulties no greater, than were to be expected in narratives originating at the time and under the circumstances historically ascribed to them, are mostly susceptible of consistent explanation, and wholly fail to invalidate the historic view of their origin and character.

4. In view of the manifold, cumulative, and convergent evidence, and with due allowance for variations inevitable during the transmission from so remote an antiquity, the fundamental historic veracity of the Hexateuch remains unshaken, and may be as frankly and implicitly accepted by the modern Christian as by Christ and his apostles and the saints of all past ages.

APPENDIX

Note i., p. 5: Professor McCurdy's statement in the Sunday School Times of May 11, 1895, is worthy of careful perusal: " The ruined cities of Babylonia have only begun to give up their longest hidden secrets; but already we have learned that the Mediterranean coast-land was, during ancient times generally, under the control of the empires of the Tigris and the Euphrates. To Babylonia is due in large measure the formation of the political environment of Israel. Many centuries before the exodus the whole western region as far as the western sea was leavened by its material and mental culture. It was sixteen centuries after the first recorded expedition from Babylonia to the West that Abraham, himself an emigrant from the banks of the lower Euphrates, entered the land of promise. It was about a thousand years later(?) that the Hebrews again entered Palestine and became a nation. Seven centuries is the outside limit of their residence in Canaan as an independent nation. During the latter half of this period they were at the mercy of the Assyrians and Babylonians. Northern Israel was abolished by the one, southern Israel was deported by the other. . . . . The anomalous régime of the Egyptians in the sixteenth and seventeenth centuries was possible by reason of the division and conflicts of Babylonia and the ambitious daughter state Assyria. Similar conditions account for the expansion of the Hittites. In the same way Israel in Canaan and the Aramean principalities in Syria found scope and opportunity for development, because the Assyrians, having become once supreme from east to west, relapsed for over a century into feebleness and inaction. The book of Kings is now intelligible throughout. Viewed from our present standpoint, the political motive of the whole great stream of events is the incessant play and interaction of the minor currents in the Palestinian states as determined in direction and destiny by the mightier sweep of Babylonian and Assyrian enterprise."

The subject is further unfolded by him at very considerable length, and is also discussed by him in the volume, "Recent Research in Bible Lands." In this volume he also characterizes the results of Egyptological research: "We have the splendid vindication of the accuracy of the writer of the account of Israel's sojourn in lower Egypt. What is said in Genesis and Exodus of the character of the country, its government and its court, and the customs of the people, are shown to be pictures faithfully drawn from the life. . . . They (the Egyptian records) give us a fairly complete conception of that eventful era, from the sixteenth to the thirteenth century, in which Palestine was being prepared to become the abode of the chosen people. They demonstrate how the result of the conflict (with Syria) was to prevent either antagonist from permanently retaining Palestine for itself, and how it was still kept as a land of promise for the impending occupation by the Hebrews."

Note ii., p. 10: The time of Sheshenk or Shishak (I.), is proximately but not yet exactly settled. Following Brugsch (Hist. of Eg., Vol. ii., p. 215), I assume the date of his accession as 966 B. C. The date of the exodus may for the present be assumed, with Lepsius (Chronologie der Aegypter, p. 314, etc.), Ebers (Durch Gosen, p. 525), and apparently Poole (Smith's Dic. of the Bible, i., p. 591), at 1314 B. C.; although Bunsen would make it 1420 (Eg. Pl., i., p. 493), as would Kuenen (Relig. of Is. i., p. 121), and Brugsch "approximately" 1300 (His. Eg., i., p. 299). From the exodus in 1314 forty years of Moses' life and twenty-five of Joshua's captaincy (Josephus, Antiq., v., 1, 29) would extend down to 1249 B. C.; and thence to Shishak's accession in 966 would be 283 years. But from Carver's death to 1897 is 276 years, a difference of only seven years.

Note iii., p. 13: Theoretically, and in a general way, Kautzsch ascribes the book to J, E, P, Dt, R, variously combined and therefore involving other hands engaged in making the combinations. But the number and complications are somewhat bewildering. Thus the twenty-four chapters present the following permutations: J alone occurs but once, E six times, R 10, P 1, ? 7, Dt 19, JE 20, RE 4, ER 1, JEP 1, (JEP) 3, (PJE) 1, (JE) 6, (Dt) 2, JE (R) 1, (R) 1, P (R) 1, R (P) 1, R (JE) 5. The parentheses enclosing the letters, and the respective positions, before or after, indicate different supposed relations and shades of influence discerned by the analyst, amounting to twenty in all. It is a liberal supply of resources.

Note iv., p. 24: Judah's territory is defined as bordered by a wilderness, the southern "tongue" of the Salt Sea, a brook, a sea, an "ascent," the northern bay of the Salt Sea, a valley, another ascent, the "stone of Bohan," a river, the waters of En-shemesh, another valley, another valley, a mountain top, a fountain, another mountain, still another and another, with a terminus on the great (Mediterranean) sea—in part. It specifies thirteen cities along the line; it repeatedly mentions the direction as northward, southward, westward; in three instances it defines the place mentioned by a second or alternative name, and in two instances by its location; and in following the line it twice specifies how it "turned about," six times how it "went up," once how it "went down," eight times how it "passed along," twice how it "was drawn," three times it "went out" or terminated, and as many "goings out,"—all in business style.

Note v., p. 30: As matter of curious interest Nowairi's account is here given from the translation contained in the Quarterly Statement of the Palestine Exploration Fund, July, 1895. The sultan of the narrative is Beybars I. of Egypt, one of the great Mohammedan leaders. This is the account:

"In the month of Jumad the First, in the year 664, the Sultan issued orders for the building of a bridge over the river Jordan. It is a river which flows through the low-lying valley of Syria, which is called the

Sharieh. The bridge is in the neighborhood of Damieh, between it and Kurawa, and there happened in connection with it a wonderful thing, the like of which was never heard of. The Sultan charged the Emir Jamal ed Din ibn Nahar with the erection of the bridge, and commanded it to be made with seven arches. Officials were assembled for the purpose, and amongst them the Emir Bedr ed Din Mohammed ibr Rahal, the Governor of Nablous. They obtained supplies, collected workmen, and erected the bridge as commanded by the Sultan. When it was completed and the people were dispersed, part of the piers gave way. The Sultan was greatly vexed and blamed the builders, and sent them back to repair the damage. They found the task very difficult, owing to the rise of the waters and the strength of the current. But in the night preceding the dawn of the 17th of the month Rabi the First of the year 666 (8th December, A. D. 1267), the water of the river ceased to flow, so that none remained in its bed. The people hurried and kindled numerous fires and cressets, and seized the opportunity offered by the occurrence. They remedied the defects in the piers and strengthened them, and effected repairs which would otherwise have been impossible. They then dispatched mounted men to ascertain the nature of the event which had occurred. The riders mounted their horses and found that a lofty mound (Kabar) which overlooked the river on the west had fallen into it and dammed it up. A 'Kabar' resembles a hill, but is not actually a hill, for water will quickly disintegrate it like unto mud. The water was held up, and had spread itself over the valley above the dam. The messengers returned with this explanation, and the water was arrested from midnight until the fourth hour of the day. Then the water prevailed upon the dam and broke it up. The water floated down in a body equal in depth to the length of a lance, but made no impression upon the building owing to the strength given to it. The water carried away the apparatus used in the work of repairs. The occurrence is one of the most wonderful of events, and the bridge is in existence to this day."

M. Clermont-Ganneau (or his representative, Col. Watson) thinks that Nowairi's account "bears the evidence of the truth on the face of it," and that he could have no knowledge of the miracle related in the Bible. An explanatory statement is given by the translator: " In a district east of Beisan, and from fifteen to twenty miles south of the sea of Galilee, the river passes through what might be described as a gorge through steep banks of marl, sometimes nearly perpendicular, which on the right or left bank exceed 150 feet in height. These marly banks are frequently undermined by the water and fall in, making it dangerous to approach the river in times of flood." "The point indicated above, east of Beisan and about twenty-five miles above Damieh, is just the place where such an accident would be most likely to occur."

Note vi., p. 51: Dillmann, in his comment on Ex. ix. 31, cites various authorities on the time of year involved in the condition of the crops specified in that verse, when the plague of the hail occurred, and reaches the result that it was in January. So also Strack. But this was the seventh of the plagues, and the remaining three were not completed till the full moon of Nisan, March or April.

Of the threatened and recorded effects of the hail, namely, the destruction of men and animals, it is not necessary to accumulate instances. Though rare, well authenticated cases are on record as having occurred in Asia, Europe and America. The present writer encountered a hail-storm of a much milder and briefer description in Cairo, December 18, 1873. It rained at intervals throughout the afternoon, and though the hail fell briskly but about two minutes, the weather was so boisterous that few went on the streets unless compelled to do so, and the dancing dervishes omitted their customary performance.

Note vii., p. 52: Thus much is unquestionably contained in the statement in Ex. xiii. 18, rendered in the R. V. "went up armed," notwithstanding a slight diversity in the precise rendering of the Hebrew חֲמֻשִׁים, which occurs only in this passage, Josh. i. 14, iv. 12, Judg. vii. 11; and in Josh. iv. 12 appears to be exchanged for חֲלֻצִים in verse 13. The Septuagint shows in these passages alike the work of different translators and the slight uncertainty in their minds, rendering in Exodus πέμπτῃ γενεᾷ, in Josh. i. 14 εὔζωνοι, in Josh. iv. 12 διεσκευασμένοι, and in Judg. vii. 11 τῶν πεντήκοντα. The Vulgate has "armed," supported by Symmachus, Aquila, and (according to Gesenius) the Syriac and Targum. Gesenius renders a little loosely, "fierce, active, eager, brave in battle"; Fuerst, "equipped, ready for battle, armed"; Ewald (Geschichte, II., p. 98), "in complete battle array" (though in his note more exactly, from a theoretical derivation, "in five divisions," quinquefied); Keil, "ready, equipped, drawn up for battle"; De Wette and Strack, "geruestet"; Dillmann, "kampfgeruestet." Whichever of these forms is adopted, all agree with the necessary implication of the several passages that there was an orderly preparation for the march, something more even than going "by their hosts."

Note viii., p. 55: M. Naville would find Migdol in a supposed fortress near the present Serapeum, Pi-hahiroth in Pikeret (a word found on a monument of Rameses II., and also in the tablet of Philadelphos), which he conjectures to designate a place northwest of it near Pithom, and Baal-zephon, "some hill like Shekh Ennedek, on the Asiatic side." (Store City of Pithom, pp. 26, 25.) This theory places the crossing north of the Bitter Lakes. Dr. Dawson puts it south of them, at a point between the railway stations Fayid and Geneffe, supposing Pi-hahiroth at "some inconsiderable ancient ruins near that place," Migdol not a fortress but a watch tower on a commanding height, which he would designate as the western peak Jebel Shebremet, more than 500 feet high, and Baal-zephon as Jebel Musheikh, the prominent northern point of Jebel er

Rahah opposite in the Arabian desert. (Modern Science in Bible Lands, pp. 388-901.)

The strongest argument for the former extension of the Red Sea to the Bitter Lakes, in historic times, is M. Naville's supposed discovery, by two Latin inscriptions at Pithom, that Pithom was also the Roman Hierapolis, and that it was but nine miles from Clysma on the Sea. But since the Itinerary of Antonine states the distance at sixty miles, M. Naville is "compelled to admit that one of the documents is wrong." He decides for the inscriptions. But as one of these was in a calcareous wall (the place of the other not mentioned), they may not be in their original place; and moreover, one is dated about 306 A. D.; and besides, the shrinkage of the Red Sea would be brought to a comparatively recent date. The identification and proximity to Clysma must be considered not absolutely proven.

On the other side the present separation of the Gulf of Suez (except as connected by the canal) from the northern lakes by such elevations of land, which M. Mauriac, engineer of the Suez Canal, considers to be a tertiary formation, must be considered a somewhat formidable objection. And this elevation would therefore have had to take place since A. D. 306. That such an elevation has taken place during that period, or since the exodus, is a thing for which one would certainly desire some definite basis of known fact.

Note ix., p. 64: We assume without discussion Jebel Musa to be Sinai, and Sufsafeh the peak from which the law was proclaimed. The Ordnance Survey would seem to have settled it,—certainly for any one who has been over the ground and made careful investigations on the spot, and with the different theories in mind. Serbal, once advocated by respectable authorities (Ebers and Lepsius), clearly does not answer the conditions. The writer climbed the mountain and examined the adjacent valleys, Ajaleh and Aleyat. It might not be an insuperable objection that the mountain is extremely difficult of ascent; but these two nearest wadies are not only too remote for hearing from the mountain or for close approach, but they are comparatively small in extent, and at present so covered with boulders and cut up by winter torrents as hardly to afford room in either of them for a dozen tents.

Equally it seemed to the writer that at Jebel Musa, the wady Sebaiyeh could not have been, as some have supposed (Kurtz, Ritter, F. A. Strauss and even Tischendorf), the place of assembling, on the south side of the mountain, instead of Er Rahah on the north side, for several conclusive reasons: its small size, being but one hundred and forty-five acres, as we found by actual measurement; its surface covered with sharp, rough stones, affording no good camping place or even standing place, while Er Rahah is entirely clear; its separation from Jebel Musa by Jebel Sebaiyeh, some eight hundred feet high, whereas Er Rahah comes to the foot of Ras Sufsafeh; its entire lack of water (except when, as apearances indicate, the heavy rains sweep over it), all the springs being on the northern side of the mountain.

Note x., p. 65: Ain Gadiz has been singularly difficult of discovery and examination. The great weight of Dr. Robinson's opinion had been cast in favor of Ain el Weibeh in the Arabah, as many as forty miles to the northeast. Rev. John Rowlands in 1842 succeeded in finding the fountain Ain Gadiz, which he enthusiastically described. Though attention and favorable opinion were drawn to this identification, no traveler was able to visit the place, owing to the fact that it is in the territory of the Azazimeh Arabs, a degraded, jealous and violent tribe, and the sheiks of the Tiyahah tribe feared and refused to conduct travelers to it. Mr. Holland and Dr. Schaff were unable to go there, even Professor Palmer was refused by his sheik, and the present writer was taken by the same sheik to a wrong place, Ain Guseimeh ("Qasaymeh," Trumbull), a notable watering place, which Sheik Soleiman solemnly persisted in declaring to be Ain Gadiz. Mr. H. C. Trumbull was fortunate in finding the two older and wily sheiks disabled from being his guides, and in inducing the young Sheik Hamdh, by means of descriptions contained in Bartlett's "Egypt to Palestine," to conduct him to the genuine Ain Gadiz. He describes it as an oasis of verdure and beauty; a carpet of grass covering the ground, fig-trees laden with nearly ripe fruit, shrubs and flowers in variety and profusion, running water gurgling under the grass, and on the northeastern side a single mass or spur of solid rock from underneath which "issued the now abundant stream." The water flowed first into a large stoned well of primitive workmanship, near which was a marble watering trough; then another and larger well and a trough, and then a large basin or pool, seemingly the principal watering place, and the appearance around as though it had been frequented by flocks and herds for centuries. "Another and larger pool, lower down the slope, was suppled with water which rippled and cascaded along its narrow bed from the upper pool; and yet beyond this westward the water gurgled away under the grass, as we had met it when we came in, and finally lost itself in the parching wady from which this oasis opened. The water itself was remarkably pure and sweet, unequaled by any we had found since leaving the Nile." The description is given (abbreviated) in the words of Trumbull, "Kadesh Barnea," pp. 272-4. The visit was brief and his notes "hurried," but of great value. It is extremely desirable that a more protracted examination, not only of the fountain but of its surroundings and eastern and southeastern connections, should be made as soon as possible.

Note xi., p. 66: Professor Palmer suggests the eleven days' stages thus: 1. To Kibroth Hattaavah, which he would find at Erweis el Ebeirig; 2, to Hazeroth, placed by him, with Robinson and Stanley, at Ain Huderah, eighteen hours from Sinai; 3, 4, 5, three days' journey for the modern traveler towards Akabah; 6, to Elath (Akabah); 7, to Ezion Gaber (Diana of the Peutinger tables), $14\frac{1}{3}$ miles; 8, Rasa of the tables,

14⅓ miles; 9, to Gypsaria of the tables, the present Contellet Garayeh, 14⅓ miles; 10, to Lysa of the tables, modern Lussan, 26⅓ miles; 11, to Ain Gadiz (apparently about 14 miles). (Desert of the Exodus, pp. 422, 514.)

Note xii., p. 74: A body of laws devised by a company of priests who felt themselves at liberty to legislate for the restored Israel, says Dr. Hayman, "should show features of plan, symmetry and order pervading it. The Priestly Code, as our critics prefer to call this ill-digested mass, the Levitical *corpus juris*, is conspicuously defective in these characteristics. Take as a test sample the book of Leviticus itself, the most homogeneous of the whole and the one least charged with the historical element. On looking at the larger members and the earlier portions of its dislocated structure, we see an attempt at method too soon abandoned and forgotten in the result. I cannot claim space to analyze it thoroughly, but will exemplify from that inner section (to which, from the recurrence of some fixed phrases, containing the word 'holy' as their key, the name 'Law of Holiness' has lately been given), reaching from chapter xvii. (or xviii.) to xxv. inclusive. Of these, chapter xvii. contains hardly any of the peculiar phrases. The critics, however, include it. But the close of a previous chapter, xi., in verses 44 and 45, has them very markedly, and is therefore a detached member of the group which I am considering. Chapter xix., headed in our A. V. 'A repetition of sundry laws,' is a mass of unconnected precepts, lacking moreover coherence with what precedes and follows. Chapter xx. is not such a cento of shreds, but of its sections some repeat previous laws, others affix penal consequences to acts already forbidden. In a digest one would expect prohibition and penalty to come together. If chapters xxiii. and xxv. were consecutive we should have in them a tolerably complete summary of the law of holy times and seasons. But chapter xxv. diverges into the redemption of landed estates, and especially those of the poor Israelite and the Levite, connected, however, by the year of Jubilee and its privileges, with the main subject. But wedged uneasily between the two chapters we have chapter xiv., itself miscellaneous, beginning with the sanctuary, its lamps, their oil, etc., then diverging into blasphemy, and embedding a *lex talionis* between the sentence on the blasphemer and his execution. As regards repetitions, the law of keeping the Sabbath Day occurs some five or six times in this book only, to say nothing of other mention of it in other books. After twice prohibiting, as it were incidentally, the eating of blood, or flesh with the blood, in chapters iv. 17, vii. 26, 27, we have the statement of the principle emphatically united with the same precept in chapter xvii. 10-14, the precept itself further recurring in chapter xix. 26, as well as three or four times in Deuteronomy; besides the original prohibition to Noah in Gen. ix. 4. Similarly, eating 'that which dieth of itself' is forbidden in this book thrice, besides one each in Exodus and Deuteronomy."

Dr. Hayman, having thus examined sections, observes that the distribution of almost any *subject* yields the same result. He pointedly inquires, "Is it conceivable that they (the supposed company of organizing scribes) would have bequeathed to their successors such a maze of jurisprudence as the Pentateuchal," and he confidently affirms that the theory leaves this striking feature of the legislation "utterly inexplicable. It subverts that primary instinct of order which governs the human mind, and that precisely at the time when it should be paramount." His entire article is weighty.

Note xiii., p. 79: That the reader may see that there is no exaggeration in these statements, Erman's brief account of a part of the jewelry found on the body of Queen Ahhotep is here submitted: "The fineness of the gold work, and the splendid coloring of the enamels, are as admirable as the tasteful forms and the certainty of the technique. Amongst them is a dagger, on the dark bronze blade of which are symbolical representations of war, a lion rushing along, and some locusts, all inlaid in gold; in the wooden handle are inserted three-cornered pieces of precious metal; three female heads in gold form the top of the handle, while a bull's head of the same precious metal conceals the place where the handle and blade unite. The sheath is of gold. One beautiful axe has a gilded bronze blade, the central space being covered with the deepest blue enamel, on which King Ahmes is represented stabbing an enemy; above him a griffin, the emblem of swiftness, hastens past. The handle of the axe is of cedar wood plated with gold, and upon it the names of the king are inlaid in colored precious stones. Gold wire is used instead of the straps which in ordinary axes bind the handle and the blade together. Perhaps the most beautiful of these precious things, however, is the golden breast-plate in the form of a little Egyptian temple. King Ahmes is standing in it; Amon and Ré pour water over him and bless him. The contours of the figures are formed with fine strips of gold, and the spaces between them are filled in with paste and colored stones. This technique, now called cloisonné, the same which has been carried to such perfection by the Chinese, was often employed by the Egyptians with great taste. The illustration heading this chapter (xviii. in the book) gives a good illustration of the character of the work, but it is impossible to represent the brilliance of the enamel, and the beauty of the threads of gold that divide the partitions."

These are but specimens of a very considerable collection, in all which gold is the precious metal, with one exception (so far as the present writer recalls): a boat of solid gold, twelve rowers of silver, the boat being mounted on a wooden truck with bronze wheels. The Dashur collection is understood to be quite as extensive. The art of gilding was also extensively practiced, apparently as early as the Middle Empire in some degree, and much more in later times. (Erman, p. 462.)

Note xiv., p. 104: To illustrate a little further the force of Mr. Poole's reasoning, an additional extract is given: "If the Hebrew documents are of the close of the period of the kings of Judah, how is it that they are true of the earlier condition, not of that which was contemporary with those kings? Why is the Egypt of the Law markedly different from the Egypt of the prophets, each condition being described consistently with its Egyptian records, themselves contemporary with the events? Why is Egypt described in the Law as one kingdom, and no hint given of the break-up of the empire into the small principalities mentioned by Isaiah (xix. 2)? Why do the proper names belong to the Ramesside and earlier age, without a single instance of those Semitic names which came into fashion with the Bubastic line in Solomon's time? Why do Zoan-Rameses and Zoar take the place of Migdol and Tahpanhes? Why are the foreign mercenaries, such as the Lubim, spoken of in the constitution of Egyptian armies in the time of the kingdom of Judah, wholly unmentioned? The relations of Egypt with foreign countries are not less characteristic. The kingdom of Ethiopia, which overshadowed Egypt from before Hezekiah's time and throughout his reign, is unmentioned in the earlier documents. The earlier Assyrian empire, which rose for a time on the fall of the Egyptian, nowhere appears."

The entire article is a powerful argument, deserving a careful perusal. It is at the same time careful and candid. He remarks that "the date of Deuteronomy is a separate question," and adds: "Leaving this problem aside, the early age of the first four books does unquestionably involve great difficulties, but not nearly so great as the hypotheses of late date when they are confronted with the Egyptian records."

In a note he makes a statement concerning Deuteronomy worth quoting: "The lamented Deutsch, remarkable among Hebraists for his acute literary perception, remarked to the writer that he could not explain the origin of Deuteronomy on any other hypothesis than its original Mosaic authorship, redaction being enough to account for its peculiarities. This opinion may not have been maintained, and therefore it is merely stated as a remarkable hint thrown out in conversation. Many scholars would not believe that Deutsch could have held the view for a moment; this is why the recollection deserves to be put on record."

Note xv., p. 132: Lefèvre proceeds thus: "Separated from these Egypto-Semites by the Himalaya and the desert, slowly increasing tribes of white men, part shepherds and part agriculturists, monogamous, worshipers of the heavenly bodies, gradually under the pressure of the Mongols leave their common country, forgetting each other as they travel, but retaining their idioms and their acquired culture exactly in *the proportion of their increasing distance*. The Celts are driven westward by the Gauls, the Gauls by the Germans, these by the Slavs and the Lithuanians, themselves urged forward and finally overrun by the Mongols and the incursion of the Huns. The future Hindus are already making their way among the affluents of the Indus. Lastly, the Greeks and Latins, passing south of the Celts, Germans and Slavs, and north of the Semitic world, follow the right bank of the Danube, and one stream of them flows towards Thrace and Thessaly, the other towards the Tiber. The Iranians alone remain, harassed by the continual attacks of the Turks; they reach Media, Persia, conquer and take possession of the old Semitic empires, and come into collision in Ionia and at Marathon with their old neighbors now forgotten, with the Hellenes, already masters of the Mediterranean basin. This large and simple view gives the true meaning of history." It unwittingly conforms in a remarkable degree not only to the recorded fact of the dispersion from near the center described, but, as may appear later, with the Scripture account of the lines of dispersion.

Note xvi., p. 150: Rawlinson adopts the identification of the Kimmerii, in their descendants, with the Cimbri and the Cymry (or Welsh) and also with the Cambri, as they were designated by the Romans, and would recognize the same fundamental name in Cumberland. The Roman historians, it will be remembered, called the modern Jutland by the name Chersonesus Cimbrica.

If we might safely follow Rawlinson's guidance, in parts of which he finds support in other authorities, the successive movements of the races westward across Europe would become somewhat obvious. For he finds the Celts among the descendants of the Kimmerii, and (supported by Niebuhr and Boeckh) the Slavs among the Scythian descendants of Magog, the Teutons among the descendants of the Thracians, whom he identifies with Tiras, locating the latter on the Bosporus, partly west of it. We should then see, not only as we do, Javan pushing gradually and surely along the Mediterranean to Greece and Italy, and Magog, as is admitted, driving Gomer northwest beyond the Euxine, but remaining in permanent possession as the Slavic race, and the Teutonic descendants of Tiras pressing their way westerly like a wedge between the now established Slavs and their driven predecessors, the Celts, until the latter were forced to the coasts of the Atlantic. But the view, however attractive, is in two of its stages too precarious at present to adopt with any confidence.

Note xvii., p. 156: The classical student does not need to be reminded of Ovid's description, Metamor. i., 242, seq. It is noticeable how distinct is the account of the flood given by Lucian, who repeatedly declares it to be Greek tradition. Thus (De Syria Dea, 12) he relates that the former race of men were destroyed for their extreme wickedness; that the earth gave forth water, great rains fell, the rivers rose, the sea swelled, till all things became water, and all men perished. Deucalion alone was saved for his piety. He built a great ark ($λάρναξ$), entered it with his wife and children, brought in by pairs hogs, horses, lions, serpents, and all other creatures, and remained there with them in a divinely established friendship so long as the waters prevailed.

Note xviii., p. 183: The older tables of great longevity have been justly criticised as resting often on insufficient evidence. Such appears to have been the case with that given by Prichard in his "Natural History of Man" (1843). He gives, after Mr. Easton, the following list of persons who had attained the ages attached: From the age of 100 to 110 inclusive, 1,310 persons; from 110 to 120 years, 267; from 120 to 130 years, 84; from 130 to 140, 26; from 140 to 150, 7; from 150 to 160, 3; from 160 to 170, 2; from 170 to 180, 3. On the other hand, in 1873 W. J. Thoms, Deputy Librarian of the British House of Lords, published a book on "Human Longevity," in which he examined and justly objected to the evidence on which very many of these instances rested; but he went to the extreme of inclining to assign to the region of fiction all or nearly all cases of alleged age greater than 105. Zoeckler in his "Urstand des Menschen" (pp. 249 seq.) shows the unreasonableness of this position, and thinks it undeniable that there are well proved instances of those who have lived to be from 120 to 130 years, and apparently very rare cases of persons who have outlived the first half of their second century. An article on this subject in Chambers' Journal in 1880 (copied into the Eclectic, Oct., 1880) contained many facts, perhaps not all carefully sifted, sustaining this position of Zoeckler. Any one who keeps a record of persons who die in this country more than a hundred years old, will weary of the task; and he will meet with apparently authenticated instances of the attainment of 112 or even 120 years and more. While, therefore, the skepticism of Thoms was uncalled for, it remains true that the greatest age now attained lies between one and two hundred years.

Note xix., p. 203: Delitzsch makes the following references: Is. xxxviii.5, Jonah ii.4, Zech.ii. 4. Strack adds to these Judg. ii. 6, 1 Ki. vii. 13. Dr. Green adopts a slightly varied but equivalent rendering: "Jehovah God, having formed, etc., brought." He adds, "In numberless passages in the English version of the Bible similar expressions are paraphrased in order to express this subordination of the first verb to the second," as, e. g., Gen. iii. 6. And as to the notion that order of mention in the Scriptures must be the order of time, he shows its absurdity by such examples as Gen. xxiv.64, 65; Ex. iv. 31; Josh. ii. 22; 1 Ki. xiii. 12; Is. xxxii. 2-5, and one or two other cases. For a fuller discussion of the alleged contradiction and of the double narrative, the reader is referred to his learned treatise.

It may be added in further explanation of the objections to a fair understanding of this artless narrative, Dr. Driver insists that while the original account of creation gives the order, vegetation, animals, man, this chapter gives it, man, vegetation, animals; and assumes to know the "progression evidently intentional on the part of the narrator." The order of temporal progression certainly does appear intentional in the first chapter of Genesis (with certain qualifications), but that the writer in referring to past facts is logically or actually held to the order of time is a view that the history of all literature contradicts. The very page in which Dr. Driver advances this notion, will not stand such a test.

Note xx., p. 206: Although it is impracticable to discuss the several theories, it may be well to mention briefly some of the more prominent and least impossible ones. It is a curious fact that less than thirty years ago the American Tract Society should have published a book in which the Nile and the Ganges were made the companions of the Euphrates and Tigris in the garden of Eden. (Studies in Bible Lands, by Rev. W. L. Gage, 1869, pp. 16-18.) Cush was of course the first stumbling block, which introduced the Nile, and then the Ganges entered easily.

A late and somewhat confident modern view is that of Friedrich Delitzsch, which has attracted no little attention. In addition to the two unquestionable rivers, he supposes two other streams to be two channels or canals branching from the Euphrates below Babylon, the one on the east, the Pallakopas (Pishon), the other on the west, the Guchanu (Gihon). He supposes the Euphrates and Tigris originally to have flowed separately to the gulf; and since the waters of the former, as it is affirmed, find their way to some degree in small streams into the latter above Babylon, the one original Euphrates passes on through four streams below Babylon, near which place he finds the garden of Eden. The theory is open to serious objections, and appears to have received more attention than assent. We may say, perhaps, that it is not impossible. It coincides in general, however, with the view of numerous other modern writers in placing the garden near or below Babylon. Some of these have approximated so near this opinion as to regard the two streams as the east and west branches of the Schatt el Arab, the united stream below the junction of the two great rivers (Bochart, and proximately Tayler Lewis); while Sir Henry Rawlinson, fixing the location in Babylonia, finds the two streams in question to be branches of the Euphrates and Tigris.

Sir J. W. Dawson (Modern Science in Bible Lands, pp. 195 seq.) with great confidence maintains that the Pison is the Karun and the Gihon is the Kerkha, two streams which rise far in the northeast and empty into the Schatt el Arab. The grave objection is that these rivers, rising in a different direction and far away from the first two, can in no sense be called divisions of one stream into four heads. Pressell anticipated this view, but not the objection, by saying that the division was not downward from the source but upward from the junction; which contravenes the description.

There is one theory which perhaps deserves more careful attention than it has received. It is the view that the locality of Eden was in Armenia, in the form stated by Pellicanus of Zurich in 1533, more thoroughly shaped and maintained by the famous Reland in 1706, and with some modifications accepted by Von Raumer, Kurtz, Baumgarten, Bunsen, Keil, Zahn, J. P. Lange, Rosenmüller, Kitto, Chesney. Oettli mentions it as one of two views both of which are favored by many circumstances and opposed by others; and Strack (in

1894) holds that it is a theory to which the biblical statements and the investigations concerning the original abode of the race "are not unfavorable." The greatest objection is removed, provided the original "river" can be understood as denoting, not a single stream, but the waters collectively, "the river system," water supply, of the region. And, aside from instances which can be adduced in support of this interpretation, there is the actual *fact* that the Euphrates and Tigris, though originating in the collective waters of the region, do not come from the same one stream. This would seem decisive. Justified by this fact, these writers fix on the Araxes, which, as Col. Chesney ascertained, rises midway between two main sources of the Euphrates, about ten miles from each, and flows a thousand miles east into the Caspian Sea. This would be the Gihon—although Michaelis made it the Pison. For the fouth river Reland selected the Phasis (Rion), flowing into the Black Sea, and found the land of Havilah, which it compasses, in the ancient Colchis, the land of the golden fleece, the consonant letters of which, with a slight transposition, somewhat closely correspond. Kitto and Chesney, however, fix in preference on the Halys (Kizil Irmak) for the fourth river, as rising nearer the sources of the others. It is also a much longer stream, equally encompasses the ancient land of gold, passing through a land of minerals, where silver mines are still known. This would include the four great rivers of the region, all rising within a comparatively short distance of one another. The interpretation encouraged by the fact is apparently sustained to some degree by linguistic usage, as in Jonah ii. 3, Ps. xxii. 4. Lange in his comment on the passage adduces several other instances bearing in the same direction. The chief objection to the interpretation is the use of the word (*nahar* in Hebrew) in a different sense from the use two verses later. It may be replied that (1) such diverse uses in even closer connections are found, e. g., "let the dead bury their dead"; (2) the Hebrew has no word or phrase corresponding to our phrase "water system" or "supply," and perhaps *nahar* comes as near as any, or nearer; (3) the facts in the actual usage here would seem to settle the question, for the Tigris is certainly a river, and the waters in which it and the Euphrates both originate are not a river. The whole subject cannot be discussed here, but a fuller, though brief statement by the present writer may be found in the American edition of Smith's Dictionary of the Bible at the end of the article," Eden." This explanation has seemed to him to have stronger claims than any other yet advanced on a difficult subject. It is to be borne in mind that Eden is a region in which the garden was situated, that the land of Havilah cannot be confidently determined, and that all attempts, like those of Sir John Dawson and others, to decide it from the products bdellium and the onyx stone are hopelessly adrift, because, after all is said, no man now knows what they were.

Note xxi., p. 223: Lenormant says: "Certain it is that at the epoch of the great influx of oriental traditions into the classic world, a representation of this nature appears upon several Roman sarcophagi, where it undoubtedly indicates the introduction of a legend analogous to the narrative of Genesis, and akin to the formation of man by Prometheus. A famous sarcophagus in the museum of the capitol exhibits, close beside the Titan, son of Japetos, who is finishing his task of moulding, the pair, man and woman, in a state of primitive nudity, standing at the foot of a tree, the man in the act of gathering fruit. A bas-relief incrusted in the wall of the little garden of Villa Albani at Rome presents the same group, but more closely conformed to the Hebrew tradition, since a great snake twists itself around the trunk of the tree under whose shadows the two mortals are standing. . . . But I find incontrovertible evidence of the existence of such a tradition in the cycle of the indigenous legends of the people of Kenaan, since the discovery of a curious vase painted in the Phenician manner, dating back to the seventh or sixth century B. C., and found by General Cesnola in one of the most ancient sepulchers of Idalium on the Island of Cyprus. We trace thereupon a tree with foliage; from the lower branches hang on either side two great bunches of fruit; a huge serpent approaches the tree with an undulating motion, and is in the act of opening his jaw to seize one of the fruits." Pp. 101, 102.

Note xxii., p. 229: "If now the term *day* is to be understood literally, it is clear that the narrative of Genesis cannot accord with the teaching of Geology; are we at liberty, then, to understand it in any other way? This question must be answered, not by a discussion as to the proper meaning of the Hebrew term employed (respecting which there is no doubt), but by inquiring whether or not it may have been used by the writer metaphorically. Although there are no precise parallels in the Old Testament for such a metaphorical use of the word, it seems on the whole reasonable to concede it here. The author, it may be supposed, while conscious that the divine operation could not be measured by human standards of time, nevertheless was desirous of accommodating artificially the period of creation to the divisions of the week; and hence adopted the term *day* in a figurative sense. If this view be correct, the term will have been used by him consciously, as a metaphor, for the purpose of his representation, it being really his intention to designate by it a period of time. The several days, with their 'evenings' and 'mornings,' will thus be the form under which the work is represented as taking place; they will not constitute part of the reality." (Driver's Sermons on the Old Testament, p. 166.)

Note xxiii., p. 236: Thus Croll quotes with approval Professor Winchell: "We have not," says Professor Winchell, "the slightest grounds for assuming that matter existed in a certain condition from all eternity, and only began undergoing its changes a few millions or billions of years ago. The essential activity of the powers ascribed to it forbids the thought. For all that we know—and indeed as the *conclusion* of all we know—primal matter began its progressive changes on the morning of its existence. As therefore the series of changes is demonstrably finite, the lifetime of matter is necessarily finite. There is no real refuge from this conclusion; for if we suppose the beginning of the present cycle to have been only the restitution of an older order effected by the operations of natural causes, and suppose—what science is unable to comprehend—that older order to be a similar reinauguration, and so on indefinitely through the past, we only postpone the predication of an absolute beginning, since, by all the admissions of modern scientific philosophy, it is a necessity of nature to run down."

Croll proceeds to say for himself, "These are consequences which necessarily follow from every theory of stellar evolution which has hitherto been advanced." And after some remarks on the impact theory, he closes thus: "We have no grounds to conclude that there is anything eternal, except God, Time and Space. But if time and space be subjective, as Kant supposes, and not modes pertaining to the existence of things in themselves, then God alone was uncreated, and *of* Him and *to* Him are all things." (Croll's Stellar Evolution, pp. 111, 112.) We are not concerned with the suggestion concerning time and space, but with the view concerning matter. Such views are not confined to these scientists.

Note xxiv., p. 251: Few things in the history of literature or science are more striking or cautionary than the great and rapid diminution of the antiquity assigned to the human race. The change in Le Conte's two editions is in point. Dr. Hunt, a president of the British Anthropological Society (cited by Southall, Recent Origin, p. 46), held that the proper date is nine million years ago. Draper (Conflict, p. 199) wanted "many hundreds of thousands of years." Lubbock (Prehistoric Times, p. 414) wants from 100,000 to 240,000. Lyell, who assigned man's appearance before the close of the glacial period, at first dated that period many hundred thousand years ago. While man's advent is still regarded as pre-glacial, the latest investigations in America tend to bring down the close of the glacial period in this country to within some eight thousand years. The results may be found in Wright's "Ice Age in North America." Prestwich says that his opinion previously expressed against Croll's view that 80,000 years intervened between paleolithic and neolithic man, and his belief that the close of the glacial period comes down to within 10,000 or 12,000 years of our times, is confirmed by these investigations. (Journal of Victoria Institute, vol. xxvii., p. 281.)

In like manner much more cautious opinions are beginning to be expressed concerning the actual antiquity of certain ancient nations to which it was customary to ascribe a kind of fabulous antiquity. Thus Max Mueller, in an article on "The Enormous Antiquity of the East" in The Nineteenth Century (May, 1891), writes: "*Authentic* history begins when we have the testimony of a cotemporary or eye-witness to the events which he relates. *Constructive* history and constructive chronology rest on deduction. The authentic history of India does not begin before the third century B. C. Constructive history places the Vedic hymns about 1,500 B. C. In Egyptian history, whatever date we accept, we must bear in mind that, like all ancient Egyptian dates, they rest on the construction which we put on Manetho's dynasties, and on the fragments of papyri, like the royal papyrus of Turin. The chronology of the Old Testament is likewise constructive. In China authentic history cannot be said to begin before the burning of the books by the Emperor Khin in 213 B. C.

"In Babylon, Nabonidus 550 B. C. lighted on the foundation stone of the Sun-god temple at Sippara, which had not been seen by any of his predecessors for 3,200 years. Hence 550+3200=3750, the time of Sargon's son, Naran Sin. But to use a foundation-stone on its own authority as a stepping-stone over a gap of 3,200 years, is purely constructive chronology."

In view of these obvious considerations, one is a

little surprised at the entire confidence with which Professor McCurdy affirms, "There is no reasonable doubt that the reckoning made by the experts of Nabonidus was correct." How do we know that there was a "reckoning" and that "experts" made it? (McCurdy's History, Prophecy and the Monuments, i., p. 97.)

In the line of caution, Professor Winchell in 1881 (Preadamite Man, p. 421) could "discover no valid ground whatever for the opinion that the stone age in Europe began more than 2500 or 3000 B. C."

Note xxv., p. 263: Thus Professor Davis thinks the form Shabbatu (or Shabattu) not certain, and that the phrase translated "rest of the heart" elsewhere denotes the appeasing the heart of the gods—which would be a more directly religious expression than the other. He, however, very fully affirms that "the seven day period was a recognized standard," and "the auspicious and sacred character of the seventh day" (pp. 32, 33).

Note xxvi., p. 263: Thomas proceeds (Le Jour du Seigneur, p. 268), "These are not the only resemblances which might be indicated. Thus the ancient Germans appear to have had the week before receiving from the Romans its mythological appellation; the Hindoos make use for many ages of the planetary week, and even in some regions specially solemnize one of its days. In reviewing the terms by which the number seven is designated in numerous languages, we become aware of curious philological facts which might become important. We should love to trace further the remarkable connection which we have already pointed out between the idea of that number and the oath."

Note xxvii., p. 270: Few persons consider how constantly and how confidently we rely on the kind of evidence which may be called traditional or prescriptive, the weight and influence of which cannot be stated in technical form. Whately has called attention to it forcibly in his little book on the evidences of Christianity. In regard to the matter of authorship Cardinal Newman in his "Grammar of Assent" (pp. 284, 286) expresses himself thus: "If we deal with arguments in the mere letter, the question of the authorship of works in any case has much difficulty. I have noticed it in the instance of Shakespeare, and of Newton. We are all certain that Johnson wrote the prose of Johnson, and Pope the poetry of Pope; but what is there but prescription, at least after cotemporaries are dead, to connect together the author of the work and the owner of the name? Our lawyers prefer the examination of present witnesses to affidavits on paper; but the tradition of "testimonia," such as are prefixed to the classics and the Fathers, together with the absence of dissentient voices, is the adequate groundwork of our belief in the history of literature." "We have no means of inferring unconditionally that Virgil's episode of Dido, or of the Sibyl, and Horace's 'Te quoque mensorem' and 'Quem tu Melpomene' belong to that Augustan age which owes its celebrity mainly to those poets. Our common sense, however, believes in their genuineness without any hesitation or reserve, as if it had been demonstrated, and not in proportion to the available evidence in its favor, or the balance of arguments."

Note xxviii., p. 310: The fact that the date of the Pentateuch or of portions of it cannot be determined by language or style is now conceded somewhat generally. Professor Robertson (p. 42) quotes Kuenen to that effect. Dr. Driver (Introduction, p. 117) speaks very decidedly, even going so far as to say that "there is no perceptible archaic flavor in the style of JE," the supposed oldest writers, and placing his argument as to their date wholly on other grounds. Dr. B. W. Bacon, who endeavors to speak for the drift of modern criticism, says (Genesis of Genesis, p. 58), "The internal evidence of the late origin of P is mainly derived from evidences of development in the legislation beyond the point of Deuteronomy and Ezekiel." In fact the arguments of the leaders of this school of interpretation direct their chief attention to what they term the historical considerations—which historical considerations, however, do not necessarily include any historical *allusions*, but are founded, as in the remark of Dr. Bacon, upon alleged marks of progress or development. Thus in a very recent commentary on Judges, the writer admits that "the author's motive, the lesson he enforces, and the way in which he makes the history teach are almost the only data at our command to ascertain the age in which he lived," but he asserts that these criteria are among the "most conclusive" and "determine beyond reasonable doubt." In regard to some fourteen chapters of which he determines the age, he confesses "there are no allusions to historical events which might serve us as a clue," and "almost the only criterion is their relation to the religious development." One thing that precludes these critics from all arguments derived from the language, is the summary manner in which they disintegrate the text.

Note xxix., p. 282: Among many other passages, the author would gladly have called attention to the phenomena exhibited in the treatment of Gen. xxii. 8-15, xxviii. 12, 13, 15-20, xxix. 24-31, xxx. 17-29; Num. x. 29–xvii., xx.–xxvi.

In so cautious a critic as Dr. Driver the reader who will take the trouble to count his tabulations of the Hexateuch, will find (besides other divisions) about fifty fragments of three or four verses, more than forty of one verse each, more than thirty of half verses, and several instances of verses divided into fragments *a*, *b* and *c* to maintain the analysis. Besides these distinct dismemberments, resort is abundantly made to "elements" not tabulated, numerous passages covered by "partly," "in the main," "additions," "a few phrases besides," "other independent sources," "other sources," passages "modeled upon the style of" a given writer, and the additional safeguard of "one of the final redactors of the Pentateuch." Here is ample room for an *aliquid ex aliquo*.

Professor Fitz Hommel, in his latest utterance, does not hesitate to express himself thus: "It is unquestionable that the higher critics have gone virtually bankrupt in their attempt to unravel, not only chapter by chapter, but verse by verse, and clause by clause, the web in which the different sources are entangled, arguing frequently from premises which are altogether false." (The Ancient Hebrew Tradition, 1897.) This comment is the more noteworthy, inasmuch as he does not assent to the denial of all "sources."

Note xxx., p. 342: Klostermann thus ridicules the process of the analysis: "For our science Moses is indeed dead; but he has found an heir of his office, though perhaps first a thousand years later, to produce the Genesis of to-day with scissors and glue-brush out of independent, collected parchments. Without further preliminary, we leap over the two thousand years and put ourselves with our Genesis behind his chair to watch him as he has so nicely pasted them together, and with kindly regard to our curiosity has preserved the colors and uncovered the seams that we may at our pleasure take them apart and group them tastefully. Yet we are at an evil disadvantage in comparison with Astruc (the early analyst). For to him Moses was a man of flesh and blood, he knew him from what he had written, and he knew his purpose. Our redactor, on the contrary, is absolutely unknown; he is everywhere and nowhere; we know not his purpose, his style, his materials. For he himself has at most written this or that line; but as soon as we will lay hold of him, one says it is but a gloss, another that it is an older addition made before his time; and so he glides away like a phantom." (Knobel, Der Pentateuch, p. 5.)

Professor Ramsay, who has done so much towards elucidating the book of Acts, describes and characterizes a similar attempt, but on a much more limited scale, to disintegrate that history: "Dr. Clemen supposes that three older documents, a history of the Hellenistic Jews, a history of Peter, and a history of Paul, were worked into one work by a Judaist-Redactor, who inserted many little touches and even passages of considerable length to give a tone favorable to the Judaizing type of Christianity; and that this completed book was again worked over by an anti-Judaist Redactor II., who inserted other parts to give a tone unfavorable to the Judaizing type of Christianity, but left the Judaic insertions. Finally a Redactor III., of neutral tone, incorporated a new document (vi. 1-6), and gave the whole its present form by a number of small touches.

"When a theory becomes so complicated as Clemen's, the humble scholar who has been trained only in philological and historical method finds himself unable to keep pace, and toils in vain behind this daring flight. We shall not at present stop to argue from examples in ancient and modern literature that a dissection of this elaborate kind cannot be carried out." And Professor Ramsay proceeds to pronounce it in this case "simply impossible." (Ramsay's St. Paul the Traveler and the Roman Citizen, pp. 12, 13.)

Note xxxi., p. 325: In the references to geographical position classed by Dr. Bacon (p. 44) as *post-Mosaic* are these: "The Pentateuch writers use invariably the stereotyped expressions for north, south, east and west, which nevertheless have no significance except for a dweller of Palestine. Thus south is literally 'Negeb-ward'; west is 'sea-ward,' toward the Mediterranean." The answer is ready, that they were used because they *were* the stereotyped Hebrew terms, and the Pentateuch, being written in the Hebrew language, must use them. The words for north (occurring in the Old Testament more than 130 times), west and south, were the only ones in common use. It is also said: "The expression 'beyond Jordan' is always shown by the context to mean eastward, whereas to Moses beyond Jordan would be west." The statement is too sweeping. The phrase is understood to have taken on a geographical signification, designating a point of compass, eastward. But the actual double usage of it, and the explanatory terms frequently connected with it in Deuteronomy and the early chapters of Joshua, go to show the ambiguity that hung over it when Moses and Joshua were themselves on the east side of the Jordan. And this curious vibration between the geographical and the general or unrestricted meaning is a strong corroboration of the narrative. Where no question would be likely to arise, "beyond Jordan" is east of Jordan, as Gen. l. 10, 11, Josh. ix. 10, xvii. 5; also in the administrative assignment of territory, or in a reference to it, the technical sense occurs—Josh. i. 14, xiv. 3. It is so used Deut. l. 5, and made distinct by being "in the plains of Moab," and Num. xxxv. 14 by being in contrast to "Canaan." In several instances a possible ambiguity is removed by adding "toward the sunrising," Josh. l. 15, xxiii. 7, Deut. iv. 41, 47, 49. Joshua on the east side of Jordan makes it clear by the same addition, it having been also used undefined in the previous verse. In Josh. xii. 1 the writer of the book adopts the same method. But Moses, in his address while east of the Jordan, naturally uses the phrase in its untechnical meaning, namely, the other side of Jordan from him, Deut. iii. 15, 20. In two notable instances where it is used in this wider sense and applied to the western region, the doubt is removed by adding "toward the going down of the sun," or "westward." A still more curious instance occurs in Num. xxxii., where in verse 32 the Reubenites and Gadites use the word in its technical sense, and in verse 19 in both senses, distinguished, however, by adding "eastward" and "forward."

An anachronism is also alleged in Gen. xl. 15, where "the land of the Hebrews" occurs. But there was an obvious reason why Joseph should not say the land of "Canaan," identifying himself with the Canaanites; and as "Abram the Hebrew" (xiv. 13) and three generations of his descendants had occupied the land of promise, the anachronism is not apparent.

Some objections as to indications of time made by the same writer may here be mentioned. The phrases "unto this day" (Gen. xxxii. 32, xxxv. 20; Deut. x.

8), and "the landmark which they of old time have set," are said to point to mementos of antiquity. But they are entirely vague, and may apply to any longer or shorter period. In Josh. xxii. 3 the interval appears to be but a few months. Gen. xv. 13, 17 has been explained in the body of this volume. On the phrase (Gen. xxxvi. 31), "before there reigned any king over Israel," as implying authorship after the monarchy was established, Dr. Briggs (Higher Criticism of the Hexateuch, p. 82), while inclined to that view, yet remarks, "We cannot deny to Moses the conception of a future kingdom in Israel. In view of the fact that the Israelites had just come out of bondage to the Egyptian kings, and that they were surrounded by nations having kings, it was natural to think of kings for Israel likewise." So also Delitzsch substantially. The statements, Gen. xii. 66, xiii. 76, "the Canaanite was then in the land," are alleged to bring down the date to the time when the Canaanites had disappeared, subsequent to Solomon. It is a large inference from a small premise. The first instance is a natural comment on the remarkableness of the promise that Abraham should possess the land of which the Canaanite was then in possession. In the second case, it may refer to the difficulty of finding pasturage, or to the danger of a quarrel between the two bodies of herdsmen when the Canaanites and Perizzites were on the ground. The comments on the character of Moses (Num. xii. 3, xxxiv. 10) may be understood as made by the one who recorded his death. The conquered "land of his possession" (Deut ii. 12) might possibly be, as Keil would have it, the portion already conquered east of the Jordan, or, in accordance with the theory of a revision, it may be one of the explanatory notes which Rosenmueller and others have recognized in several passages, especially in Deuteronomy, which interrupt the direct narrative. (See Speaker's Commentary, i., p. 810.) The singular precariousness of this method is shown in the attempt to find an anachronism by identifying the Agag of Num. xxiv. 7

with the Agag of 1 Sam. xv. 23; whereas Dillmann (on Num. xxxiv. 7), speaking of the latter, says, "Whether another also still bore the name, or Agag was a title of all Amalekite kings (Ros., Win., Ges., Hgst., K. and others), is wholly unknown to us."

These are given us as "examples of a class." One is surprised that so slender a kind and array of anachronisms can be alleged against a book with such a history.

Note xxxii., p. 310: It is highly suggestive to see in a condensed form the summary mode in which Kuenen deals with the Hexateuch. Without making an exhaustive count, the reader will find in the volume, besides numerous statements to the same effect but in less compact form, the following terms applied to various parts of the Hexateuch:

"Glosses, interpolations, insertions, additions," 86 times; "amplifications, redactions, corrections, expansions, supplements, alterations, remodelings," 29 times; "later strata, another hand, other hands, foreign elements, another source, later origin," 34 times; "unhistorical, fiction, fictitious, absurd, impossible" (or equivalent terms), 22 times; "recast, retouched, worked over," 20 times; "manipulated, corrupt, harmonizing artifices, patch-work, literary artifices, tacked on," 15 times; "fused, welded, amalgamated, combined, compiled, incorporated, remodeled," 16 times; besides other similar terms, a free use of "contradictions," and the general statement that "the redaction was *a long and continuous process.*"

This is but a partial enumeration and is far from giving an adequate exhibition of the process claimed. For we read not alone of single changes, but of long continued operations, described in such terms as these: "Subsequently filled and expanded, gradually elaborated, product of continuous redaction, gradually accumulated, later expansions have risen successively, successive filling in and amplification, repeated manipulation and expansion, the result of imitation, largely remodeled and further altered when fused, stories have passed through many phases, have undergone more than one recension, indications of various accounts, several successive recensions and not much of the original narrative remaining, drastic recension, completely recast, drastic treatment, imitated him, collection brought together by a redactor who fitted it into a framework of his own, put together and worked up and certain foreign elements afterwards inserted, underwent a rather complicated literary process of which we know nothing, several hands at work on the same lines, the editor running them into his own mould, a compound narrative, a composite narrative, diversity of sources, interpolated and recast again and again, an absolutely unhistorical invention framed to defend the doctrine of a unique sanctuary, additions to bring the account into a semblance of agreement with the current belief, purposely altered to bring it into harmony," and so on *ad libitum*. It is well to get a bird's-eye view of the method in which one of the two great lights of the latest theory proceeds. Wellhausen's method, though perhaps less minute, is equally summary. The marvel is how, after all these "drastic" processes, Kuenen can pretend to find J E D and P. They would seem to have been thoroughly and continuously welded, fused and worked over.

Since the discovery of the long lost Diatesseron (Harmony of the Gospels) of Tatian, and its publication in 1888, an effort has been made to find in it some aid and comfort for the analysis of the Pentateuch, thus:

"If the Syrian church had been left to itself, without constant contact with the greater church to the west, the knowledge of the separate gospels might have been lost even among the learned. The parallel to the history of the Pentateuch would then have been complete." (Journal of Biblical Literature, 1890, p. 209.)

But the entire absence of the conditions covered by the two words "if" and "then" not only prevents the "parallel" from being "complete," but vacates it of every essential resemblance that would make it a parallel to "the history of the Pentateuch" as postulated in the critical analysis. For—

1. We have and always have had actual "knowledge" of separate gospels. We never have had knowledge nor hint of separate documents compiled to form the Pentateuch as a whole.
2. The church has always had the gospels themselves in their separate form. It has never had nor known of J E D P R, etc., in separate form.
3. The writers of the four gospels are all historically known personages. J E D P, etc., are one and all unknown to history or tradition.
4. We have external means of knowing proximately the time, and more or less credible evidence of the circumstances, of the origin of our gospels; as to the time or circumstances of J and the rest, no external indications whatever.
5. The two methods, alike only in the bald and superficial fact that Tatian made a compilation, are radically different in character. The writer in the Journal distinctly states that Tatian's method was "to preserve every detail found in any one of the sources, and yet avoid repetitions and hard transitions"; (2) that "the author has added nothing which was not contained in his sources"; (3) that he "has changed them as little as possible," and only by phrases of "transition or connection" (though in one case unfortunately, between Matt. i. 1 and Luke ii. 39)—the only considerable omission, except repetitions, being the two difficult genealogies. Contrast, on the other hand, not only the constant liberties taken by R in his many forms, but the wholesale fabrications by D and P, of transactions, discourses, and even legislations; and could two proceedings be more *essentially* diverse?
6. Equally in conflict with any parallelism but of contrast is the confessed inability to detect the component parts of the Diatesseron without possessing the gospels themselves. The Journal writer "confidently" admits, as he must, that except in case of John's gospel (which, not being synoptic, could be used without disintegration), "we should not be able to analyze the Composite Gospel (of Tatian) with as much success

as we have had with the Pentateuch." A necessary but damaging admission; imaginary writers can be analyzed, actual ones cannot.

In what respect does Tatian help Kuenen, Cornill or Driver?

Note xxxiii., p. 106: The discussion of this inscription of Menephtha is continued from time to time, with an agreement as to the mention of Israel, and some difference in rendering the associated words, and on the question whether it refers to Israel as being in Egypt or in Palestine. And it is recognized as not only a mention of Israel, but as a boast of triumph over him.

INDEX OF PRINCIPAL AUTHORS CITED OR REFERRED TO IN THIS VOLUME

Addis, W. E., The Documents of the Hexateuch, 1893.
Armstrong, C., Names and Places in the Old and New Testaments, 1889.

Bacon, Benjamin B., The Genesis of Genesis, 1892.
Baxter, W. L., Wellhausen's "One God, One Sanctuary"; The Thinker, 1893-1894.
Bartlett, W. H., Forty Days in the Desert, 1862.
Bissell, Edwin C., Genesis Printed in Colors, 1892.
Bliss, F. J., A Mound of Many Cities, 1894.
Blomfield, A., The Old Testament and the New Criticism, 1893.
Boscawen, W. St. Chad, The Bible and the Monuments, 1895.
Briggs, C. A., The Higher Criticism of the Hexateuch, 1893.
Bunsen, Christian C. J., Egypt's Place in Universal History, 1858-1867.
    Bibelwerk, volumes 1st and 2nd, 1858-1860.

Cave, Alfred, The Inspiration of the Old Testament, 2nd ed., 1888.
Cesnola, Louis P., Cyprus, 2nd ed., 1878.
Chesney, Francis R., Survey of the Euphrates and Tigris, 1850.
Conder, Claude R., Tent Work in Palestine, 1878.
    Heth and Moab, 1885.
    The Tell Amarna Tablets, 1892.
Cornill, Carl Heinrich, Einleitung in das Alte Testament, 1891.
Cotta, Bernard von, Die Geologie der Gegenwart, 1878.
Croll, James, Stellar Evolution, 1891.

Dana, James D., Manual of Geology, 4th ed., 1895.

Davis, John D., Genesis and Semitic Tradition, 1894.
Dawson, Sir J. W., The Origin of the World, 1877.
>Modern Science in Bible Lands, 1889.
>The Meeting Place of Geology and History, 1894.
Delitzsch, Franz, New Commentary on Genesis, English translation, 1889.
Delitzsch, Friedrich, Wo lag das Paradies, 1881.
Dillmann, August, Die Genesis, sechste auflage, 1892.
>Exodus und Leviticus, 1880.
Draper, J. W., The Conflict of Religion and Science, 1875.
Driver, S. R., Notes on the Hebrew Text of Samuel, 1890.
>Introduction to the Literature of the Old Testament, 1891.
>Sermons on the Old Testament, 1892.
>Commentary on Deuteronomy, 1895.

Ebers, Georg, Aegypten und die Bücher Mose's, 1868.
>"Joseph," Smith's Dictionary of the Bible, 2nd ed., 1893.
Ebrard, J. H. A., Christian Apologetics, English translation, 1886.
Edersheim, Alfred, Prophecy and History in Relation to the Messiah, 1895.
Edwards, Amelia B., Pharaohs, Fellahs and Explorers, 1892.
Ellicott, C. J., Christus Comprobator, 1892.
Erman, Adolph, Life in Ancient Egypt, 1894.
Ewald, Heinrich, Geschichte von Israel, dritte ausgabe, 1864.

Geikie, Archibald, Text Book of Geology, 1893.
Girard, Raymond de, Le Deluge, 1892, 1893, 1895.
Girdlestone, R. B., The Foundations of the Bible, 1890.
Godet, F., Creation and Life, 1882.
Green, Wm. Henry, The Higher Criticism of the Pentateuch, 1895.
>The Unity of the Book of Genesis, 1895.

Gray, Asa, Natural Science and Religion, 1880.
Guyot, Arnold, The Earth and Man.
    Creation, 1884.

Harper, H. A., The Bible and Modern Discoveries, 1890.
Hilprecht, Herman V., Explorations in Babylonia (Recent Researches in Bible Lands), 1896.
Hitchcock, Charles H., The Geology of New Hampshire, 1874-1878.
Holzinger, H., Einleitung in den Hexateuch, 1893.
Hommel, Fitz, Discoveries in Arabia (Recent Researches in Bible Lands), 1896.
    The Ancient Hebrew Tradition, 1897.
Howorth, Sir Henry H., The Mammoth and the Flood, 1887.
Huxley, T. H., Science and Hebrew Tradition, 1894.

James, Sir Henry, Notes on the Great Pyramid, 1869.
Joly, N., Man before Metals, 1883.

Kalisch, M. M., Commentary on Genesis, 1858.
    Commentary on Exodus, 1855.
Kautsch, E., and Socin, A., Die Genesis, 1888.
Kittel, R., History of the Hebrews, English translation, 1895.
Klostermann, August, Der Pentateuch, 1893.
Knötel, H. J. R., Homeros der Blinde von Chios, 1894-1895.
Kuenen, A., The Hexateuch, English translation, 1886.
    The Religion of Israel, English translation, 1874-1883.

Ladd, George T., The Doctrine of Sacred Scripture, 1883.
Layard, Austin H., Nineveh and its Remains, 1849.
    Babylon and Nineveh, 1853.
Leathes, Stanley, The Law in the Prophets, 1891.
Le Conte, Joseph, Elements of Geology, revised edition, 1891.
Lefèvre, André, Race and Language, 1894.

Lenormant, François, The Beginnings of History (Brown's translation), 1882.
Lex Mosaica, by various writers, 1894.
Lightfoot, J. B., Essays on "Supernatural Religion," 1889.
Loftus, W. K., Travels in Chaldea and Susiana, 1857.
Lyell, Sir Charles, The Antiquity of Man, 1878.
  Principles of Geology, 11th ed., 1878.
Lubbock, Sir John, Prehistoric Times, 1872.

Mariette, Auguste, Aperçu de L'Histoire D'Egypte, 1872.
Maspero, G., Places Captured by Sheshenk, Jour. Victoria Institute, 1894.
  Egyptian Archæology, 1887.
  The Struggle of the Nations, 1897.
McCoan, J. C., Egypt, 1877.
McCurdy, J. F., History, Prophecy and the Monuments, 1894, 1896.

Nadaillac, Marquis de, Prehistoric Peoples, 1892.
Naville, Edouard, The Store City of Pithom, 1885.
  Goshen, 1887.

Oettli, Samuel, Das Deuteronomium, und die Bücher Joshua und Richter, 1893.

Palmer, E. H., The Desert of the Exodus, 1871.
Petrie, W. M., Tell el Hesy, 1891.
  The Story of a "Tell" (The City and the Land), 1892.
  Egypt and Israel, Contemporary Review, May, 1896.
  History of Egypt, 1896.
Pinches, T. G., "Eden," Smith's History of the Bible, 2nd ed.
Poole, R. S., Ancient Egypt, Contemporary Review, March, 1879.
Prestwich, Joseph, The Tradition of the Flood, Jour. Victoria Institute, 1894.

Quatrefages, A. de, The Human Species, 1879.

Records of the Past, various writers, 1875-1881.
  New Series, 1888-1892.
Rawlinson, George, The History of Herodotus, 1858-1860.
  The History of the Nations, 1878.
Reusch, Fr. H., Nature and the Bible, English translation, 1886.
Robertson, James, The Early Religion of Israel, 1892.
Robinson, Edward, Biblical Researches, 1841-1852.
Ryle, Herbert E., The Canon of the Old Testament, 1892.
  The Early Narratives of Genesis, 1892.
Sanday, W., Inspiration, 2nd ed., 1894.
Sayce, A. H., The Ancient Empires of the East, 1884.
Schrader, E., Die Keilinschriften und das Alte Testament, 2nd ed., 1884.
Schuchardt, C., Schliemann's Excavations, 1891.
Smith, George, The Chaldean Genesis, Sayce's edition, 1880.
  Delitzsch's Edition, 1876.
Smend, R., and Socin, A., Die Inschrift des Konigs Mesa, 1886.
Southall, James C., The Recent Origin of Man, 1875.
Strack, H. L., Genesis, Exodus und Leviticus, 1894.
  Einleitung in das Alte Testament, vierte auflage, 1895.

Tait, P. G., Recent Advances in Physical Science, 3rd ed., 1885.
Thomas, Louis, Le Jour du Seigneur, 1892.
Thomson, W. M., The Land and The Book, popular edition, 1880.
Tomkins, Henry G., The Times of Abraham, 1878.
Tristram, H. B., Natural History of the Bible, 1868.
  The Land of Israel, 2nd ed., 1866.
  The Natural History of Palestine (The City and the Land), 1892.
Trumbull, H. Clay, Kadesh Barnea, 1879.

Watson, F., The Book of Genesis a True History, 1894.

Westphal, Alexander, Les Sources du Pentateuch, 1888-1892.
Wilkinson, J. G., The Ancient Egyptians, Birch's ed., 1883.
Winchell, Alexander, Preadamites, 1881.
Winckler, Hugo, The Tell Amarna Letters, 1896.
Wright, G. Frederick, The Ice Age in North America, 1889.
Wright, William, The Empire of the Hittites, 1884.
    The Hittites (The City and the Land), 1892.

Zenos, Andrew C., The Elements of the Higher Criticism, 1895.
Zöckler, O., Die Lehre vom Urstand des Menschen, 1879.

INDEX

Aaron..............327, seq.
Abiathar................339
Abiri, The................39
Abraham........35,48,92,96,
  111,113,116,120,121,122,124
Accad...............118,145
Achan...........20,31,41,45
Achsah....................26
Achor..................... 8
Ahab..............6,7,330
Ahhotep...................80
Ahiab...................339
Ai...............18,20,31,45
Ain, Berwad, 60; Hawwarah,
  60; Musa, 59
Amenophis IV.......16,34,48
Amorites............36,40,42
Amos.....87,275-277,332-335
Amraphel................118
Anachronisms, Alleged.....
 323-325,386-389
Analysis, Critical........
 295-310,361,384-390
Animal Life.......249, seq.
Antediluvian Life, Length of
 178-186
Antiquity of the Human
  Race.............380-382
Arabia, Its Early Civiliza-
  tion..................9,35
Aramaic Language........36
Arioch.......117,118,119,124
Ark, The............157, 164
Arts, The Early....192, seq.
Ashteroth Karnaim.......119
Askelon (Ascalon)........
  .....16, 28, 35, 38, 42, 117
Assyrian Discoveries......5,6
Augustine................252

Authorship, Evidence of...
 269,272
Azekah...................20

Baal-zephon..............56
Babel..............126-128
Babylonia, Relations to Pal-
  estine.................359
Babylonian Discoveries, 5;
  Garment, 20; Conquests, 117
"Badgers' Skins"..........77
Balaam..........48, 68, 324
Bede....................252
Beirut........16, 35, 41, 43
Berosus................127
Beth-horon..............9, 45
Bethlehem..............127
Beth-shan................41
Bezaleel.................77
Biographies in the Hexa-
  teuch..............112-114
Birs Nimrud.........126,128
Bitumen........120,121,157
Bochim.................328
"Book-town"..............16
Boulak Museum..........79
Boundaries, Tribal.......361
Bradford's History of Plym-
  outh.........85, 288 seq.
Bricks, Egyptian, 87, 88;
  Babylonian, 126.
Bronze........78,82,194,195

Cain, Cainites....188,192,198
Calah...................146
Camels in Egypt.........93
Canaan, Language of .....
 43,111,283
Canaanites....26,28,32,36,38

Canal, Sweet water, 53; Suez, 54, 56.
Candor of narratives.... 28, 31
Carchemish 9
Caspian Sea, depression of. 172
Cattle..................... 248
Cereals 130
Chaeremon................. 44
Chaloof................. 55, 56
Changes of level.... 168, seq.
Chaos................. 236, 238
Charcoal................... 71
Chariots .. 21, 41, 42, 54, 93, 95
Chemosh 7
Chedorlaomer ... 118, 119, 121
Chittim................... 148
City, Cain's.......... 191, 192
Civilization, in Canaan, 42; around Israel............ 10
Chronicler, The..........
.... 6, 9, 328, 343, 344
"Codes," a loose title.. 347-348
Confusion of tongues.. 132, 133
Conquest of Palestine......
.... 14, 19, 20, 21, 29
Contemporaneousness, Marks of.......... 18, 19, 277
Continents 239
Contradictions created. 320, 321
Copper............ 42, 194, 195
Creation narrative, its aim and method, 227-234; not duplicated, 201, 202; confirmed in detail..... 255, 256
Creation, Classic story, 257; Chaldean, 25; defects of................ 258, 259
"Creeping thing"..... 248, 249
Crossing the Jordan......
.... 45, 46, 48, 361-365
Cush..................... 264
Curse, The........ 224, seq.

Dahariyeh................. 26
Damieh................... 30
Dan............... 18, 120, 121
Daughters of men.... 187, 188
David.......... 340, 341, 342
Day, Creation. 234, 252, 253, 379

"Day, To this"........... 18
Dead Sea................. 29
Death 223
Debir 16, 25, 26
Deluge, Traditions of, 151, seq.; extent, 163, seq.; possibility, 170; method, 171-178.
Deluge narrative, definite, 156; consistent, 156, 157; contemporary, 158.
Dibon 67
Dispersion, The..........
... 129-132, 144, 149, 372, 373
Documents in Genesis.. 2, 200
Dodanim................. 149

Ebal 21, 22, 380
Eden 270
Edom................... 29
Egypt, Accurate account of
.... 85-88, 360, 370, 371
Egyptian words........ 94, 96
Elam........ 118, 119, 142, 204
Elim.................. 59, 61
Elishah................ 148
Ellasar................. 118
Elohim.................. 43
Encampment by the Sea, 61; at Sinai, 66.
Engedi................. 120
English Bible, Revision of. 283
Enoch 181
Enos 180
Erech............. 125, 145
Esau............ 48, 112, 115
Etham.................. 54
Evidence, Traditional.... 382
Exodus, The, 50 seq.; preparations, 51, seq., 363; stations, 69, 367.
Ezra 78, 287, 288

Famines 89
Feasts, observed, 332-335; abuse condemned, 335, 336.
Feiran.................. 52
Fenced cities.......... 7, 9, 40
Fire................... 191

INDEX

Firmament............238, 239
Flying creatures..........245
Food supply, miraculous
.... 66, 67
Fortresses.................38
Fruit, The forbidden...208, 209

Galeed, Jegur-sahadutha..111
Gardens....................42
Gerizim..............21, 280
Gezer..................26, 35
Gibeon, Gibeonites........
..20, 22, 31, 45, 46, 319, 328, 331
Gideon..............340, 341
Gilgal.........14, 18, 20, 25, 31
Gold..........41, 42, 78, 79, 80
Golden Age...............214
Gomer....................146
Goshen................53, 100
Gomorrah.................14
Great Eastern, The.......157
Great Deep, The.........168

Ham........ 134, 135, 144, 149
Haran......... 121, 124, 125
Hazezon Tamar..........121
Hazor........16, 25, 35, 38, 117
Hebrew language........111
Hebrews........ ... 105, 106
Hebron............25, 96, 123
Heshbon..................67
Hesiod...................215
Hezekiah......6, 8, 40, 280, 330
Hexateuch, Two theories
of, 1-3; its truth assailed,
312; sustained, 357-358.
"Hill of Aaron"............65
Hissarlik............195, 196
Hittites..........26, 27, 28,
36, 37, 38, 39, 41, 54, 96-99, 359
Homer..........3, 28, 196, 249
Hophni...................339
Hor......................73
Horeb..............65, 286
Hormah..................29
Horses............41, 42, 93
Hosea........275, 276, 331-335
Huleh....................21
Hyksos............89, 105

Idioms, Canaanite........ 43
Imposition, Priestly, im-
practicable.........355-357
Inscriptions, Arabian, 9;
Assyrian, 98; Moabite, 7,
283; at Magarah, 40; at
Siloam, 8; of Shishak, 8;
of Menephtah, 106.
Iron.......... 81, 82, 195, 197
Isaac................48, 114
Ishmael.................114
Israel, Kings of, mentioned
in Assyria...............6

Jabal....................192
Jacob..... 48, 111, 112, 114, 115
Japheth... 134, 135, 141, 146, 149
Jashar, Book of..........284
Javan.......... ....147, 148
Jericho................19,
23, 31, 40, 41, 42, 45, 46, 68, 324
Jeroboam....330, 331, 340, 343
Jerusalem.................
......9, 16, 25, 35, 39, 117, 120
Jezreel...................41
Jewelry...........78-80, 369
Joppa................16, 35
Jordan...................
..18, 19, 22, 30, 31, 32, 45, 46, 48
Joshua, Character of......33
Joseph...................
...43, 44, 45, 90, 110, 111, 115
Josephus............9, 44, 45
Josiah....................9
Jubilee year............354
Judah, Kings of, mentioned
in Assyria. 6
Junius..................202

Kadesh..............29,
50, 65, 66, 67, 120, 121, 186, 220
Kedesh..................25
Kimmerii............146, 372
Kiriathaim..............119
Kirjath-jearim............25
Kirjath-sepher. 116
Knötel on Homer........3, 4
Koyunjik.................6

INDEX

Lachish, 16, 117; siege of, 6; excavations at, 40.
Lamech, 181; his family, 192; his song, 197, 198.
Language, Variant 300
Larsa 125
Law, Non-observance of 317, 318
Law, The, given 365
Lebanon 27
Legislation, successive and interrupted, 64, 349-352, 368; order of, 354.
Leshem 18, 27
Level, Changes of ... 168, seq.
Levites and priests ... 342-345
Life, Length of ...... 183, seq.
Light 237
Life in Egypt 85-88
Longevity 374
Lot 113

Machpelah 126
Madai 147
Magarah, Wady 40
Magog 147
Makkedah 16, 20, 35, 41, 117
Man in paradise, 190; two-fold nature, 199; condition and traits, 208; capacity and dominion, 251, 252; his prohibition, 209.
Manetho 44
Manna 71
Manoah 300, 341
Marah 60
Marriage, Ideal 210, 212
Megiddo 32
Memorials .... 280, seq.
Menephtah ... 106, 107, 108, 393
Merom 21, 37, 38, 40, 41
Mesha 7
Methuselah 183
Micah 339, 340, 343
Migdol 54, 55, 56
Mines 194
Misrephoth 21, 27
Mizpeh, Mispah 21, 27, 328
Moab, Moabites 7, 29, 48, 67, 68, 69, 81, 82, 283

Mohar 93
Moses, 11, 16, 49, 50, 270, 271, 273 seq.; 280, 281, 288, 355.
Mosul 207
Music, Instruments of 193
Mulberries 42

Nabonidus 7
Naharain 82
Names, Palestinian 24, 25, 27, 34
Nebo 63
Nimrud 82, 126
Nineveh 196
Noah 113, 133, 134, 181
Nob 331
Numbers, uncertain 179
Nuffar 195

Observances, commemorative 104
Olives 42, 185
Ophrah 328
Outline descriptions. 245, 250
Orontes, The 41, 54
Ovid 190, 215
Oxen 42
Oxford Essays 232

Paradise, rivers, 205 seq.; locality, 375, 378.
Palm trees 61
Papyrus 3
Pentaur, Poem of, the .. 41, 54
Pharaoh-necho 9
Phenicia 39, 41
Pi-hahiroth 55, 56
Pisgah 68
Pithom 53, 54, 88, 100
Plagues, The, 91, 92; time of, 363.
Plymouth colony 10, 11, 85
Pottery, Early use of 191
Precious stones 78-80
Priests, priesthood, 227 seq., 338-340.

Quails 72

Rahab .... 46, R.

INDEX

Rahah, Wady er.... 59, 60, 64
Ramah................ 2
Rameses.............. 53
Rameses II., 38, 42, 54, 80, 98,
.... 100
Records, Assyrian, 6; pre-Mosaic, 2.
Rehoboam............. 9, 40
Rephidim............. 63
Reptiles............. 246
Red Sea, Crossing of.....
.... 48, 53, 54, 57, 58, 59
Revision of English Bible, 285; of Hebrew Bible, 286.
"Rib"................ 210
Rithmah.............. 71

Sabbath.............. 266
Sacrifices.... 330-332, 341-342
Samaritan Pentateuch. 179, 273
Samuel...... 328, 331, 339, 340
Sarabit el Khadim..... 40, 195
Sargon I., 97; Sargon II.,
.... 98, 142
Satan................ 218
Saul................. 340
"Seed," The.......... 225
Seir................. 65
Sennacherib.......... 6
Septuagint, The...... 16, 17
Serapeum............. 55, 56
Serbonian Bog........ 55
Serpent, 73; traditions of, 220, seq.
Seti I............... 53
Sethites............. 187, 188
Sex.................. 209
Shabbatu............. 263, 282
Shalmanezer.......... 6, 98
Sharahen............. 18
Shechem..............
.... 17, 21, 43, 46, 318, 329, 331
Shem........ 134, 135, 144, 149
Shiloh........... 319, 328, 331
Shinar.... 118, 126, 129, 144, 145
Ships................ 42
Shishak.............. 8, 9, 360
Shittim wood......... 70
Sidon.. 16, 21, 27, 38, 42, 117, 142

Silence, Argument from....
.... 315, 316
Siloam inscription....... 7, 8
Sin, Wilderness of....... 62
Sin and penalty......... 216
Sinai................. 64
Slave............... 43, 354
Solomon............. 340, 342
Sons of God......... 186-188
Stretched out creatures (monsters)............ 246
South Country........... 66
Species destroyed.... 249, 250
Stations 69
Style, popular and phenomenal, 214; does not fix date, 322, 383.
Succoth.............. 53, 100
Suez Canal......... 54, 55, 57
Sufsafeh 64
Sun and moon.... 234, 242, 243

Tabernacle, The, its construction............ 77, 78
Table of Nations.... 137 seq.
Targum................ 16
Tarshish........... 146, 148
Tatian's Diatesseron.. 390, 391
Tell Amarna tablets. 16, 34, 36, 39, 99, 101, 111, 117, 119,
.... 143, 183
Tell el Hesy........ 33, 35, 40
Tell el Maskutah......... 53
Temptation, The..... 217-223
Tents................ 192
Thebes............... 8
Thothmes III..........
.. 18, 34, 38, 82, 98, 119, 123. 196
Tidal................. 119
Tiglath-pileser......... 6
Timsah, Lake......... 55, 56
Tiras................ 147
Torah, The........... 11
Tree, Sacred......... 37, 38
Tribute of Hezekiah, 6; of Moabite king, 7.
Trumpets............. 41
Tumilat, Wady....... 53, 101
Two Brothers, Tale of..... 90

Tyre.. 16,27,28,35,38,42,43, ...117,135,142

Ur..................123,125
Usertesen I............. ..98

Vegetable life............24
Vineyards................42

Wady, Ed Deir, 64; Er Rahab, 64; Feiran, 63; Gharandel, 61; Hamr, 63; Hibran, 64; Leja, 64; Magarah, 193,194; Nukhl, 64; Saal, 71; Sebayeh, 64;

Shellal, 63; Tayibeh, 61; Tumilat, 53,100.
Wagons..................63
Water, courses at Jerusalem, 8; supply in the desert, 67.
Weaving................193
Week, The..........264 seq.
Wells of Moses.........59,60
Wilderness of Sin.........62
Wine............75,133,134
Woman 209-211
Writing..... 15,16,17,25,41,78

Zephath...............29,66
Zoar....................121

www.ingramcontent.com/pod-product-compliance
Lightning Source LLC
Chambersburg PA
CBHW030558300426
44111CB00009B/1022